NUTRITIONAL NEEDS
AND ASSESSMENT
OF NORMAL GROWTH

Nutritional Needs and Assessment of Normal Growth, Seventh Nestlé Nutrition Workshop, Rome, Italy, May 30–June 1, 1983

Conference participants *(from left to right)*: S. Nordio, L. Franguelli, L. A. Barness, Samudsin, J. C. Waterlow, N. Butte, W. C. L. Yip, A. Marini, H. A. Kader, M. Roulet, E. DeMaeyer, F. Falkner, E. Marcondez, J. Senterre, M. Gracey, A. Briend, M. Pierson, C. M. Anderson, R. G. Whitehead, G. Zoppi, P. R. Guesry, A. Rubino, A. Latronico, A. Lechtig, L. Mata.

Nutritional Needs and Assessment of Normal Growth

Editors

Michael Gracey, M.D.,
Ph.D., F.R.A.C.P.
Associate Professor of Child Health
University of Western Australia
Princess Margaret Children's
Medical Research Foundation
Perth, Western Australia

Frank Falkner, M.D.,
F.R.C.P.
Professor of Maternal and Child Health
School of Public Health
University of California at Berkeley
Berkeley, California,
Department of Pediatrics
University of California at San Francisco
San Francisco, California

Nestlé Nutrition
Workshop Series
Volume 7

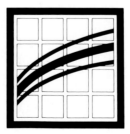

NESTLÉ NUTRITION

RAVEN PRESS ■ NEW YORK

Raven Press, 1140 Avenue of the Americas, New York, New York 10036

Made in the United States of America

Library of Congress Cataloging in Publication Data
Main entry under title:

Nutritional needs and assessment of normal growth.

(Nestlé Nutrition workshop series ; v. 7)
Based on the 7th Nestlé Nutrition workshop, held in
Rome, Italy, May 30–June 1, 1983.
Includes bibliographies and index.
1. Infants—Nutrition—Congresses. 2. Infants—Growth—
Congresses. I. Gracey, Michael. II. Falkner, Frank T.,
1918–   . III. Nestlé Nutrition S.A. IV. Series.
[DNLM: 1. Child Development—congresses.   2. Fetus—physi-
ology—congresses.   3. Growth—congresses.   4. Infant
Nutrition—congresses. W1 NE228 v.7 / WS115 N9855 1983]
RJ216.N86   1985   613.2   84-27526
ISBN 0-88167-044-8 (Raven Press)

Preface

Volume 7 of the *Nestlé Nutrition Workshop Series* reviews the most recent advances in knowledge about such important, basic questions concerning growth and nutrition in infancy and childhood as, "What is normal growth?" "How can it best be assessed?" "What are the nutritional needs which must be met to support normal growth in infants and children?" Special emphasis throughout the volume is placed on the practical application of new knowledge and, particularly, on the nutritional needs and problems of vulnerable infants in developing countries.

This volume brings together contributions by acknowledged experts and research workers from Europe, the United States, Britain, Australia, Asia, Africa, and Latin America. Their chapters review the most recently conducted research and field studies and the literature on the nutritional needs of infants and young children and how these can be provided and monitored in real-life situations, especially in areas of the world where undernutrition is still prevalent. Volume 7 commences with contributions on the nutritional requirements for fetal growth and for healthy neonates, then proceeds to the nutritional requirements for low birth weight infants.

A major problem area for nutritionists has been methodology available to study nutrient and energy intakes in the first months of life. This is covered in chapters on measured energy and nutrient intakes to 4 months and by a thorough literature review on lactational performance and the discussions that follow each chapter. The book then considers how growth can be monitored in practical terms *in utero* and throughout childhood. A review of child-growth studies done in Australia over the past 50 years and the prospective Perth Child Growth Study highlight the need to select appropriate growth "standards" and reference values because of secular trends in growth that have occurred over recent decades. These are crucial issues and introduce the final two chapters, which consider environmental factors, such as housing, hygiene, and infectious disease and their impact on growth patterns and the impact of nutritional supplementation on growth outcome. This is still a contentious but extremely important subject because of the prevalence of maternal and infant undernutrition in developing countries and the need to improve fetal outcomes in pregnancy and to improve patterns of growth in children living in the poorer parts of the world. Constraints on government and other institutional budgets make it imperative that the limited resources available for health programs are spent in the most cost-effective ways. This puts nutritional rehabilitation under administrative and scientific scrutiny.

This book is designed as a practical guide and relevant literature review for workers in various disciplines (e.g., clinical science, nutrition, public health) involved in the nutrition of infants and young children. Because of the wide range of subjects and disciplines involved, it should be of particular use to allied health personnel, such as nutritionists, dietitians, and maternal and child health nurses who would otherwise have difficulty obtaining primary sources of literature covered in the book. This will make it especially useful to health workers in developing countries and other areas where access to libraries is limited.

The volume will be of particular value to pediatricians and other doctors interested in the nutritional needs and difficulties facing pregnant and lactating mothers and infants and young children in underdeveloped countries. It should also be of interest to a wider audience of pediatricians, general practitioners, specialist physicians, nurses, and medical students concerned with maternal and child health.

MICHAEL GRACEY
FRANK FALKNER

Foreword

Growth is the key outcome measurement for all clinicians dealing with infants and young children. For many years, in fact, the nutritional requirements of infants have been set by measuring the intake of breastfed infants who were growing normally. The genetic, metabolic, nutritional, and environmental factors that influence growth have long preoccupied scientists working in this area and formed the basis for the Seventh Nestlé Nutrition Workshop. Many topics, such as secular trends and the crucial question of the universality of growth standards, have been addressed, as well as the value of classic standards established on a small number of infants who may have been overfed.

Contributors had experience working in many different parts of the world, from Africa to Australia. All focused on the nutritional needs and growth outcome for infants in both health and disease.

We hope this volume of the Nestlé Nutrition Workshop Series will prove useful to all who have an interest in pediatrics and growth.

PIERRE R. GUESRY, M.D.
Vice President
Nestlé Products Technical
Assistance Co. Ltd.

Acknowledgments

The contributions in this volume were presented at the Seventh Nestlé Nutrition Workshop, *Nutritional Needs and Assessment of Normal Growth*, held in Rome, Italy, May 30–June 1, 1983.

Warm thanks are due to Monsieur Y. Barbieux and Dr. Pierre Guesry, Nestlé Nutrition, Vevey, who organized and supported, and also spoilt, the participants; to the Academia Lancisiana in Rome who were our gracious hosts in their delightful historical premises; to the Rome Academy of Pediatrics; and to the ever-patient and laborious Mrs. Verna Hevron and Ms. Karen Phelps for their secretarial expertise. We also thank Dr. Edouard DeMaeyer for his expert help in editing the manuscript and the discussion segments that follow the presentations. And, finally, we thank the contributors and discussants themselves, whose Workshop it was.

Contents

Normal Fetal Growth Regulation: Nutritional Aspects 1
André Briend

Nutrition for Healthy Neonates 23
Lewis A. Barness

Nutritional Requirements of Low Birthweight Infants 45
Jacques Senterre and Jacques Rigo

Energy and Protein Intakes of Exclusively Breastfed Infants
   During the First Four Months of Life 63
Nancy F. Butte and Cutberto Garza

Human Lactation, Infant Feeding, and Growth:
   Secular Trends 85
R. G. Whitehead and A. A. Paul

Monitoring Growth 123
Frank Falkner

Studies of Growth of Australian Infants 139
Michael Gracey and Nancy E. Hitchcock

Environmental Factors Affecting Nutrition and Growth 165
Leonardo Mata

Early Malnutrition, Growth, and Development 185
Aaron Lechtig

Subject Index 221

Contributors

*Lewis A. Barness
College of Medicine
Department of Pediatrics, Box 15
University of South Florida Medical
  Center
12901 North 30th Street
Tampa, Florida 33612

*André Briend
ICCDR, B
G.P.O. Box 128
Dhaka-2, Bangladesh

*Nancy F. Butte
Lactation Program
Medical Towers Building
Suite 501
608 Fannin
Houston, Texas 77030

*Frank Falkner
School of Public Health
Maternal and Child Health Program
University of California at Berkeley
Earl Warren Hall
Berkeley, California 94720

Cutberto Garza
Children's Nutrition Research Center
Department of Pediatrics
Baylor College of Medicine
Texas Children's Hospital
Houston, Texas 77030

*Michael Gracey
Gastroenterology and Nutrition Research
  Unit
Princess Margaret Children's Medical
  Research Foundation (Inc.)
G.P.O. Box D184
Perth, Western Australia 6001

Nancy E. Hitchcock
Gastroenterology and Nutrition Research
  Unit
Princess Margaret Children's Medical
  Research Foundation (Inc.)
G.P.O. Box D184
Perth, Western Australia 6001

*Aaron Lechtig
Edificio Seguradoras
13 Andar, SBS
Brazilia 70-072, Brazil

*Leonardo Mata
Instituto de Investigaciones en Salud
  (INISA)
Universidad de Costa Rica
Ciudad Universitaria Rodrigo Facio
San Pedro, Costa Rica

A. A. Paul
Medical Research Council Dunn
  Nutrition Unit
Downhams Lane
Milton Road
Cambridge CB4 1XJ, United Kingdom

Jacques Rigo
Department of Pediatrics
State University of Liège
Bavière Hospital
B-4020 Liège, Belgium

---

*Workshop participant.

*Jacques Senterre
Department of Pediatrics
State University of Liège
Bavière Hospital
B-4020 Liège, Belgium

*R. G. Whitehead
Medical Research Council Dunn
 Nutrition Unit
Downhams Lane
Milton Road
Cambridge CB4 1XJ, United Kingdom

Invited Attendees

C. M. Anderson/*Perth, Australia*
S. Balakrishnan/*Johore Baru, Malaysia*
E. DeMaeyer/*Geneva, Switzerland*
D. Gaburro/*Verona, Italy*
M. Giovannini/*Milan, Italy*
H. A. Kader/*Kuala Lumpur, Maylaysia*
E. Marcondez/*Sao Paulo, Brazil*
A. Marini/*Milan, Italy*

S. Nordio/*Trieste, Italy*
M. Pierson/*Nancy, France*
M. Roulet/*Lausanne, Switzerland*
A. Rubino/*Naples, Italy*
Samsudin/*Jakarta, Indonesia*
J. C. Waterlow/*London, England*
W. C. L. Yip/*Singapore*
G. Zoppi/*Verona, Italy*

Nestlé Participants

Pierre R. Guesry
Vice President
Nestlé Products Technical
Assistance Co. Ltd.
La Tour de Peilz, Switzerland

Yves Barbieux
Senior Vice President
Nestlé Products Technical
Assistance Co. Ltd.
La Tour de Peilz, Switzerland

Nestlé Nutrition Workshop Series

Volume 7: Nutritional Needs and Assessment of Normal Growth
Michael Gracey and Frank Falkner, Editors; 240 pp., 1985

Volume 6: Chronic Diarrhea in Children
Emanuel Lebenthal, Editor; 496 pp., 1984

Volume 5: Human Milk Banking
A. F. Williams and J. D. Baum, Editors; 216 pp., 1984

Volume 4: Iron Nutrition in Infancy and Childhood
Abraham Stekel, Editor; 218 pp., 1984

Volume 3: Nutritional Adaptation of the Gastrointestinal Tract of the Newborn
Norman Kretchmer and Alexandre Minkowsi, Editors; 244 pp.1983

Volume 2: Acute Diarrhea: Its Nutritional Consequences in Children
Joseph A. Bellanti, Editor; 240 pp., 1983

Volume 1: Maternal Nutrition in Pregnancy—Eating for Two?
John Dobbing, Editor (Academic Press); 210 pp., 1981

Forthcoming Volumes

Volume 8: Trace Minerals
R. K. Chandra, Editor

Volume 9: Maternal Nutrition and Lactational Infertility
John Dobbing, Editor

Volume 10: Weaning: Why, What, and When?
A. Ballabriga and J. Rey, Editors

Volume 11: Feeding the Sick Infant
L. Stern, Editor

Volume 12: Neurobiological Development
A. Minkowski, P. Evrard, G. Lyon, and J. P. Changeux, Editors

Nutritional Needs and Assessment of Normal Growth, edited by M. Gracey and F. Falkner. Nestlé Nutrition, Vevey/Raven Press, New York © 1985.

Normal Fetal Growth Regulation: Nutritional Aspects

André Briend

ORSTOM Nutrition, 75008, Paris, France

NORMAL FETAL GROWTH

To determine the mean fetal growth curve in the human species is theoretically impossible; it would require a precise measurement of fetal weight *in utero* during the entire fetal life. Fetal growth curves used in clinical practice are based on data obtained from liveborn infants of different gestational ages. Presumably, they provide reasonable estimates of the general pattern of fetal growth, although it is not valid to derive velocity growth curves from cross-sectional data. Longitudinal ultrasound studies on large numbers of patients have now been obtained and have provided no evidence that babies with larger heads or who are large for dates have a significantly shorter duration of gestation (1). All the fetal growth curves obtained by this technique have the same general pattern: they show a regular and rapid growth during the second trimester of intrauterine life, followed by a slight faltering, which becomes more pronounced just before term (2). This faltering in the fetal growth curve does not seem to be an artifact due to the cross-sectional nature of the data collected at birth. This is also apparent on head growth curves, which can be derived from longitudinal measurements made *in utero* by echography (3).

After delivery, the newborn infant grows faster than just before birth and seems to "catch up" after the preterm growth faltering. This results in a marked irregularity of growth during the perinatal period (4), which is apparent on velocity curves (Fig. 1).

To explain this irregularity, it has been suggested that near term, fetal growth is not optimal and is limited by some unknown maternal factor, in the absence of which the growth curve would have no linear deviation during the perinatal period (2).

That human growth might be suboptimal in the perinatal period is also suggested by epidemiological evidence. In all populations, perinatal mortality is related to birthweight by a U-shaped curve with high values for small birthweights, a minimum in the medium range, and again high mortality for larger newborn infants (5). Birthweight associated with the lowest level of perinatal mortality may be considered as being the "optimal birthweight." In all the statistics published so far,

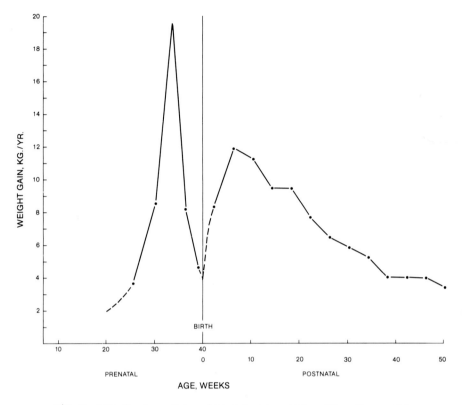

FIG. 1.   Velocity of growth in weight of singleton children. [From Tanner (4).]

this optimal birthweight is higher than the mean birthweight (6–12), suggesting that the mean fetal growth results in lower than optimal birthweights.

   To determine normal fetal growth in the human, therefore, is a doubly insoluble problem. First, it is impossible to measure fetal growth directly; even if this were possible, mean growth curves would presumably not reflect optimal fetal growth. In addition, optimal birthweight associated with the lowest perinatal mortality seems to vary considerably from one ethnic group to the other, from one population to the other, and even within the same ethnic group between socioeconomic classes. It would be between 3,800 and 4,000 g for white Americans (6), approximately 2,950 g in the poorest social groups in India (11) but 3,380 g in the upper middle class (11), 3,050 g in Ghana (10), and between 3,500 and 4,000 g in Nigeria (9). The wide range of these figures shows how difficult it is to interpret birthweight statistics. When the level of perinatal mortality for every birthweight class is not known, which is frequently the case in developing countries, it is impossible to know whether the mean fetal growth is normal: in other words, if the difference "optimal birthweight − mean birthweight" is in the usual range or, on the contrary, if there is a real problem of fetal growth retardation in a population.

In the absence of precise data on the value of optimal birthweight, it may be wiser to consider with skepticism the classic idea that a mean birthweight below the standards of industrialized countries is synonymous with insufficient fetal growth. Many nutritionists insist that the same growth standards should be adopted for all populations (13): ethnic factors seem to have little influence, if any, on growth potential before puberty (14,15). To advocate different birthweight standards for every population may seem to be a return to the past, when the extent of malnutrition in a given population could be minimized by using local standards, which included a significant number of malnourished children. Ethnic factors, however, may have an influence on postpubertal growth (14,15). Maternal size is not uniform in different populations and is known to have a more pronounced influence on fetal growth than the genetic factor. There is an important correlation between half-sibs with a common mother ($r = 0.581$), while birthweights of half-sibs with a common father are almost unrelated (16). One cannot expect to have similar birthweight statistics in populations with different maternal sizes, even though, as is likely to be the case, growth potential is the same for all during fetal life.

FACTORS LIMITING FETAL GROWTH

That fetal growth might be limited by some maternal factor does not seem to be specific to humans. In most species, the fetus rarely fully expresses its genetically determined potential for growth (17).

The classic demonstration was made as early as 1938 by crossing Shire horse with Shetland ponies (18). The birthweights of foals born to Shetland dams were similar to those of pure Shetland, while foals born to Shire dams were of similar birthweights to purebred Shires. This maternal influence, independent of genetic factors, was confirmed more recently by experiments of transplantation of fertilized eggs. Eggs of normal sized pigs transplanted into dwarf sows produced lighter than usual piglets. When the experiment is reversed, that is, when eggs from dwarf sows are transferred to normal sized mothers, the piglets are about twice the size of dwarf piglets (19). A similar predominant maternal influence on birthweight has been observed in sheep (20) and rabbits (21).

Comparative physiology provides some clue to the nature of this maternal regulation. Widdowson (22) first suggested that placental blood flow might be the main regulator of fetal growth, since plasma concentration of nutrients does not vary markedly between species, whereas placental blood flows are very different. This hypothesis is supported by the allometric relationship between maternal and fetal weight. When comparing species of different sizes, the relationship between physiological variables and body weight is not necessarily linear (23,24). The best example is basal metabolic rate, which is much lower per unit of body weight in larger species. Some variables, such as energy reserves or muscular mass, are related to body weight, whereas others, such as blood flows, are related to body surface area; others, such as blood pressure, are independent of physical size.

These relationships can be predicted by mathematical calculations, which were discovered as early as the 17th century by Galileo (23). Thus it can be demonstrated that plasma concentration of nutrients is independent of body size, as pointed out by Widdowson (22). In mathematical terms, the relationship between a physiological variable and body weight can be described by the general equation:

$$X = \text{body weight}^a$$

The coefficient a is called the "allometry coefficient," and the variable X is related linearly to body weight if $a = 1$, to the maternal surface area if $a = 0.73$, and is independent of body size if $a = 0$. This allometry coefficient can be estimated from observed values of a given variable in different species. This approach was used by Battaglia and Meschia (25) to determine the relationship between maternal and fetal size. The authors showed that fetal weight (or litter weight for polytoccus species) is related to maternal weight by the equation:

$$\text{Fetal weight} = (\text{maternal weight})^{0.75}$$

This suggests that fetal growth is regulated by an unknown factor related to body-surface area. These authors suggested that fetal growth might be limited by the fact that the fetal oxygen supply should remain only a small fraction of the total maternal oxygen uptake. A limitation of fetal size by the maternal capacity to provide the fetus with oxygen is supported by the persistence of a prolonged lactation period among placental mammals. Lactation presumably appeared earlier than placentation in mammalian evolution (26). When it appeared in early mammals, placentation offered a selective advantage, since the fetus *in utero* is strongly protected against the external environment. That lactation persisted despite the lack of protection offered to the fetus suggests that the mother's capacity to keep the fetus *in utero* is limited by an unknown factor, which could be the oxygen supply to the fetus. All the other nutrients needed for growth are provided by the mother during lactation.

That maternal nutritional reserves do not intervene in interspecies regulation of birthweight and that a factor related to maternal capacity to provide oxygen to the fetus is more likely to be involved suggest that it could be the same within the human species. To speculate on the allometric relationship between maternal and neonatal size in humans is hardly feasible, however. Lean body mass is related to the square of the height and not to its cube as a result of changing morphology in individuals of different sizes. This makes the interpretation of allometric data more difficult than in comparative physiology. It is well known, however, that birthweight is not proportional to maternal weight, as would be expected if maternal nutritional reserves regulated fetal growth. Mean birthweights of term newborn infants for different classes of maternal body weight calculated from Aberdeen standards in the United Kingdom (27) are reported in Table 1.

Heavier women have lighter newborn infants per unit of body weight. The lower birthweight compared to maternal body weight in heavier women has been long noticed but has been interpreted in nutritional terms (28). It has been postulated

TABLE 1. *Birthweight/maternal weight ratio[a]*

Maternal weight at midpregnancy (kg)	Mean birthweight (kg)	Ratio	Maternal weight at midpregnancy (kg)	Mean birthweight (kg)	Ratio
35	2.91	0.083	60	3.46	0.057
40	3.03	0.076	65	3.555	0.054
45	3.145	0.070	70	3.645	0.052
50	3.255	0.065	75	3.73	0.049
55	3.36	0.061	80	3.815	0.047

[a]Calculated from data of Thomson et al. (27).

TABLE 2. *Factors related to birthweight in Dakar, Senegal[a]*

Variable	Regression coefficient	t
Maternal weight (kg)	19	17.1
Triceps skinfold (mm)	− 17	8.5
Sex of the newborn	− 126	8.2
Parity	163	7.2

[a]Sample size, 2,456; $p < 0.001$.

that when the mother has low energy stores, there is suboptimal fetal growth with a competition between the deposition of maternal nutritional reserves and fetal needs. When the mother is well nourished, however, the fetus reaches optimal growth and the surplus of nutrients can be stored by the mother without any major further increase of birthweight. This interpretation, postulating a competition between maternal fat reserves and fetal growth with a priority either for the fetus or for the mother, depending on the availability of nutrients, would imply that birthweight would be positively related to maternal fat reserves. If this nutritional interpretation were true, low birthweights should be more frequent among women with low fat stores, whereas fatter women should have bigger newborns. We tested this hypothesis in a survey on birthweight in an underprivileged population of the periphery of Dakar. Results are reported in Table 2. Maternal triceps skinfold, which may be considered a rough estimate of maternal fat reserves, was negatively related to birthweight when adjusted for maternal body weight. In other words, birthweight was lower when maternal fat stores were higher. This result was statistically highly significant.

This result may seem surprising. Most nutritionists would assert that a good maternal nutritional status (i.e., solid energy reserves) is necessary for normal fetal growth. It seems that this inverse ralationship between maternal fat stores and birthweight has long been noticed. Classically, it is well recognized that maternal height has a noticeable influence on birthweight and that this relationship is independent of maternal weight (27,29). We also found this relationship in our sample (Table 3): adjusted for maternal weight, birthweight is higher in taller women. However, if the influence of maternal height, weight, and triceps skinfold is tested simultaneously, the relationship between maternal height and birthweight is no more significant (Table 2). This suggests that the relationship between maternal height and birthweight would only reflect the negative relationship between maternal fat stores and birthweight; for a given weight, taller women are slimmer.

The inverse relationship between maternal fat stores and birthweight is hardly compatible with the hypothesis that fetal growth is suboptimal when the mother has low energy reserves. It is difficult to explain in nutritional terms why heavier women have proportionally smaller newborns. A vascular interpretation is more attractive. All the oxygen consumed by the fetus is brought to the placenta by uterine blood flow. Uterine blood flow, as any blood flow (24), is likely to be comparatively smaller in heavier women. We suggest that fetal oxygenation limits fetal size in humans.

PLACENTAL BLOOD FLOW AND FETAL METABOLISM REGULATION

All clinical situations resulting in fetal hypoxia are associated with fetal growth retardation. When the pregnancy takes place at high altitude, the birthweight is depressed by about 100 g per 1,000 m of altitude (30). Severe maternal anemia resulting in tissue hypoxia is associated with low birthweight. When the hematocrit is below 30%, birthweight is depressed by about 100 g per 2% decrease in the packed cell volume (31). Tissue hypoxia resulting from narcotic use might be responsible for the birthweight reduction observed in drug addicts (30). Tobacco consumption is also associated with intrauterine growth retardation. This may be caused by a reduced transfer of oxygen to the fetus by a double mechanism. First, carbon dioxide causes a minor but chronic hypoxia; second, nicotine has a vaso-constrictor effect, thus reducing placental blood flow (30). The hypothesis of a decreased infant birthweight among smokers as a result of a decreased food intake does not seem tenable. There is a depression of birthweight even when maternal food intakes are maintained (32).

These observations support the hypothesis that oxygen supply to the uterus controls fetal growth. The relationship between oxygen supply and fetal size,

TABLE 3. *Influence of maternal weight and height on birthweight in Dakar, Senegal*[a]

Variable	Regression coefficient	t
Maternal weight (kg)	10.5	11.6
Parity	170	7.0
Maternal height (cm)	6.2	3.9

[a]Sample size, 2,456; $p < 0.001$.

however, is not straightforward. First, there is no evidence that the fetus is suffering from metabolic acidosis, as would be expected if its metabolism were limited by oxygen availability. This has been shown in the ewe, the cow, the mare, and in humans (33–35). Moreover, the fetus is a consumer and not a producer of lactic acid, which means that its metabolism is mainly aerobic (25). Finally, giving pure oxygen to the mother does not increase fetal oxygen consumption, which suggests that, under usual conditions, all metabolic fetal needs are met (36). Apparently, fetal metabolism is regulated by some unknown mechanism, keeping the oxygen demand below the amount brought by the uteroplacental blood flow.

Glucose is intriguing with respect to fetal nutrition because it is the only major substrate of oxidative metabolism that is not transferred actively across the placenta (37). This is in marked contrast with other essential nutrients, such as amino acids, vitamins, and minerals. One may wonder why such an active mechanism did not appear during evolution. A possible explanation could be that the absence of an active placental uptake makes glucose a potential regulator, which could adjust fetal metabolism and fetal oxygen demand to placental blood flow. A transfer of glucose to the fetus by passive diffusion implies that the amount of glucose crossing the placenta at any time is determined by physical factors and is mainly dependent on placental blood flow under usual conditions when maternal and fetal blood glucose levels are tightly controlled. A regulation of fetal metabolism by the rate of glucose transfer would make oxygen demand indirectly related to uteroplacental blood flow. This would mean that even in the absence of any sign of fetal hypoxia, fetal metabolism could be adjusted to oxygen availability.

Glucose regulates fetal metabolism at two levels. First, it is the main substrate of fetal oxidative metabolism (25). In animals, it has been estimated that, under basal conditions, 50% of fetal oxygen is used to oxidize the glucose consumed by the fetus and directly transferred from maternal circulation. Another 25% is used to oxidize lactate produced by the placenta from maternal glucose. Second, glucose stimulates fetal insulin production, which seems to act as a "fetal growth hormone," since it stimulates both fat and protein synthesis (17). Among the factors that may cause the birthweight to deviate from the mean, fetal insulin secretion seems to induce the widest variations. When the mother has a poorly controlled diabetes, a state in which fetal hyperinsulinemia is known to be present, birthweights approaching 6,000 g are not exceptional. On the other hand, diabetic newborn infants from normal mothers but who had a deficient insulin production during fetal life have a severe intrauterine growth retardation and birthweights as low as 1,250 g are reported in the literature (17).

The hypothesis of an adjustment of fetal oxygen demand by glucose transfer is further supported by experiments in sheep which show that making the fetus hyperglycemic results in a definite increase of the plasma lactate of the fetus (38) and in metabolic acidosis (39). In conclusion, if oxygen availability seems to be the factor limiting fetal size, glucose is likely to be the regulator adjusting fetal metabolism to placental blood flow and indirectly to oxygen supply.

ORIGIN OF PRETERM FETAL GROWTH FALTERING

The preterm growth faltering observed in man is intriguing. After birth, growth accelerates through "catch up" growth, as may be seen after an episode of malnutrition (4). Since fetal growth seems independent of maternal nutritional reserves, it is unlikely that the factor limiting fetal growth is nutritional. Moreover, this fetal growth faltering has been described in well-fed populations with no problems of food availability (2). Tanner (4) suggested that this could be an adaptation of the species to make delivery easier. This does not explain, however, why this growth faltering results in lower than optimal birthweights. Moreover, if this were a genetic adaptation of the species, one should observe growth irregularity in preterm newborn infants approaching their estimated date of delivery. This is not the case: growth curves of preterm newborn infants do not falter before 40 weeks of gestational age (40).

This growth irregularity appears much more like an imperfection of the species than an adaptation. According to the laws of evolution, this type of minor imperfection can occur when there is a rapid change in the genetic heritage, giving an important selective advantage to the species. This has suggested the hypothesis that the slight preterm growth faltering could be an imperfection appearing as a result of the acquisition of upright posture (41). This human acquisition with large selective advantages results in perturbations of the cardiovascular system and of the supply of blood flow to the uterus. This could explain why the organism is not able to sustain fetal growth at an optimal level up to the end of intrauterine life. Upright posture is associated with a marked lumbar lordosis, which compresses the aorta before the origin of the uterine arteries. It also results in a decrease of plasma volume and cardiac output, which is corrected by an increased sympathetic activity and does not seem to protect the fetus (42).

Recently, this hypothesis has been questioned, since there is no preterm faltering of abdominal growth curves measured *in utero* by ultrasound (1). If this fetal growth faltering is attributable to a reduced placental blood flow, abdominal growth should be more affected than fetal head growth, which does not appear to be the case. Actually, fetal growth curves (1,3) are incompatible not only with the above hypothesis but also with the most widely used fetal growth standards. Before 35 weeks of pregnancy, fetal weekly weight gain is estimated to be approximately 300 g and only 100 g between 39 and 40 weeks (43). Ultrasound estimates suggest that fetal head growth velocity peaks at 25 g per week at 30 weeks of gestational age and falls to 15 g per week before term (1). Obviously, fetal head growth faltering does not explain fetal weight gain faltering. Presumably, all organs have a low growth velocity before birth, yet abdominal growth continues steadily. Abdominal circumference measurements *in utero* are influenced by fetal position (3), which is constantly changing during fetal life. It is more reasonable, therefore, to doubt the general shape of intrauterine abdominal curves. Otherwise, one should have to admit that the 200 g per week decrease of fetal velocity results mainly from the growth faltering of nonabdominal organs, which is not supported by postmortem studies of growth-retarded stillborns or neonates (44).

African women have a pronounced lumbar lordosis. They give birth to newborn infants lighter than Europeans; this has often been interpreted in nutritional terms. In Table 4, however, we report the birthweight of African babies in a periurban community with no problems of food availability. Birthweights were calculated for different classes of maternal weights which, one may assume, reduces or even eliminates the nutritional factor. These values were obtained with a regression equation derived from our data and compared to Aberdeen standards (27). The difference in birthweight is, on the average, 375 g. This difference may be attributable to an increased compression of uterine arteries by a marked lumbar lordosis. None of the other factors known to influence birthweight could account for such a difference. This may be indirect evidence that the acquisition of lumbar lordosis results in impaired fetal growth.

THE FETUS AS NUTRITIONAL VICTIM

That fetal growth seems to be unrelated to maternal energy reserves and to depend mainly on the mother's ability to provide oxygen is in agreement with the idea of the fetus being a perfect nutritional parasite. Under certain circumstances, however, fetal growth seems to be sacrificed to protect maternal nutritional reserves.

During the Dutch famine of 1944–1945, there was a sharp birthweight depression of more than 300 g when the mean maternal weight after delivery decreased only 2.5 kg (45). According to usual standards of birthweights related to maternal weight (27), such a minor variation of maternal weight should have resulted in a birthweight depression of less than 50 g.

What was observed in Holland during the famine occurs every year in many rural Third World communities when there is a food shortage just before the harvest, when mothers must sustain heavy physical activity. This phenomenon was described by Prentice et al. (46,47) in The Gambia. Their data show that during the rainy season, there is a depression of birthweight of 160 g when the mothers on average are 3 kg lighter. According to birthweight standards from Dakar, which

TABLE 4. *Comparison of birthweight in different classes of maternal body weight in Dakar and in Aberdeen[a]*

Maternal weight (kg)	Birthweight (g)		Maternal weight (kg)	Birthweight (g)	
	Dakar	Aberdeen[b]		Dakar	Aberdeen[b]
35	2,730	2,910	60	3,050	3,460
40	2,790	3,030	65	3,110	3,555
45	2,855	3,145	70	3,175	3,645
50	2,920	3,255	75	3,240	3,730
55	2,980	3,360	80	3,305	3,815

[a]All parity groups
[b]Data from Thomson et al. (27).

were collected in an ethnically similar population, this diminution of maternal weight should have resulted in a birthweight depression of only 60 g (see Table 2).

Several years ago, a high-protein low-carbohydrate diet was supposed to reduce the incidence of preeclampsia. In Motherwell, Scotland, the obstetrician in charge of the only maternity hospital between 1938 and 1977 insisted that all pregnant women, even in the absence of any sign of preeclampsia, should follow this diet, which resulted in an acute decrease of maternal total energy intake (48). At 20 weeks of pregnancy, women were slightly lighter than in Aberdeen, a nearby community where the diet was not prescribed but which was similar to Motherwell in all other respects. Although this difference of maternal weight was not significant, birthweights in the two communities were very different: newborn infants in Motherwell on average were 300 g lighter. According to Aberdeen standards (27), this birthweight difference is usually observed when differences of maternal weight of approximately 15 kg are seen.

Contrary to previous traditional thought, these observations suggest that the fetus is not a parasite but is a victim when there is decreased maternal food intake. This is not contradictory with our hypothesis about fetal growth regulation—that birthweight might decrease when maternal energy reserves are hardly depressed. This may even be considered evidence of birthweight regulation independent of maternal reserves.

Acute food shortage is the common characteristic of all situations, suggesting that the fetus is a victim when the mother is malnourished. Metabolic adjustments occurring during an acute depression of food intake were studied extensively in animals. These result in faltering of fetal growth, presumably by the following mechanism (25,49). Maternal fasting is associated with a decrease of maternal glucose plasma levels. Since glucose crosses the placenta by a facilitated diffusion mechanism, this results in fetal hypoglycemia. Fetal insulin production is depressed, and there is a reduction of fetal metabolism and growth.

That glucose could regulate fetal metabolism makes the fetus sensitive to maternal fasting, regardless of the extent of maternal fat reserves. In mammals, there is no enzymatic system allowing a transformation of fatty acids into glucose (49). When the 70 or 90 g of hepatic glycogen reserves are exhausted, that is, after a few hours, fasting results in hypoglycemia. Keeping glucose to a tolerable level is possible only by gluconeogenesis from muscle amino acid. During maternal fasting, the fetus can presumably use some alternate fuels, such as fatty and ketonic bodies (25,49). These substances do not stimulate fetal insulin production, however, and allow only limited fetal metabolic activity. The slowing down of fetal metabolism in only a few hours, well before maternal energy reserves are seriously depressed, suggests that during fasting, the conservation of maternal energy reserves is a priority compared to sustaining optimal fetal metabolism.

All the metabolic adjustments that occur during maternal fasting are associated with modifications of cardiovascular physiology, which combine with the depressed plasma nutrient levels to decrease the nutrient flow in the placenta. In man, fasting results in decreased blood volume (50), decreased cardiac volume, and lowered blood pressure (51). These vascular modifications are likely to reduce placental blood flow. They occur well before maternal energy reserves are seriously depressed. In animals, the same physiological adjustments to fasting have been reported, and their effects on placental perfusion have been measured. In pregnant rats (52), when maternal food intake is reduced by 50%, there is an inadequate plasma volume expansion during pregnancy, a reduced cardiac output, and a reduced placental blood flow. In the pregnant ewe (53), the cardiac output remains unchanged compared to controls when food intake is reduced, but there is a redistribution of cardiac output toward the liver at the expense of uteroplacental blood flow, which decreases by about 25%.

When the cardiovascular function is deficient, the organism usually reacts by an activation of the sympathetic nervous system with an increased secretion of catecholamines. The type of vascular redistribution observed in the pregnant ewe during fasting suggests that this reaction is also activated by acute malnutrition (53). The involvement of the sympathetic nervous system would make the fetus a victim during maternal fasting. This reaction is activated in emergency situations only, when maternal life is in danger. Animal experiments suggest that it does not protect placental perfusion (42). Hard muscular work could have the same effect (54). Physical activity, especially if performed in a hot environment, results in increased sympathetic nervous activity, which likely provokes a reduced placental blood flow (42).

THE FETUS AS PERFECT PARASITE

If one excepts fasting, during which maternal metabolism is disturbed, the plasma level of glucose is under the tight control of a complex hormonal mechanism. If fetal growth is regulated by the placental glucose flow, this control makes the fetus a perfect parasite, especially when considering that it plays a role in regulating maternal hormonal balance.

At the beginning of pregnancy, when fetal energy needs are minimal, progesterone produced by the placenta results in maternal fat storage following an increased dietary intake and a reduction in energy expenditure (30). Progressively, during the third trimester of pregnancy, this deposition of fat decreases; this has been attributed to a progesterone antagonist, estriol, also produced by the fetoplacental unit (55). At the end of pregnancy, there is a lipolysis, with fasting plasma fatty acid levels up to 5 times those observed in nonpregnant women. This appears to be due to the action of human placental lactogen (HPL), which induces an increased peripheral resistance to insulin (55). This alteration in fat metabolism provides an alternative fuel source for the energy needs of maternal tissues and so spares glucose for use by the fetus. At this stage, the fetus seems to have an absolute priority over the deposition of fat by the mother. Since there is an increased peripheral resistance to insulin, the mother can lay down fat only when there is a frank hyperglycemic peak, during which the fetus itself becomes hyperglycemic and fetal growth is stimulated by an increased fetal insulin production. The fetus might also be able to stimulate muscle protein breakdown by a hormonal mechanism and to reuse muscle amino acids for the synthesis of new tissues.

At the end of pregnancy, there is a raised excretion of 3-methylhistidine by the mother, which seems to reflect an increased muscle catabolism (55). This increased amino acid turnover probably is related to an upsurge in estrogen production by the fetoplacental unit. It may protect the fetus against the variations of maternal protein intake, muscle mass being a virtually limitless reserve of amino acids, which can be transformed rapidly and efficiently into fetal proteins.

In conclusion, under usual conditions, the fetus may be considered as a perfect parasite. In contrast, when there is maternal fasting and when the mother becomes hypoglycemic, there is a depression of cardiovascular function and the fetus is victimized.

ENERGY REQUIREMENTS OF PREGNANT WOMEN

According to FAO/WHO recommendations (56), a pregnant woman should receive a daily supplement of 1.2 MJ (or 285 kcal), which amounts to a total of 335 MJ for the entire period of pregnancy (80,000 kcal). This is in addition to a diet providing 9.2 MJ per day (2,200 kcal) and is equivalent to a total daily intake of 10.4 MJ (2,485 kcal).

In most developing countries, food intakes of pregnant women are much lower. In West Africa and in India, for instance, daily energy intakes of about 1,400 kcal are often reported, and a daily intake below 2,000 kcal appears to be the rule in most developing tropical countries (46). This difference between observed energy intakes and internationally recommended values is reported constantly from one survey to another; it is difficult to believe that it results from an underestimation of food consumption.

This difference may be interpreted in several ways. Women can be considered as having grossly insufficient energy intakes. This would imply that they produce a fraction of the energy they need from fat stores or, alternatively, that they reduce their energy expenditure by feeding a small fetus with reduced energy needs.

The first interpretation would mean that in societies where energy intakes are low, and pregnancies are frequent and followed by a prolonged energy-demanding lactation, there should be a progressive deterioration of maternal nutritional status with parity. In West Africa, where all these conditions are met, one should observe a rapid maternal wasting in rural zones, since most women are energy deficient according to international standards. This is far from being the case, however. Table 5 shows the mean body weights of a sample of rural women in the poorest zones of Upper Volta and Mali. Their weight remains constant with parity, although the survey showed that the average interval between two deliveries was approximately 2.4 years. In rural Gambia, similar results were obtained from a smaller sample (47). It seems that despite energy intakes well below internationally recommended allowances, these women are in energy balance during all their reproductive years.

Pregnancy and lactation are notably successful in populations with low energy intakes. The main difference compared to affluent societies is that mean birthweight

TABLE 5. *Body weight and parity in rural Sahelian women[a]*

Parity group	No. of women (N = 460)	Weight (kg) Mean	SD	Parity group	No. of women (N = 460)	Weight (kg) Mean	SD
0	60	49.7	8.4	5	46	53.5	6.7
1	56	52.5	8.1	6	43	52.5	6.0
2	52	52.8	7.3	7	34	52.2	6.1
3	67	53.2	6.3	8	27	53.9	6.6
4	42	51.5	6.3	9 and over	33	54.7	6.2

[a]Data from E. Bénéfice and A. Briend *(unpublished data).*

is lower (47). This does not mean that there is a birthweight deficit, however. To interpret a low mean birthweight, one must compare it with the local optimal birthweight associated with the lowest perinatal mortality. Our data on the relationship between perinatal mortality and birthweight in poor communities with no possibility of cesarean section suggest that this deficit, if present, may be much lower than usually assumed by a crude comparison of mean birthweights with European standards.

A low mean birthweight may be seen from a teleological point of view as a maternal adaptation to produce an infant with lower nutritional needs when food is scarce. It may seem more advantageous for the species that a mother give birth to a small baby with low energy needs rather than to a normal sized baby (57). This interpretation is debatable: after birth, the mother can tap the energy she needs for lactation from her fat stores, in contrast to what happens during pregnancy. Adjusting the size of the newborn to maternal lactating capacities would imply a regulation of birthweight by maternal fat stores, which does not seem to be the case.

So far, there is no evidence that energy intakes below internationally recommended allowances result in altered reproductive ability. An alternative interpretation must be sought considering that these women are able to give birth to a child every 2 years, to breastfeed him for 18 months or more without losing weight during the reproductive years, and have energy intakes nearly 4 MJ (1,000 kcal) below their theoretical requirements. A possible conclusion is that their needs are overestimated.

To estimate the energy cost of pregnancy, several approaches are possible. One can observe healthy, well-nourished pregnant women, estimate the energy value of the tissues synthesized by the mother and the fetus, and add to it the energy required to cover the extra metabolic needs. This approach, used by the 1973 WHO/FAO committee (56), has several limitations. First, the women who were used to calculate the recommended allowances had newborns with a birthweight higher than the mean birthweight observed in less affluent communities. This resulted in higher estimates of energy requirements. It seems inappropriate to set these as international standards, since mean birthweights observed in industrialized countries are higher than optimal birthweight in other communities. On the other hand, it is by no means clear whether the women consumed during pregnancy the exact quantity of energy they needed and no more. Approximately half the energy needs estimated by FAO/WHO are intended to cover the cost of the deposition of 3.5 kg of fat by the mother, which is supposed to be a prerequisite for good lactation. Most women in poor societies do not lay down that much fat and yet breastfeed their babies successfully (47). One wonders whether all this extra fat is necessary.

An epidemiological approach would be more appropriate to estimate the energy needs of pregnant women. Theoretically, the ideal method would be to observe pregnancy in populations with various energy intakes, to determine at which level pregnancy is less successful, and to test whether energy supplementation will improve its outcome.

Increasing maternal energy intake does seem to improve fetal growth in situations of acute food shortage. In The Gambia, the birthweight depression observed during the rainy season could be corrected by an appropriate nutritional intervention (58). In chronic situations, where maternal energy intakes are low but regular, the situation is not as clear.

One of the first supplementation studies carried out in Guatemala (59) on women who had energy intakes below 1500 kcal before intervention is often quoted as evidence that energy supplementation in undernourished populations increases birthweight. It is not clear, however, whether this study, conducted in a rural community, dealt with a chronic situation and if the reported effects of food supplementation were due to the correction of periods of acute shortage occurring throughout the year.

This intervention initially was designed to test the influence of a protein supplement on fetal growth. The supplement was distributed in two of four experimental villages. At the end of the intervention, when it appeared that this protein supplement had no effect on birthweight, the data were used to test whether there was a relationship between energy supplementation during pregnancy and birthweight. In the original publication, there was a small correlation ($r = 0.135$) which, taking into account the large sample size, was statistically significant. The authors deduced from this result that there was a causal link between energy supplementation and increased birthweight. The design of the study, however, did not allow this conclusion. The protein supplement was randomly given, but the energy supplement was determined by the mothers themselves. In other words, this study, as far as energy was concerned, was not a supplementation of randomly selected women but an observation of self-selected patients. A bias due to the selection of women who tended to have heavier newborns must be considered. The authors tried to overcome this problem by testing whether this relationship might be explained by the effect of some confounding factor.

The potential confounding variables that were analyzed accounted for only 16% of birthweight variance. None was related to maternal cardiovascular characteristics, which were the most likely to influence birthweight. A noncausal interpretation of the observed correlation between birthweight and energy supplementation was not ruled out. To estimate *a posteriori* the results of this intervention, the best approach would be to compare the mean birthweight in the villages before and after supplementation. This estimation from available data (59) gives an increase of mean birthweight of about 50 g. A similar increase of mean birthweight was also observed in most nutritional experiments carried out in women with low energy intakes in Colombia (60), Taiwan (61), New York (62), and Montreal (63). There was no increase of the mean birthweight during the dry season in The Gambia (58).

All these interventions had a low efficiency (64). On average, the increase of birthweight was about 30 g for 10,000 kcal, which is extremely low considering that according to international estimates (56), the energy cost of a normal pregnancy resulting in the birth of a 3,300 g newborn is 40,000 kcal, if one excludes the cost of maternal fat deposition. Obviously, a minor fraction of the energy supplement is used for fetal growth. This does not support the hypothesis that these interventions increased the mean birthweight by correcting a fetal energy deficit, especially when one considers that when there is no acute maternal wasting, the fetus seems to have priority over the constitution of maternal energy stores.

Presumably, the effect of these supplementations on birthweight is to result in higher postprandial hyperglycemic peaks, which promote the synthesis of fetal tissues through the secretion of insulin by the fetus. Since maternal glucose level is tightly controlled in normal nondiabetic women, the effect of such supplementations is bound to be limited.

In principle, women involved in supplementation studies were given as much food as they wanted. Assuming that the small birthweight increase resulting from supplementation was associated with lower perinatal mortality, the food intake after supplementation would be equivalent to the energy needs of the mothers. In none of these studies did energy intake after supplementation approach the internationally recommended allowances. In Guatemala (59), after supplementation, women consumed an average of 1,525 kcal/day; in Colombia (60), 1,765 kcal; and in The Gambia, 1,900 kcal (58). This suggests that if international allowances were derived from observations on Third World women eating *ad libitum*, the conclusion would be that pregnant women in affluent societies eat too much.

There is evidence that internationally recommended energy intakes for pregnant women are overestimated. There is no solid epidemiological basis, however, to give more reasonable estimates. The small birthweight increase obtained by maternal supplementation in populations with low energy intakes is not sufficient to conclude that these women are energy deficient.

PRIORITIES

In communities where cereals are the staple food, there is no evidence that increasing protein intake results in an improved pregnancy outcome (59). Even among the poorest, increasing the maternal protein intake during pregnancy is not a priority. No intervention has been attempted to increase the protein intake of women living on a diet with roots as a staple food and who are the most likely to have insufficient protein intake.

With respect to energy, the present attitude of most international bodies, namely, that increasing maternal energy intake is a priority in communities with a low mean birthweight, must be debated. It is controversial to consider that fetal growth is independent of maternal energy reserves, the reverse opinion being almost a dogma among nutritionists. This, however, is our conclusion; it implies a less straightforward attitude toward maternal energy supplementation.

In communities where there is an acute food shortage, such as observed in many Third World rural communities before harvest or during wars or natural cataclysms, giving food to pregnant women is a priority. There is much evidence that in these situations, the fetus is a victim and suffers severely, well before maternal nutritional reserves are seriously depressed. If women take part in heavy agricultural work, they should stop working or reduce their activity at the end of pregnancy. This could be even more important than giving them extra food: it is possible that muscular work results in reduced uteroplacental blood flow, even if the mother is not malnourished (42). "Rest is best" could be the most appropriate message for these communities.

In communities with chronically low energy intakes below those internationally recommended and where the mean birthweight is lower than Western standards, the need for an untargeted maternal supplementation is debatable. Recommended food intakes may be overestimated, and birthweight standards from affluent societies may be irrelevant in these communities.

In poor countries with limited health budgets, any nutritional program competes with other programs. What is the priority? To give the possibility to all women living in developing countries to deliver their babies under hygienic conditions with a possibility of cesarean section and blood transfusion when needed, even in the most remote areas? Or to insist on these women receiving an energy intake equivalent to the theoretically estimated needs? We know that in terms of maternal and neonatal mortality, the first option is rewarding. So far, there is no evidence that random nutritional intervention, when there is no acute food shortage, has much effect.

REFERENCES

1. Meire HB. Ultrasound assessment of fetal growth. Br Med Bull 1981;37:253–58.
2. Gruenwald P, ed. The placenta and its maternal supply line. Lancaster: Medical and Technical Publishing Co., 1975:1–17.
3. Campbell S. Fetal growth. In: Beart RW, Nathnielsz P, eds. Fetal physiology and medicine. London: WB Saunders, 1976:271–301.
4. Tanner JM. Foetus into man: physical growth from conception to maturity. London: Open Books, 1978:37–51.
5. Van Valen L, Mellin GW. Selection in natural populations—New York babies (fetal life study). Ann Hum Genet 1967;31:109–27.
6. Chinnici JP, Sansing G. Mortality rates, optimal and discriminating birth weights between white and non-white single births in Virginia (1955–1973). Hum Biol 1977;49:335–48.

7. Ellis WS. Mortality and birth weight in Philadelphia Blacks: an example of stabilizing selection. Am J Phys Anthrop 1973;38:145–9.
8. Goldstein H. Factors related to birth weight and perinatal mortality. Br Med Bull 1981;37:259–64.
9. Harrison KA. Approaches to reducing maternal and perinatal mortality in Africa. In: Philpott RH, ed. Maternity services in the developing world—What the community needs. London: Royal College of Obstetricians and Gynaecologists, 1979:52–69.
10. Hollingsworth MJ. Observations on the birth weights and survival of African babies: single births. Ann Hum Genet 1965;28:291–300.
11. Jayant K. Birth weight and some other factors in relation to infant survival. A study of an Indian sample. Ann Hum Genet 1964;27:261–7.
12. Lubchenco LO, Brazie JV. Neonatal mortality rate: relationship to birth weight and gestational age. J Pediatr 1972;81:814–22.
13. Habicht JP, Martorell R, Yarbrough C, Malina RM, Klein RE. Height and weight standards for pre-school children. How relevant are ethnic differences in growth potential? Lancet 1974;I:611–5.
14. Eveleth PB, Tanner JM. Worldwide variations in human growth. London: Cambridge University Press, 1976.
15. Rona RJ. Genetic and environmental factors in the control of growth in childhood. Br Med Bull 1981;37:265–72.
16. Morton NE. The inheritance of human birth weight. Ann Hum Genet 1955;20:125–34.
17. Liggins GC. The drive to fetal growth. In: Beard RW, Nathanilesz, P, eds. Fetal physiology and medicine. London: WB Saunders, 1976:254–70.
18. Walton A, Hammond J. Maternal effects on growth and conformation in Shire horse—Shetland poney crosses. Proc R Soc Lond 1938;125B:311–35.
19. Smidt D, Steinbach J, Scheven B. Die Beeinflussung der prä- und postnatalen Entwicklung durch Grösse und Korpergewicht der Mutter, dargestellt an Ergebnissen reziproker Eitransplantationen zwischen Zwergschweinen und grossen Hausschweinen. Monatsschr Kinderheilkd 1967;115:533.
20. Hunter GL. Maternal influence on size in sheep. J Agric Sci 1956;48:36–60.
21. Venge O. Maternal influence on birth weight in rabbits. Acta Zool 1950;31:1–8.
22. Widdowson EM. How the fetus is fed. Proc Nutr Soc 1969;28:17–24.
23. Astrand PO, Rodahl K. Textbook of work physiology. New York: McGraw-Hill, 1977;369–88.
24. Gunther B. Dimensional analysis and theory of biological similarity. Phys Rev 1975;55:659–99.
25. Battaglia FC, Meschia G. Principal substrates of fetal metabolism. Phys Rev 1978;58:499–527.
26. Jelliffe DB, Jelliffe EFP. Human milk in the modern world. Oxford: Oxford University Press, 1978.
27. Thomson AM, Billewicz WZ, Hytten FE. The assessment of fetal growth. J Obstet Gynaecol Br Cwlth 1968;75:903–16.
28. Rosso P. Nutrition and maternal-fetal exchange. Am J Clin Nutr 1981;34:744–55.
29. Hytten FE, Leitch I. The physiology of human pregnancy. 2nd ed. Oxford: Blackwell Scientific Publications, 1971.
30. Hytten FE, Chamberlain G, eds. Clinical physiology in obstetrics. Oxford: Blackwell Scientific Publications, 1980.
31. Harrison KA, Ibeziako PA. Maternal anaemia and fetal birth weight. J Obstet Gynaecol Br Cwlth 1973;80:798–804.
32. Haworth JC, Ellestad-Sayed JJ, King J, Dilling LA. Fetal growth retardation in cigarette smoking mothers is not due to decreased maternal food intake. Am J Obstet Gynecol 1980;137:719–23.
33. Comline RS, Silver M. A comparative study of blood gas tensions, oxygen affinity and red cell 2,3 DPG concentrations in foetal and maternal blood in the mare, cow and sow. J Physiol Lond 1974;242:805–26.
34. Comline RS, Silver M. Placental transfer of blood gases. Br Med Bull 1975;31:25–31.
35. Rooth G, Jacobson L, Heinrich J, Seidenschnur G. The acid-base status of the fetus during normal labor. In: Longo LD, Bartels H, eds. Respiratory gas exchange and blood flow in the placenta. Washington DC: Dept. Health, Education and Welfare, 1972:477–86.
36. Battaglia FC, Meschia G, Makowski E, Bowes W. The effect of maternal oxygen inhalation upon fetal oxygenation. J Clin Invest 1968;47:548–55.
37. Hytten FE. Nutrition in pregnancy. In: Talhamer O, Baumgarten K, Pollack A, eds. 6th European Congress of Perinatal Medicine. Sttuttgart: Thieme Publishers, 1979:34–43.

38. Shelley HJ, Basset JM, Milner RDG. Control of carbohydrate metabolism in the fetus and newborn. Br Med Bull 1975;31:37–43.
39. Robillard JE, Sessions C, Kenedy RL, Smith FG. Metabolic effects of constant hypertonic glucose infusion in well oxygenated fetuses. Am J Obstet Gynecol 1977:130:199–203.
40. Brandt I. Growth dynamics of low birth weight infants with emphasis on the perinatal period. In: Falkner F, Tanner JM, eds. Human growth vol. 2. New York:Plenum, 1978:557–617.
41. Briend A. Fetal malnutrition—the price of upright posture? Br Med J 1979;2:317–9.
42. Briend A. Maternal physical activity, birth weight and perinatal mortality. Med. Hypotheses 1980;6:1157–1170.
43. Tanner JM, Thomson AM. Standards for birth weight at gestation periods from 32 to 42 weeks, allowing for maternal height and weight. Arch Dis Child 1970;45:566–9.
44. Naeye RL. Malnutrition as a probable cause of fetal growth retardation. Arch Pathol 1965;79:284–91.
45. Stein Z, Susser M, Saenger G, Marolla F. Famine and human development. New York: Oxford University Press, 1975.
46. Prentice AM. Variations in maternal dietary intake, birth weight and breast milk output in the Gambia. In: Aebi H, Whitehead RG, eds. Maternal nutrition during pregnancy and lactation. Bern: Hans Huber, 1980:167–83.
47. Prentice AM, Whitehead RG, Roberts SB, Paul AA. Long term energy balance in child bearing Gambian women. Am J Clin Nutr 1981;34:2790–9.
48. Kerr JF, Campbell-Brown BM, Johstone FD. Dieting in pregnancy: a study of the effects of a high protein low carbohydrate diet on birth weight in an obstetric population. In: Sutherland HW, Stowers JM, eds. Carbohydrate metabolism in pregnancy and the newborn. Berlin: Springer Verlag, 1979:518–34.
49. Adam PA, Felig P. Carbohydrate, fat and amino acid metabolism in the pregnant women and fetus. In: Falkner F, Tanner JM, eds. Human growth vol. 1. New York: Plenum, 1978;461–547.
50. Bloom WL, Azar G, Smith EG. Changes in heart size and plasma volume during fasting. Metabolism 1966;15:409–13.
51. Gottdiener JS, Gross HA, Henry WL, Borer JS, Ebert MH. Effects of self induced starvation on cardiac size and function in anorexia nervosa. Circulation 1978;58:425–33.
52. Kava R, Rosso P. Effects of food restriction on cardiac output and blood flow to the uterus and placenta in the pregnant rat. J Nutr 1980;110:2350–4.
53. Morris PH, Rosenfeld CR, Crandell SS, Adcock III EW. Effects of fasting on uterine blood flow and substrate uptake in sheep. J Nutr 1980;110:2433–43.
54. Tafari N, Naeye RL, Gobezie A. Effects of maternal malnutrition and heavy physical work during pregnancy on birth weight. Br J Obstet Gynaecol 1980;87:222–6.
55. Naismith DJ. Endocrine factors in the control of nutrient utilisation in pregnancy. In: Aebi H, Whitehead RG, eds. Maternal nutrition during pregnancy and lactation. Bern: Hans Huber, 1980:16–26.
56. FAO/WHO. Energy and protein requirements. Geneva: WHO tech. rep. series 522, 1973.
57. Rosso P, Gramoy C. Nutrition and pregnancy. In: Winick M, ed. Nutrition, pre- and postnatal development. New York: Plenum, 1979:133–228.
58. Prentice AM, Whitehead RG, Watkinson M, Lamb WH, Cole TJ. Prenatal dietary supplementation of African women and birth weight. Lancet 1983;1:489–92.
59. Lechtig A, Habicht JP, Delgado H, Klein RE, Yarbrough C, Martorell R. Effect of food supplementation during pregnancy on birth weight. Pediatrics 1975;56:508–20.
60. Mora JO, Paredes B, Wagner M, de Navarro L, Suescun J, Christiansen N, Herrera MG. Nutritional supplementation and the outcome of pregnancy. I Birth weight. Am J Clin Nutr 1979;32:455–62.
61. Mac Donald EC, Pollit E, Mueller WH, Hsueh AM, Sherwin R. The Bacon Chow study: Maternal nutritional supplementation and birth weight. Am J Clin Nutr 1981;34:2133–44.
62. Rush D, Stein Z, Susser M. A randomized controlled trial of prenatal nutritional supplementation in New York City. Pediatrics 1980;65:683–97.
63. Rush D. Nutritional services during pregnancy and birth weight. A retrospective matched-pair analysis. Can Med Assoc J 1980;125:567–76.
64. Stein Z, Susser M, Rush D. Prenatal nutrition and birth weight: experiments and quasi experiments in the past decade. J Reprod Med 1978;21:287–99.

DISCUSSION

Dr. Waterlow: From the data you have produced, the evidence suggests that the birth-weight of the baby is related to the mother's lean body mass. This would explain the kind of relationship you have shown to both weight and height.

Dr. Lechtig: The hypothesis that maternal nutrition is related to fetal growth does not exclude the importance of other factors on fetal growth, such as diarrhea during pregnancy, intrauterine infections, bacteriuria, smoking, and hard physical work. These factors usually interact in a complex way, and most act through nutritional mechanisms.

In large samples from Latin American populations, there is evidence of a consistent association between subcutaneous fat and arm muscle measurements with birthweight, after controlling for maternal height and sex of the baby. These data suggest that maternal "reserves" could be used to some extent for fetal growth.

In the human species, the reproductive process has a remarkable capacity to adapt to chronic, moderate deficits in dietary intake. The price, however, is low weight gain during pregnancy, low birthweight, postnatal stunting, low maternal height, lower nutrient require-ments, and some degree of suboptimal mental development. This adaptation process, however successful it is to keep the species alive in an unfavorable environment, should not be a reason for not improving the dietary intake in these populations.

Finally, a question: did you explore the contribution of weight gain during pregnancy to birthweight prediction in addition to that of prepregnancy weight? Were there any significant interactions between both independent variables?

Dr. Briend: The results you quote about the relationship between maternal skinfold and birthweight do not seem to be in conflict with my data. I observed a negative correlation between these two variables after controlling for maternal weight and not for maternal height. That an even stronger association exists between birthweight and the indicators of lean body mass is in support of my hypothesis of an indirect regulation of birthweight by lean body mass.

I have no personal data on the relationship between maternal weight gain during pregnancy and birthweight. In most studies published so far, there is a strong correlation between these two variables. It is unwise, however, to take for granted that this relationship should be interpreted in nutritional terms only. Water storage and plasma volume expansion are both related to birthweight and to maternal weight gain. This suggests that the relationship between maternal weight gain and birthweight might be indirect and due mainly to the interaction of an unknown vascular variable.

Dr. Lechtig: Most of the mechanisms responsible for the effect of intense physical activity during pregnancy on birthweight are of a nutritional nature, for example, higher energy expenditure or lower provision of blood nutrients to the cells. Thus data supporting an effect of physical activity on birthweight do not conflict; indeed, it may contribute evidence to the nutritional hypothesis. In poor populations, resting daily during 2 to 3 hr may be equivalent to supplementing 100 to 200 kcal per day.

Dr. Waterlow: Would Dr. Lechtig or Dr. Briend expect a Guatemalan woman who is very small to produce under normal circumstances a child of the same birthweight as a tall West African woman? I am not suggesting that these are ethnic differences in birthweight, because the small size of the Guatemalan woman is probably largely imposed by environmental influences in the past, but is a 2.5 kg baby from a small mother necessarily any worse than a 3 kg baby from a larger mother?

Dr. Lechtig: As mentioned in my chapter, one way of estimating impact on birthweight is through changes in the proportion of low birthweight babies. Its public health significance arises from the known relationship between low weight at birth and higher risk of infant and neonatal mortality. We have found in a sample of Guatemalan babies that about 90% of neonatal deaths occurred in the group of low birthweight infants. Thus it appears that in poor populations, when a baby weighs less than 2.5 kg at birth, his risk of dying is notably higher than that of babies with a higher birthweight. Although maternal height, parity, birth interval, and other characteristics influence the magnitude of the association between low birthweight and risk of death, they do not change the basic conclusion.

Although maternal height is associated with birthweight, short mothers (less than 147 cm) may show less than 5% of low birthweight babies when they are supplemented during pregnancy or pertain to the high socioeconomic group in rural villages.

Also, tall mothers (≥ 147 cm) may have as high as 20% of low birthweight babies when they pertain to the low socioeconomic group and do not have appropriate food supplementation during pregnancy. Therefore, although short mothers show a trend toward lower birthweight babies, they are able to decrease the proportion of these babies down to figures usually seen in middle class, white populations in the United States.

I would also like to point out that the average increase in birthweight needed to decrease the proportion of low birthweight babies is relatively small. In most poor populations, it ranges between 100 and 300 g. Under these circumstances, the maximum increment expected in head circumference (about 1 cm) would not be enough to significantly increase the risk of cephalopelvic disproportion. This may be the reason for not observing an increase in the incidence of cephalopelvic disproportion after successful nutritional interventions.

Dr. Briend: To estimate the impact of a nutritional intervention, one must take into account the situation of the community where it takes place. If there is an acute food shortage, the intervention is bound to be effective. In situations where food intake is low but regular, the effects of such an intervention are not so clear. This was apparent in The Gambia, where food supplementation was effective in increasing birthweight only during the rainy season, before the harvest.

Dr. Whitehead: I will briefly summarize what we have recently published in *The Lancet.* When food intake during pregnancy in rural Gambian mothers is 1,600 kcal/kg/day or more, the average birthweight of babies is remarkably normal. It is only during times of the year when average energy intakes fall well below this average, particularly during the last trimester, that birthweight is seriously affected. If a dietary supplement is given to the mother during this period of extreme food deprivation, then a significant increase in birthweight can be produced. In our study, this increase was on average 225 g; we also reduced the incidence of small-for-dates babies from 30% down to about 5%. Our data thus demonstrate the tremendous ability of a mother to adapt to low energy intakes as well as the fact that there is a threshold to this adaptation below which the growth and development of the fetus are adversely affected.

Dr. Briend: Is this a threshold effect or an acute shortage effect? If the intake of a mother who is obese and whose intake is adjusted to 2,200 kcal drops to 1,800 kcal, she would still be well above the mean energy intake observed in The Gambia; this fasting effect, however, will reduce blood volume and blood perfusion of the placenta.

Dr. Whitehead: We do not suggest that the "threshold" value we found in The Gambia is applicable all over the world. It is important that this phenomenon be studied in a number of countries with differing socioeconomic backgrounds. We must also know more about the range of individual requirements within these environments. Only when we have all this information at our disposal will we be able to provide recommended dietary allowances for pregnant women with a greater degree of confidence than we can at the moment.

Dr. Mata: Dr. Briend's chapter enlightens us on the physiological approach to understanding the genesis of low birthweight in developing countries. There is much skepticism about the relationship between diet in pregnancy and birthweight. For instance, Australian workers cannot explain the relatively good birthweight of infants from aboriginal women in the presence of poor food intake during pregnancy and low pregnancy weight gain. What is fascinating in Dr. Briend's chapter is the emphasis given to uteroplacental blood flow in the dynamics of fetal growth. In our studies with Mayan women, who consume 1,800 to 2,000 kcal normally, but who are very short, no correlation was observed between low birthweight and pregnancy diet, but a correlation was noted with maternal weight and especially with height. Over 4 years, during which 40% of the entire village population consumed the best possible mixture of soya flour supplemented with lysine, vitamins, and iron, no changes were induced in birthweight or in postnatal physical growth. On the other hand, women in the Guatemalan highlands spend half their time inside homes, cooking and inhaling smoke from the hearth, a situation that may contribute to the high incidence of intrauterine growth retardation. This risk has disappeared in Costa Rica and Panama (due to electrification), where a drop in the incidence of low birthweight has occurred within the last two or three decades. Furthermore, is anxiety due to scarcity of food during the dry season a factor? If so, how can we measure stress? Stress might explain the increase of low birthweight and infant mortality in recent times in virtually all the socialist countries, particularly in the USSR. Infant mortality in the USSR in 1981 was about 34 per 1,000, while it is declining, for instance, in Sri Lanka, Costa Rica, and in Cuba, countries that certainly are poor, and where the diet has not changed significantly in the last 15 years. These controversial issues should be taken into consideration in future studies, and should focus on lifestyles of people, infection, and other variables that nutritionists usually do not measure.

Dr. Waterlow: Dr. Briend has produced a detailed study from which he has made certain propositions about the regulation of birthweight. The conclusion that I draw from his chapter is that the most convincing regulator of birthweight at the physiological level might well be the infant's insulin secretion, since this is an anabolic hormone for all nutrients; and that the infant's insulin secretion might be influenced by the maternal blood glucose level. This leads me to the question: in the intervention studies, such as those in the Gambia, is there any relationship between the intake of the supplement and maternal blood glucose levels?

Dr. Whitehead: Data of the type you require are at present being prepared for publication. You know, of course, that we have published this type of data covering lactation. We have suggested that the high level of circulating energy metabolites in the blood is related to the greater sense of health and well-being which the mothers claim when their diet is being supplemented.

Dr. Waterlow: I repeat my question: Do measurements of blood glucose in women provide an indication of (a) those who are at risk if they had low glucose levels, and (b) whether a supplementary program was needed or was likely to work?

Dr. Whitehead: So far we have emphasized the importance of regularly weighing women during the course of pregnancy. Such measurements are simple and can be informative. The problem with routine measurements of biochemical components, such as blood glucose, is that the collection of the blood must be done under highly standardized conditions; otherwise, misleading values can be obtained.

Nutritional Needs and Assessment of Normal Growth, edited by M. Gracey and F. Falkner. Nestlé Nutrition, Vevey/Raven Press, New York © 1985.

Nutrition for Healthy Neonates

Lewis A. Barness

College of Medicine, Department of Pediatrics, University of South Florida, Tampa, Florida 33612

For many years, nutrition of the breastfed infant growing at a satisfactory rate has been the standard against which nutritional requirements have been set. While recognizing the importance of genetic, metabolic, and environmental influences in producing significant differences, the notion of "adequate breastfeeding" has been subjected to intensive study as carefully obtained data have revealed wide variations in nutrient intake of some breastfed infants. Not only is the total volume of intake variable, but also the composition of breast milk has been found to vary more widely than previously suspected (1).

Recommendations for nutrition of healthy neonates must take into account several factors. Infants grow at different rates, influenced in part by nutrition. While usual recommendations are safe, sufficient, and practical for almost all infants, they may be excessive or deficient for a few. Where ranges are accepted, the minima probably include a small safety factor.

WATER

Water requirements are related to caloric consumption, environmental temperature, activity, rate of growth, and specific gravity of the urine. Water is required for maintenance, excretion of excess protein, electrolyte intake, and changes in body composition. Water constitutes approximately 78% of body weight at birth and decreases to about 60% by the end of the first year (2). Average water requirements for age (Table 1) and for urine specific gravity (Table 2) reflect the needs of unstressed infants. In the basal state, requirements are 30 ml as skin loss,

TABLE 1. *Average water requirements[a]*

Age	Weight (kg)	Water (ml/kg)	Age	Weight (kg)	Water (ml/kg)
3 days	3.0	80–100	6 months	7.3	130–155
10 days	3.2	125–150	9 months	8.6	125–145
3 months	5.4	140–160	1 year	9.5	120–135

[a]From ref. 84.

TABLE 2. *Average water requirements[a]*

Urine (specific gravity)	3-kg Infant (300 kcal)		
	ml	ml/100 kcal	ml/kg
1,005	650	217	220
1,015	339	113	116
1,020	300	100	100
1,030	264	88	91

[a]From ref. 84.

TABLE 3. *Energy expenditure[a]*

State	0–2 Months (kcal/kg)
Basal	48
Activity	15
Stress, waste	30[b]
Thermal	30[b]
Growth	33
	126

[a]From ref. 9.
[b]Thermal requirements may increase from 2 kcal/kg/hr at 32°C to 4 kcal/kg/hr at 28°C.

15 ml through the respiratory tract, and 50 to 70 ml/100 kcal for excretion of nonconcentrated urine. Allowance for activity increases this estimate by 50% to 150 to 200 ml/100 kcal. Infants who consume 150 to 200 ml/kg/day of human milk thus require no supplemental water from birth to the end of the first year if no other osmotically active foods or fluids are given.

While many breastfed infants in tropical and subtropical areas may be offered water, many are also given supplemental foods. Because of the risk to the infant of contaminated water, adherence to nonsupplementation of water or food during early infancy, as long as breastfeeding supplies sufficient calories for growth, provides a safety factor to infants even in the warmest climates (3).

ENERGY

Energy needs for the term infant during the first year vary according to age and weight. Estimated energy requirements during the rapid growth period of the first 2 months may be as high as 126 kcal/kg/day (Table 3). In the neonatal period, energy requirements are somewhat lower on a weight basis since the body contains more metabolically inactive water than later, as the infant begins to change body composition. The National Academy of Sciences–National Research Council (NAS-NRC) (4) has recommended an average of 115 kcal/kg/day for the first 6 months and 105 kcal/kg/day for the next 6 months. Term infants in the first 3 days of life consume 40 to 90 kcal/kg/day and on subsequent days 110 to 120 kcal/kg/day. Basal metabolism accounts for 35 to 40% of this energy, and 10 to 30% is utilized for growth (Table 4).

Threefold differences have been found in energy intake in infants fed either human milk (5) or formula (6). Stewart (6) found a range of intakes of 56 to 152 kcal/kg/day in a group of infants studied at 3-month intervals with total average intakes slowly declining with age. Dewey and Lonnerdal (5) found that intakes averaged 107 kcal/kg/day at 1 month and declined to 85 kcal/kg/day at 5 to 6 months in infants fed breast milk.

Whitehead et al. (7) calculated the energy needs of infants in Cambridge from periodically measured breast milk intakes. All infants were growing within the 5th and 95th percentiles of the National Center for Health Statistics (NCHS) standards, most along the 50th percentile. They found the mean energy intakes in boys at 2 months to be 104 kcal/kg, at 3 months 97, at 4 months 91, at 5 months 89, at 6 months 87, and at 8 months 89 kcal/kg. They suggest, therefore, that breast milk as a sole food is adequate up to 6 months, and that an explanation for the increased needs after 6 months is related to the infant's increased activity. Waterlow and Thomson (8) found that ranges of intake of breast milk and weight gain would indicate that breast milk alone could be sufficient for infants for 2 to 6 months.

Consideration has been given to caloric utilization related to ambient temperature. Widdowson (9) indicates that nude infants (age not stated) at 32°C consume 2 kcal/kg/hr, whereas those at 28°C consume 4 kcal/kg/hr. (The thermoneutral zone for adults is 26–28°C.) The difference in basal caloric utilization at these two temperatures is approximately 50 kcal/kg/day, or about one-half the total recommended caloric intake. Likewise, crying may increase basal energy expenditure three- to fourfold, and other forms of stresses in infancy increase energy utilization.

Requirements for growth as estimated from increments in body protein and fat are 33 kcal/kg/day at 0 to 2 months, 18 kcal/kg/day at 2 to 4 months, and 7 kcal to 3 kcal/kg/day from 4 months to 1 year. To this, some small cost should be added for the metabolism of foods consumed (10).

TABLE 4. *Estimated energy requirements[a]*

State	Term infants (kcal/kg/24 hr)		
	0–2 months	3–4 months	5–12 months
Basal	48	48	48
Activity	45	40	48
Stress, waste	45	40	48
Growth	33	18	4
	126	106	100

[a]From ref. 9.

Payne and Waterlow (11) suggest that the energy cost of heat production under basal conditions, specific dynamic effect of the digestion and absorption of food, the cost of resynthesizing food, and minimal muscular activity is 1.5 times the basal metabolic rate. For growth during the first year, they calculate that 5 kcal/g of new tissue added is needed, and 5 to 7% of the energy ingested is lost in the stools.

Energy requirements are met primarily by carbohydrate and fat. Ingested protein may also be used for energy, particularly if other sources of energy are limited. If carbohydrates or fats are limited, energy requirements for maintenance take precedence over protein needs for growth.

Energy requirements can be estimated from surface area or by direct measurement of energy consumption, losses, and utilization but are best determined by observing the growth pattern, including length, weight, and head circumference, the sense of well-being, and satiety of the infant. Chessex et al. (12) have shown that the relationship between heart rate and metabolic rate offers a simple method of estimating energy requirements, particularly in the low birthweight newborn. Metabolic rate, calculated from oxygen uptake and respiratory quotient was compared with heart rate. For each beat, approximately 50 μl oxygen/kg are consumed, and 0.258 ± 0.3 kcal/kg (1.1 J/kg) are expended. Spady et al. (13) measured energy expenditure of infants by the heart rate method and found an average figure of 92 kcal/kg/day, of which 10 kcal was considered to be due to activity and 5 kcal/g to weight gain (14).

Lemons et al. (15) indicate that the reported energy content of infant formulas depends on the method used to measure or calculate caloric value. The manufacturer's label is intended to reflect metabolizable energy, the gross energy minus the energy lost via urine, feces, and so on when fed to humans. Gross energy is either calculated from heat of combustion of components or determined by bomb calorimetry. Bomb calorimetry results may be as much as 9% higher than those listed on the label of the 12 United States infant formulas studied. Since the calculations for bioavailable energy (protein, 4 kcal/g; carbohydrate, 4 kcal/g; and fat, 9 kcal/g) are based on utilization of foods by adults, and since it is speculated that newborn infants do not utilize foods with the same efficiency as adults, energy requirements based on data from ingested nutrients must be considered estimates. In addition, digestibility varies. Carbohydrates average 98%, fats 95%, and protein 92% digestibility, but these values vary depending on the food source. Nonetheless, protein, fat, carbohydrate, and energy contents of many formulas have been developed to approximate the composition of pooled human milk.

PROTEIN

Pooled mature human milk contains an average of 0.9 g protein, peptides, and amino acids and 0.2 g non-amino acid nitrogen/100 ml (16). The protein content may be somewhat decreased in malnourished women; normally, it slowly falls during the first 4 months in the well-nourished woman and falls slightly further after 6 months. Conversely, in women who lactate preterm, protein content is somewhat higher (17).

Protein requirements are based on needs for growth and obligatory losses of nitrogen in urine, feces, and skin and its appendages. Protein is required as well for synthesis of hormones, enzymes, sols for maintenance of osmotic pressure gradients, and for the synthesis of other body proteins. While no body pool of proteins or amino acids exists, in the protein-deficient child, proteins are lost first from the muscles, liver, and intestines and later from the viscera, and utilized for energy.

Protein quality depends on digestibility, absorbability, and distribution of amino acids. The essential amino acids (Table 5), if limited, affect tissue and organ growth, height, weight, and head circumference. Some prematurely born infants also require cystine, tyrosine, and perhaps taurine. Human milk contains 91 mg methionine and 120 mg cystine/g total nitrogen. Cow's milk and formulas made from cow's milk with a whey/casein ratio of 18:82 contain 180 mg methionine and 60 mg cystine. Formulas with demineralized whey contain approximately 108 mg cystine and 156 mg methionine (18). Taurine, formerly considered a waste product of sulfur metabolism, has known effects on eye abnormalities in some animals. Because of its presence in human milk and absence in many formulas, attention has been directed to its possible essentiality in human infants, particularly in relation to fat metabolism (19) and bile acids (20). Taurine stimulates activity of human pancreatic lipases and is used in the conjugation of bile acids.

If one or more essential amino acids are present in excess, the amino acid imbalance causes similar defects in protein production or utilization. Excessive protein intake, especially in the small infant, causes an amino acid excess, which must be metabolized and eliminated, and may result in stress on liver and kidney functions as the amino acids are deaminated (21).

TABLE 5. *Estimated amino acid requirements of infants and children[a]*

Amino acid	Infants[b] (mg/kg body wgt/day)	Children[c] (mg/kg body wgt/day)
Histidine	33	Unknown
Isoleucine	83	28
Leucine	135	42
Lysine	99	44
Total S-containing amino acid (methionine and cystine)	49	22
Total aromatic amino acid (phenylalanine and tyrosine)	141	22
Threonine	68	28
Tryptophan	21	4
Valine	92	25

[a]From ref. 4.
[b]4–6 months.
[c]10–12 years.

In calculating protein requirements based on human milk intake, factors other than digestibility must be considered. Many nitrogen-containing components of human milk contain factors that serve purposes other than those related to protein alone. Human colostrum contains approximately 2.5 g/dl protein and mature milk, 0.9 g/dl. Casein constitutes approximately 20% of the protein of human milk and has a lower phosphorus content and more amino sugars and sialic acid than cow's milk casein (22). The non-protein-nitrogen-containing compounds constitute approximately 25% of the total nitrogen of human milk.

Chan and Waterlow (23) found that in infants recovering from malnutrition, the nitrogen of cow's milk was utilized with almost 100% efficiency. Picou and Phillips (24) found that urea can be utilized for protein synthesis when total nitrogen intake is low. The utilization of these nitrogen-containing compounds in healthy neonates, however, has not been demonstrated.

Lactoferrin, as well as other constituents (Table 6), are antibacterial (25). The enteromammary immune system allows the mother to come into contact with antigens to which the infant has been exposed. When these antigens reach the intestinal tract, they stimulate production of specific immunoglobulin A(IgA) antibodies. Lymphoblasts or lymphocytes migrate into the circulation and into the mammary glands, thence into the milk and into the infant gastrointestinal tract. The major immunoglobulin in human milk, secretory IgA, provides antimicrobial protection for mucous membranes (26). Breast milk lymphocytes, neutrophils, macrophages, and lysozyme protect the infant from infection and may protect the mother's breast. Macrophages appear to synthesize lactoferrin and components of complement (27) and other proteins and prostaglandin E_2. These cells actively phagocytize zymosan particles (28). Bifidus factor from human milk suppresses multiplication of *E. coli* (26).

The secretory IgA has an apparent barrier effect in addition to an antiinfectious effect (29) and may be important in preventing the infant from absorbing antigens

TABLE 6. *Protein constituents of milk*

Constituent	Milk (g/dl)	
	Human	Cow
Casein	0.2	2.7
Whey	0.7	0.6
α-Lactalbumin	0.26	0.11
Lactoferrin	0.17	Trace
β-Lactalbumin	0	0.36
Lysozyme	0.05	Trace
Albumin	0.05	0.04
IgA	0.10	0.003
Peroxidase	Trace	
Bifidus factor	Trace	
Nonprotein nitrogen	0.20	0.03

that may later be detrimental, or may slow the absorption of antigens in order to improve the antibody response of infants (30). Udall and Walker (31) have studied the transport of macromolecules across the intestinal tract. This transport is facilitated early in life, may be related to development of food allergy, and is modified by abnormalities of gastric, pancreatic, and small intestine function. Secretory IgA, however, is excreted in significant amounts and may not be utilizable entirely as a nutrient (32).

Both human and cow's milk contain many enzymes, the significance of which is not entirely clear. Bile salt-stimulated lipase, protease, and lysozyme apparently aid in digestion. Lactoperoxidase and xanthine oxidase, present in human milk as traces, are present in significant quantities in cow's milk (33).

Colostrum contains protease inhibitors which may alter the protein absorption from early human milk (34). Protease inhibitors may be increased in protein-energy malnutrition, thus decreasing catabolism during states of deficiency of essential amino acids (35).

Several biological indices are used to determine the nutritive value of proteins, such as the protein efficiency ratio (PER), biological value (BV), net protein utilization (NPU), or a provisional optimal amino acid pattern, as suggested by FAO/WHO. The PER is defined as the weight gained per gram of protein consumed. The BV is the amount of nitrogen retained compared to nitrogen absorbed. The NPU is the percentage of ingested nitrogen retained and includes digestibility and utilization of absorbed amino acids. Tests for adequacy of protein quantity and quality in the human being include nitrogen balance, rate of growth, body composition, serum albumin levels, 3-methylhistidine excretion, and serum levels of proteins with high turnover rates, such as transferrin, prealbumin, and retinol-binding protein. Cellular immunity is decreased in protein malnutrition. Plasma concentrations of essential compared to nonessential amino acids may be disproportionately decreased in protein deficiency states (36). The well-known late effects of protein deficiency include edema with low serum albumin, fall in hemoglobin level, skin discoloration and rash, perhaps increased rate of infections, and poor response to infections.

Zoppi et al. (37) studied the immunocompetence of infants fed formulas containing cow's milk protein at 2.0 and 4.0 g/kg/day, and soya protein at 2.0 and 5.0 g/kg/day for 5 months. Those fed the formulas with soya protein had lower immunoglobulins, transferrin, several complement fractions, and T-lymphocyte reactivity; they also had more minor infections. Tikanoja et al. (38) note that all plasma amino acids, except alanine and glycine, rise in the newborn after an adequate protein meal consisting of either breast milk or formula. The essential amino acids show the greatest rise. Glycine falls and alanine rises continuously but slowly in a pattern different from the rapid rise of the essential amino acids.

Body protein increases approximately 3.5 g/day from 0 to 4 months of age, and 3.1 g/day for the next 8 months (9). Widdowson (9) calculated the daily protein requirement to be 1.6 g/kg/day, as follows:

	g Protein
2 mg N/basal kcal (catabolism) = 2 × 48 kcal/kg/day = 96 mg N =	0.6
Mean amount of protein laid down	2.9
Mean amount of protein for maintenance, waste, etc.	3.06
	6.56

Mean body weight, 5.1 kg; 6.56/5.1 = 1.3 g/kg/day plus 30% for inefficiency of utilization, feces, skin = 1.6 g/kg/day.

Nitrogen requirements to obtain satisfactory growth in children appear to be consistently higher by about 30% than calculations based on obligatory losses and growth, even when high quality proteins are consumed (39). To this amount, another 30% is added, which represents twice the coefficient of variation to cover the variability in individual infants.

Nearly two-thirds of the protein requirement in the first month is needed for growth, and about 10% is needed for growth in the 1-year old (38,39). King et al. (40) recommend that children in Africa start cereal by 4 months of age and a better protein source by 6 months.

Infants fed human milk thrive when consuming 150 to 200 ml/kg/day, implying a requirement of 1.3 to 1.8 g protein, peptides, and amino acids and 0.3 to 0.4 g nonamino acid nitrogen/kg/day. The BV of human milk protein is higher than that of other proteins fed infants, and most formulas are adjusted to provide 2.3 g/100 kcal compared with 1.6 g/100 kcal in human milk. The American Academy of Pediatrics Committee on Nutrition (41) proposed a minimum protein intake of 1.8 g/100 kcal with a PER at least equal to that of casein. Huang et al. (42) calculated from the regression equation based on balance studies that infants at approximately 1 year required approximately 100 mg/kg/day nitrogen for maintenance. Excessive protein intake may be accompanied by signs of protein intoxication, such as lethargy, hyperammonemia, dehydration, and diarrhea. The American Academy of Pediatrics Committee on Nutrition recommends a maximum protein intake of 4.5 g/100 kcal/day.

Minima, maxima, and optimal protein intake for well prematurely born infants are much less well defined, particularly since optimal growth rates for premature infants are not defined. Nonetheless, growth rates similar to those expected in the third trimester of pregnancy are achievable with protein intakes similar to those of term infants. Many investigators, however, recommend protein intakes about 20% higher than those specified for term infants. Fresh human milk from the infant's own mother produces satisfactory growth in these infants (43).

LIPIDS

Human mature milk provides about 40 to 50% of energy as fat (3–4 g/100 ml). Milk from poorly nourished mothers may contain as little as 1.5 g/100 ml. A minimum of 30% of the energy as fat appears desirable not only to satisfy energy needs but also to facilitate absorption of essential fatty acids, fat-soluble vitamins, and calcium and other minerals, and also to balance the diet to conserve other nutrients which might otherwise be used for energy (44). At least 10% of the fatty acids should be polyunsaturated; they are usually in the form of linoleic acid (41). Linolenic acid also appears to be essential; it is present in most vegetable oils except safflower oil (45). Precise requirements of linolenic acid are unknown. Sufficient linoleate and linolenate may be absorbed through the skin by inunction, if necessary (46).

Cow's milk, which contains about 1% polyunsaturated fatty acids, has been fed to infants, reportedly without evidence of signs of essential fatty acid deficiency. When unmodified cow's milk formulas were widely used in the United States, eczematoid skin lesions were recognized more frequently in infants than today. Many causes of eczema-like lesions are recognized, including deficiencies of essential fatty acid, biotin, vitamin E, and zinc, and perhaps food and environmental allergies and some as yet unrecognized factors. It is tempting to suggest that the relative disappearance of eczema in recent years is due in part to the use of formulas in which the cow's milk fat has been partially replaced by vegetable oils.

Human milk contains other long chain polyenoates (47), and these influence the composition of cell membranes (48). Essential fatty acids are necessary not only for growth but also for function and maintenance of cell membranes, lipotropic activity, synthesis of prostaglandins, reproduction, and cholesterol metabolism (49).

Excessive polyenoates, however, increase the requirement for vitamin E (49). The American Academy of Pediatrics Committee on Nutrition recommends that formulas for term infants contain 0.7 IU vitamin E/g linoleic acid.

Infants absorb 85 to 90% of breast milk fat (49). Lingual lipase is responsible for 50 to 70% of the digestion, and the balance is accomplished by human milk-bile salt-stimulated lipase (50). Heat treatment of pooled mature human milk decreases fat absorption, with a decrease in nitrogen retention.

In studies conducted by Watkins et al. (51), newborn full-term infants excreted 13.6% of the fat in formulas containing vegetable oils. Fomon (49) found that term infants fed formulas containing butterfat excreted as much as 30% of the fat. Tomarelli et al. (52) suggest that at least part of the difference in absorbability of fat in the young infant is related to the position of palmitic acid in triglycerides. The palmitic acid in human milk is mainly esterified in the 2-position and is almost equally esterified in all three positions of glycerol in butterfat.

Medium chain triglycerides require no reesterification or chylomicron formation and move directly from intestinal mucosal cells; they are complexed with albumin and proceed directly through the portal vein and are metabolized in the liver. Approximately 10% of human milk or cow's milk fat consists of medium chain triglycerides. Cow's milk fat contains more short chain (4:0, 6:0) and medium chain (8:0, 10:0) fatty acids (53). Since these are frequently more easily absorbable than longer chain fatty acids, they may be useful in infants with limited ability to absorb fat (54).

Low-fat diets have been fed to normal infants who appear to continue to grow normally with a decrease in subcutaneous fat. Svanberg et al. (16) suggest that this is attributable not to energy difference but to change in body composition. Until more is known about the requirements of nervous tissue in the preweaning infant, however, it is not prudent to feed low-fat diets during this period. Rats weaned prematurely to a low-fat diet had decreased learning and memory and degeneration of the testes (55). Similar data are not available in humans.

Human milk contains 10 times as much cholesterol as formulas prepared from cow's milk or soybeans; it also contains long chain polyenoates not found in animal or vegetable milks. The long chain polyenoates in breastfed infants are reflected in the red cell membrane composition at 4 to 6 months. Their significance remains unclear.

Human milk contains phospholipids, a source of choline, believed to be necessary for the infant. It also contains carnitine, necessary for fat transport, and enhances oxygen consumption from neonatal adipose tissue (56). While carnitine is absent in formulas prepared from vegetables, the infant is apparently able to synthesize sufficient quantities so that fat utilization appears to be adequate, at least in infants born at term.

CARBOHYDRATES

Protein sparing, antiketogenesis, and electrolyte conservation result when as little as 15% of total energy requirements are met by carbohydrates. Most of the carbohydrate in human milk is lactose. Lactose helps preserve an acid flora in the lower intestine, decreasing gram-negative bacilli as the concentration of the gram-positive lactobacilli increases. Acidity, probably due to fermentation of lactose through much of the length of the intestine, increases absorbability of calcium, magnesium, and many other trace minerals (57).

About 10% of the carbohydrate in human milk is in the form of oligo- and polysaccharides, which include N-acetylneuraminic acid. The latter is a growth factor for lactobacilli, but its function in infants is not well characterized (58).

Lactase develops late in gestation and is not fully developed in the term infant. Its relatively low concentration in the newborn does not lead to any apparent difficulty, although the early soft stools of the breastfed infant may indicate some decrease in carbohydrate absorption.

Lactose intolerance develops as a racial phenomenon usually at 2 to 3 years of age in certain racial groups. Secondary lactose intolerance may develop for a short time after episodes of diarrhea. During periods immediately following a diarrheal episode, it may be prudent to exclude lactose from the infant diet (59). In those populations that become intolerant to lactose in later life, no precautions are usually necessary during infancy, since the lack of lactase occurs after this age.

Galactosemia is an absolute contraindication to the inclusion of lactose or galactose in the diet. In children with galactosemia, the diet should be supplemented with other carbohydrates.

VITAMINS AND MINERALS

Requirements for vitamins and minerals are estimated from multiple influences (Table 7). Evidence of deficiency states indicates a critical lack of one or more of

TABLE 7. *Nutrient levels of infant formulas*[a]

Nutrient	Committee on Nutrition 1976 recommendations (per 100 kcal)	
	Minimum	Maximum
Protein (g)	1.8	4.5
Fat		
g	3.3	6.0
% cal	30.0	54.0
Essential fatty acids		
linoleate		
% cal	3.0	—
mg	300.0	—
Vitamins		
A (IU)	250.0 (75 μg)[b]	750.0 (225 μg)[b]
D (IU)	40.0	100.0
K (μg)	4.0	—
E (IU)	0.3[c]	—
C (ascorbic acid) (mg)	8.0	—
B_1 (thiamine) (μg)	40.0	—
B_2 (riboflavin) (μg)	60.0	—
B_6 (pyridoxine) (μg)	35.0[d]	—
B_{12} (μg)	0.15	
Niacin		
(μg)	250.0	—
(μg equiv)	—	
Folic acid (μg)	4.0	—
Pantothenic acid (μg)	300.0	—
Biotin (μg)	1.5	—
Choline (mg)	7.0	—
Inositol (mg)	4.0	—
Minerals		
Calcium (mg)	50.0[e]	—
Phosphorus (mg)	25.0[e]	—
Magnesium (mg)	6.0	—
Iron (mg)	0.15	—
Iodine (μg)	5.0	—
Zinc (mg)	0.5	—
Copper (μg)	60.0	—
Manganese (μg)	5.0	—
Sodium (mg)	20.0 (6 mEq)[f]	60.0 (17 mEq)
Potassium (mg)	80.0 (14 mEq)[f]	200.0 (34 mEq)
Chloride (mg)	55.0 (11 mEq)[f]	150.0 (29 mEq)

[a]From ref. 41.
[b]Retinol equivalents.
[c]With 0.7 IU/g linoleic acid.
[d]With 15 μg/g protein in formula.
[e]Calcium/phosphorus ratio must be no less than 1.1 and no more than 2.0.
[f]Milliequivalent for 670 kcal/liter of formula.

these trace substances. Blood levels are poor indicators of deficiency or excess of most vitamins and minerals, as they are frequently influenced by the most recent intake, and rates of storage in various organs or tissues vary. Determination of mineral status by uptake of trace minerals by red blood cells may have similar limitations (60,61).

Excretion following a loading dose is useful for some trace substances, but frequently such a test is difficult to obtain or to interpret. Determinations of tissue concentrations usually require knowledge of the normal distribution of the element in question and biopsy of the tissue. Rate of growth, while easy to observe in animals, is usually a crude test in humans and, because of the long duration needed to determine growth rate changes, may be harmful in infants. Where specific metabolic pathways are known for trace elements that act as coenzymes, exquisitely accurate determinations of deficiencies can be made. Unfortunately, such determinations are available for relatively few of the trace elements.

Propionic or other hydroxy acid excretion (Tables 8–10) is a good test for biotin deficiency (62). Methylmalonate excretion is an excellent test for vitamin B_{12} deficiency (63) and has been used in infants who develop seizures and acidosis (64). Xanthurenic acid excretion is a fair test for vitamin B_6 deficiency (65). Formiminoglutamic acid excretion has been used for detection of folic acid deficiency (66). Pyruvate-lactate ratio in blood or urine has been used for vitamin B_1 deficiency (67). Vitamin C deficiency has been detected by measuring urinary tyrosine metabolites (68), and vitamin D deficiency by measuring serum 25- or 1,25-dihydroxycholecalciferol (69) (HCC, DHCC). The former, 25-HCC, apparently is more closely related to body stores, while activity is more closely related to

TABLE 8. *Representative metabolic tests for trace element status*

Element	Test	Element	Test
Thiamine	Pyruvate	B_{12}	Methylmalonate
Pyridoxine	Xanthurenate	Biotin	Propionate
Folate	FIGLU[a]	Ascorbate	Phenol

[a]Formiminoglutamic acid.

TABLE 9. *Representative enzyme tests for trace element status*

Element	Enzyme
Riboflavin	Growth-stimulating hormone reductase
Vitamin K	Prothrombin
Selenium	GSH oxidase
Zinc	Alkaline phosphatase
Molybdenum	Xanthine oxidase

TABLE 10. *Representative other than blood-level tests for trace-element status*

Element	Test
Vitamin D	25-HCC, 1,25-DHCC
Vitamin E	Peroxide hemolysis
Chromium	Glucose tolerance
Iodine	T_4
Iron	Hemoglobin

1,25-DHCC concentrations. Vitamin E status utilizes *in vitro* peroxide hemolysis as a test with specificity, after effects of recent ingestion of tocopherol are excluded (70).

Some enzymes can be measured directly. Riboflavin status has been estimated by measuring erythrocyte glutathione reductase (71) and vitamin K by measuring prothrombin time. Other tests have been proposed, but for most suspected deficiencies, response to administration of the element remains the test most often used.

Since requirements for many of the trace elements are related to the normal metabolic rate of growing infants, the American Academy of Pediatrics Committee of Nutrition has elected to express requirements on the basis of energy intake by the infant (Table 7). Many of these requirements are estimates and await better tests; in many cases, they are based on the amount found in breast milk. Breast milk from the healthy, well-fed mother is believed to contain sufficient trace elements, except vitamin D and, in some areas, fluoride. Selenium, chromium, and molybdenum are recognized as essential (4), although they are not included in Table 7.

Trace elements, like essential amino acids, are needed in balance. For example, zinc excess may cause copper deficiency; manganese excess may inhibit iron absorption; and other competitions are recognized (72). In addition, excess of many of these substances may cause other evidence of toxicity. Excesses of any single vitamin or mineral may be as toxic or harmful as a deficiency. Data on maximum intake, unfortunately, are available for even fewer of the trace substances than data on minimum intake. Recommendations as listed in Table 7 are for well infants; at times of illness, requirements for individual nutrients may increase at rates different from those required for normal growth.

Requirements of many of the trace substances for the well-fed child are subject to modification by some feeding practices utilizing the major dietary foodstuffs. For example, young infants who ingest large amounts of cow's milk may become anemic not only because of lack of dietary iron but also because of occult bleeding, perhaps due to toxic, enzymatic, or immunologic factors (73). Similarly, early introduction of supplemental feeds is said to reduce absorption of iron from other foods (74). Calcium, magnesium, and fat-soluble vitamin absorption is closely linked to fat absorption (75), important in the normal neonate or preterm infant who absorbs some fats poorly. Alteration in trace element requirements may be detectable only by the development of obvious deficiency states.

Many other trace substances are present in human milk. Among these, thyroxine, cortisol (76), prolactin (77), and epidermal growth factor (78) have been identified. Their significance and importance, when they are taken orally with food, are not clear. Epidermal growth factor may hasten repair of an injured intestinal mucosa; prostaglandin E_2 (79) has been suggested as a possible zinc ligand (80). Orally administered hormones have well-documented effects. Whether these trace substances are required, modify utilization of foods, or are complementary but not essential is unknown.

The National Academy of Sciences (81) identified five areas of functional competence likely to be affected by malnutrition: cognitive ability, disease response, reproductive competence, physical activity, and work and social/behavioral performance. While several of these categories are not applicable to infants, Solomons and Allen (82) believe that these can be studied functionally at the cellular level.

SUMMARY

While it has been recognized almost from time immemorial that human milk from the well-nourished mother seems to meet all the nutritional requirements of the healthy infant, and since formulas roughly based on the composition of pooled human milk likewise seem to meet the nutritional requirements of healthy infants, nutrient requirements must be estimated and interpreted with caution. Within the constraints of the definition of normal growth, as previously discussed, water intakes of 120 to 175 ml/kg/day suffice for most healthy infants. As supplemental feedings are given, water requirements increase. Calorie intakes of approximately 50 to 150 kcal/kg/day have been reported to satisfy needs of healthy, breastfed infants in the first year and support growth rates only roughly proportional to caloric intake. Protein intake of approximately 1.6 to 2.0 g/kg/day, or more appropriately of 1.6 to 2.3 g/100 kcal/day, seems to satisfy the needs of most growing infants during the first year, providing the protein is of a quality approaching that of human milk and that the balance of calories is almost equally distributed between fat and carbohydrate.

Ranges of requirements are large and can serve only as a rough guide for individual infants. Health, well-being, activity, and learning ability are the goals of proper nutrition of the infant. These sometimes require sophisticated observations to determine adequacy of feeds and frequently are influenced by factors other than nutrition, which may be as important, or even more, than nutrition. In summary:

1. Growth rates in "normal" individuals are multiple, and requirements vary widely.
2. Genetic, metabolic, and environmental factors greatly affect requirements.
3. Activity of infants, subject to emotional, innate, and environmental influences, alters requirements.
4. Mother's milk output, which may vary independently of infant factors, alters requirements.

5. Factors in human milk, identified or as yet unidentified, may alter digestion and may influence requirements calculated for nonhuman milk.
6. Factors in human milk serve nonnutritional functions. Some of these factors are poorly absorbed but usually are included as nutrients in calculations of requirements.
7. Requirements generally have been computed in areas where foods are plentiful and applied to areas where foods are less available. As the population of the earth increases, food may become generally less available, and humans may adapt to requirements entirely different from those presently estimated.

The benchmark for nutritional requirements of the full-term infant remains milk from the infant's healthy, well-nourished mother. The multipurpose factors in human milk may be of such significance that calculations of protein and calorie requirements based on human milk are applicable only to human milk. These factors may so modify digestion and absorption that factors such as BV, PER, and others are inadequate for calculation purposes to convert human milk protein to any other protein.

Nourishment of the mother cannot begin only after delivery. The well-nourished parturient compared with the poorly nourished one produces not only more milk for longer periods of time, but also milk with other trace substances, which may alter the utilization of foods or are growth factors for the infant.

Supplemental feedings may be necessary as early as 2 to 3 months after birth for those infants whose mothers have not been well-nourished. If supplements are required, they must be adequate in protein and calories.

Although probably overemphasized, mothers should not be exposed to poisons or drugs which may be transmitted through the milk. While the toxins that may be transmitted through the breast should be avoided if possible, usually the infant has been exposed to the same toxins in even higher concentration as a fetus.

A relaxed mother appears to be beneficial to the baby, since such a mother seems better able to nurse. The importance of oral ingestion probably involves many beneficial nutritive and nonnutritive factors, as emphasized by reports of more rapid growth of preterm infants after nonnutritive sucking (83).

While human milk supplies the nutrients in the desired quantity for the infant, if this milk is not available, nutrients must be supplied in a similar pattern to that present in breast milk. Unless evidence develops to the contrary, the quantity and quality of nutrients in human milk should be mimicked. Further studies of human milk may reveal other requirements. Hence, studies on the composition of human milk continue to be desirable.

REFERENCES

1. Rattigan S, Ghisalberti AV, Hartmann PE. Breast milk production in Australian women. Br J Nutr 1981; 45:243–49.
2. Friis-Hansen B. Body water compartments in children. Pediatrics 1961;28:169–81.
3. Goldberg NM, Adams E. Supplementary water for breast-fed babies in a hot and dry climate—not really a necessity. Arch Dis Child 1983;58:73–4.

4. Food and Nutrition Board. Recommended dietary allowances. 9th ed. Natl. Acad. Sci. Washington D.C. 1980.
5. Dewey KG, Lonnerdal B. Nutrition, growth and fatness of breast-fed infants from one to six months. Fed Proc 1982;41:352.
6. Stewart RA. Infant and child feeding. Bond et al., ed. New York: Academic Press, 1981:123–33.
7. Whitehead RG, Paul AA, Cole TJ. How much breast milk do babies need? Acta Pediatr Scand. (Suppl.) 1982;299:43–50.
8. Waterlow JC, Thomson AM. Observations on the adequacy of breast feeding. Lancet 1979;2:238–41.
9. Widdowson EM. Nutrition. In: Davis JA, Dobbing J, eds. Scientific foundation of pediatrics. 2nd ed. Baltimore: University Park Press, 1981:41–53.
10. Sauer PJ, Pearse RG, Dane HJ, Visser HKA. The energy cost of growth estimated from simultaneous direct and indirect calorimetry of infants less than 2500 g. In: H. K. A. Visser, ed. Nutrition and metabolism of the fetus and infant. V nutricia symposium, Hague: Martinus Nijhoff, 1979:93–107.
11. Payne PR, Waterlow JC. Relative energy requirements for maintenance, growth and physical activity. Lancet 1971;2:210–2.
12. Chessex P, Reichman BL, Verellen GJE, et al. Relation between heart rate and energy expenditure in the newborn. Pediatr Res 1981;15:1077–82.
13. Spady DW, Payne PR, Picou D, Waterlow JC. Energy balance during recovery from malnutrition. Am J Clin Nutr 1976;29:1073–88.
14. Waterlow JC, Hill AA, Spady DW. Energy costs and protein requirements for catch-up growth in children. In: Wilkinson, AW, ed. Early nutrition and later development. Tunbridge Wells, Pitman, 1976:175–89.
15. Lemons JA, Moorhead H, Jansen RD, Schreiner RL. The energy content of infant formulas. Early Hum Dev 1982;6:305–8.
16. Svanberg U, Gebre-Medhin M, Ljungquist B, Olsson M. Breast milk composition in Ethiopian and Swedish mothers. III. Amino acids and other nitrogenous substances. Am J Clin Nutr 1977;30:399–507.
17. Lemons JA, Moye L, Hall D, Simmons N. Differences in the composition of preterm and term human milk during early lactation. Pediatr Res 1982;16:113–7.
18. Gurr MI. Review of the progress of dairy science. Human and artificial milks for infant feeding. J Dairy Res 1977;48:419–554.
19. Naismith DJ, Cashel K. Taurine in breast milk: a role in fat utilization. Proc Nutr Soc 1979;38:105A.
20. Watkins JB, Jarvenpaa AL, Raiha N, Gaull GE. Regulation of bile acid pool size: role of taurine conjugates. Pediatr Res 1979;13:410.
21. Barness LA, Baker K, Guilbert P, Torres FE, Gyorgy P. Nitrogen metabolism of infants fed human and cow's milk. Pediatrics 1957;51:28–39.
22. Alois C, Blanc B. Milk proteins: biochemical and biological aspects. World Rev Nutr Diet 1975;20:66–166.
23. Chan H, Waterlow JC. The protein requirements of infants at the age of about one year. Br J Nutr 1966;20:775–82.
24. Picou D, Phillips M. Urea metabolism in malnourished and recovered children receiving a high or low protein diet. Am J Clin Nutr 1972;25:1261–6.
25. Arnold RR, Cole MF, McGhee JR. A bacterial effect for human lactoferrin. Science 1977;197:263–5.
26. Goldman AS, Garza C, Nichols BL, Goldblum RM. Immunological components in human milk during the first year of lactation. J Pediatr 1982;100:563–7.
27. Pittard WB. Breast milk immunology. Am J Dis Child 1979;133:83–7.
28. Blau H, Parswell JH, Levandon M, Davidson J, Kohen F, Ramot B. Studies on human milk macrophages: effect of activation on phagocytosis and secretion of prostaglandin E_2 and lysozyme. Pediatr Res 1983;17:241–5.
29. Vukavic T. Intestinal absorption of IgA in the newborn. J Pediatr Gastroenterol Nutr 1983;2:248–51.
30. Udall JN, Pang K, Fritze L, Kleinman R, Walker WA. Development of gastrointestinal mucosal barrier. Pediatr Res 1981;15:241–4.

31. Udall JN, Walker WA. Physiologic and pathologic basis for the transport of macromolecules across the intestinal tract. J Pediatr Gastroenterol Nutr 1982;1:295–301.
32. Haneberg B. Immunoglobulins in feces from infants fed human or bovine milk. Scand J Immunol 1974;3:191–7.
33. Shahani KM, Kwan AJ, Friend BA. Role and significance of enzymes in human milk. Am J Clin Nutr 1980;33:1861–8.
34. Lindberg T, Ohlsson K, Westron B. Protease inhibitors and their relation to protease activity in human milk. Pediatr Res 1982;16:479–83.
35. Schelp FP, Migasewa P, Pongpaew P, Schreuro WHP. Are proteinase inhibitors a factor for the derangement of homeostasis in protein-energy malnutrition? Am J Clin Nutr 1978;31:451–6.
36. Antener I, Tonney G, Verwilghen AM, Mauron J. Biochemical study of malnutrition IV. Determination of the amino acids in the serum, erythrocytes, urine and stool ultrafiltrates. Int J Vitam Nutr Res 1981;51:64–78.
37. Zoppi G, Girosa F, Pezzini A, et al. Immunocompetence and dietary protein intake in early infancy. J Pediatr Gastroenterol Nutr 1982;1:175–82.
38. Tikanoja T, Siwell D, Viikari N, Jarvenpaa AL. Plasma amino acids in term neonates after a feed of human milk or formula. Acta Paediatr Scand 1982;71:391–7.
39. FAO Nutrition Report Series No. 52. Energy and protein requirements. Food and Agricultural Organization, Rome. 1973.
40. King M, King F, Morley D, Burgess L, Burgess A. Nutrition for developing countries, Nairobi. Oxford University Press, 1972.
41. American Academy of Pediatrics Committee on Nutrition. Commentary on breast feeding and infant formulas, including proposed standards for formulas. Pediatrics 1976;57:278–85.
42. Huang PC, Lin CP, Hsu JY. Protein requirements of normal infants at the age of about 1 year: maintenance nitrogen requirements and obligatory nitrogen losses. J Nutr 1980;110:1727–35.
43. Gross SJ. Growth and biochemical response of preterm infants fed human milk or modified infant formula. N Engl J Med 1983;308:237–41.
44. Alfin-Slater RB, Aftergood L. Fats and other lipids. In: Goodhart RS, Shils ME, eds. Lipids in modern nutrition in health and disease. 5th ed. Philadelphia: Lea & Febiger, 1980:134–6.
45. Holman RT, Johnson SB, Hatch TF. A case of human linolenic acid deficiency involving neurological abnormalities. Am J Clin Nutr 1982;35:615–23.
46. Friedman Z, Shochat SJ, Maisels J, Marks KH, Lamberth EL. Correction of essential fatty acid deficiency in newborn infants by cutaneous application of sunflower seed oil. Pediatrics 1976;58:650–4.
47. Putnam JC, Carlson SE, Devoe PW, Barness LA. The effect of variations in dietary fatty acids on the fatty acid composition of erythrocyte phosphatidylcholine and phosphatidylethanolamine in human infants. Am J Clin Nutr 1982;36:106–14.
48. Carlson SE, Devoe PW, Barness LA. The effect of infant diets with different polyunsaturated to saturated fat ratios on circulating high density lipoproteins. Pediatr Gastro Nutr 1982;1:303–9.
49. Fomon SJ, ed. Fat. In: Infant nutrition, 2nd ed. Philadelphia: WB Saunders, 1974:168.
50. Hamosh M. Lingual and breast milk lipases. Adv Pediatr 1982;29:33.
51. Watkins JB, Bliss CM, Donaldson RM, Lester R. Characterization of newborn fecal lipid. Pediatrics 1974;53:511–5.
52. Tomarelli RM, Meyer BJ, Weaber JR, Bernhart FW. Effect of positional distribution on the absorption of the fatty acids of human milk and infant formulas. J Nutr 1968;95:583–90.
53. Jensen RG, Hagerty MM, McMahon KE. Lipids of human milk and infant formulas: a review. Am J Clin Nutr 1978;31:990–1016.
54. Tantibhedhyangkul P, Hashim S. Medium chain triglyceride feeding in premature infants: effects on fat and nitrogen absorption. Pediatrics 1975;55:359–70.
55. Hahn P, Koldovsky O. Development of metabolic processes and their adaptation during postnatal life. In: Bajusz, E, ed. Physiology and pathology of adaptation mechanisms. Oxford: Pergamon, 1969:48–74.
56. Novak M, Penn-Walker D, Monkus EF. Oxidation of fatty acids by mitochondria from newborn subcutaneous (white) adipose tissue. Biol Neonate 1975;25:95–107.
57. Zeigler EE, Fomon SJ. Lactose enhances mineral absorption in infancy. J Pediatr Gastroent Nutr 1983;2:288–94.
58. Gauhe A, Gyorgy P, Hoover JRE, et al. Bifidus factor. IV. Preparations obtained from human milk. Arch Biochem Biophys 1954;48:214–24.

59. American Academy of Pediatrics. Committee on Nutrition. The practical significance of lactose intolerance in children. Pediatrics 1978;62:240–5.

60. Burk RF, Pearson WN, Wood RP, Viteri F. Blood-selenium levels and in vitro red blood cell uptake of ⁷⁵Se in Kwashiorkor. Am J Clin Nutr 1967;20:723–33.

61. Berry RK, Bell MC, Wright PL. Influence of dietary calcium, zinc and oil upon the in vitro uptake of zinc-65 by porcine blood cells. J Nutr 1966;88:284–90.

62. Tanaka K, Isselbacher KJ. Experimental B-hydroxy isovaleric aciduria induced by biotin deficiency. Lancet 1970;2:930–1.

63. Barness LA, Young D, Mellman WJ, Kahn SB, Williams WJ. Methylmalonate excretion in a patient with pernicious anemia. N Engl J Med 1963;268:144–6.

64. Higginbottom MC, Sweetman L, Nylan WL. Syndrome of methylmalonic aciduria, homocystinuria, megaloblastic anemia and neurologic abnormalities in vitamin B_{12} deficient breast-fed infant of a strict vegetarian. N Engl J Med 1978;299:317–23.

65. Cinnamon AD, Beaton JR. Biochemical assessment of vitamin B_6 status in man. Am J Clin Nutr 1970;23:696–702.

66. Hansen HA. On the diagnosis of folic acid deficiency. Acta Obstet Gynecol Scand 1967;46(suppl 7):13–37.

67. Sauberlich HE. Biochemical alterations in thiamine deficiency—Their interpretation. Am J Clin Nutr 1967;20:528–42.

68. Cornely DA, Barness LA, Gyorgy P. Effect of lactose on nitrogen metabolism and phenol excretion in infants. J Pediatr 1957;51:40–5.

69. DeLuca HF. The vitamin D system in the regulation of calcium and phosphorus metabolism. Nutr Rev 1979;37:161.

70. Oski FA, Barness LA. Vitamin E deficiency: a previously unrecognized cause of hemolytic anemia in the premature infant. J Pediatr 1966;70:211–20.

71. Tillotson JA, Baker EM. An enzymatic measurement of the riboflavin status in man. Am J Clin Nutr 1972;25:425–9.

72. Solomons NW, Jacob RA. Studies on the bioavailability of zinc in humans: effects of heme and non-heme iron on the absorption of zinc. Am J Clin Nutr 1981;34:475–82.

73. Eastham EJ, Walker WA. Effect of cow's milk on the gastrointestinal tract: a persistent dilemma for the pediatrician. Pediatrics 1977;60:477–81.

74. Oski FA, Landaw SA. Inhibition of iron absorption from human milk by baby food. Am J Dis Child 1980;134:459–60.

75. Barness LA, Morrow G, Silverio J, Finnegan L, Heitman SE. Calcium and fat absorption from infant formulas with different fat blends. Pediatrics 1974;54:217–24.

76. Kulski JK, Hartman PE. Changes in the concentration of cortisol in milk during different stages of human lactation. Aust J Exp Biol Med Sci 1981;59:769–78.

77. Weichert CE. Prolactin cycling and the management of breast-feeding failure. Adv Pediatr 1980;27:391–407.

78. Carpenter G. Epidermal growth factor is a major growth-promoting agent in human milk. Science 1980;210:198–9.

79. Reid B, Smith H, Friedman Z. Prostaglandins in human milk. Pediatrics 1980;66:870–2.

80. Evans GW, Johnson PE. Prostaglandin E_2: the zinc-binding ligand in human breast-milk. Am J Clin Nutr 1977;30:611–3.

81. National Academy of Sciences. World food and nutrition study. Washington, D.C., 1977.

82. Solomons NW, Allen LH. The functional assessment of nutritional status: principles, practice and potential. Nutr Rev 1983;41:33–50.

83. Field T, Ignatoff E, Strevger S, et al. Nonnutritive sucking during tube feedings: effects on preterm neonates in an intensive care unit. Pediatrics 1982;70:381–4.

84. American Academy of Pediatrics Committee on Nutrition. Water requirement in relation to osmolar load as it applies to infant feeding. Pediatrics 1957;19:339–43.

DISCUSSION

Dr. Zoppi: We have been the first investigators (Udall JN. Dietary proteins, serum immunoglobulins and antigens. J Pediatr Gastroenterol Nutr 1982;1:155–6) to examine environmental factors that may stimulate the production by the infant of increased amounts of immunoglobulin. We have shown (Zoppi G, et al. Gammaglobulin level and dietary protein intake during the first year of life. Pediatrics 1978;62:1010–8; Zoppi G, et al. Gammaglobulin level and soy protein intake in early infancy. Eur J Pediatr 1979;131:61–9; Zoppi G, et al. Immunocompetence and dietary protein intake in early infancy. J Pediatr Gastroenterol Nutr 1982;1:175–82; Zoppi G, et al. Diet and antibody response to vaccinations in healthy infants. Lancet 1983;2:11–3) that an intake of less than 3 g/kg/day of animal protein or more than 4 g/kg/day of protein of vegetable origin (soya) results in: (a) a low blood level of gammaglobulin, IgG, and the complement fractions C3, C1 INA, and C3 PA; (b) an impairment of T-lymphocyte markers and reactivity; and (c) a low antibody response to poliovirus, diphtheria, and pertussis.

Dr. Rubino: I am concerned about the risks of recommending avoiding lactose after an episode of acute diarrhea. I agree that for the first few hours, only glucose-electrolyte solution should be given by mouth, but when the refeeding stage starts, then the question is whether or not to give a lactose-free diet. Since there are only a limited number of patients with lactose intolerance after acute gastroenteritis, I suggest treating each child individually and selecting the diet on the basis of a simple test, such as, for instance, measuring the reducing substances in the stools.

Dr. Barness: A baby who has diarrhea for more than 5 days is likely to become lactose intolerant.

Dr. Gracey: Removal of lactose from the diet has different implications in different parts of the world, and the issue of discontinuation of breastfeeding is important in developing countries where malnutrition and diarrhea are prevalent. Prof. Anderson, would you comment on this in relation to the remarks by Dr. Barness?

Dr. Anderson: I agree with Dr. Gracey; one must consider generalized recommendations in a global setting. Finding an inexpensive, readily available, and nutritious lactose-free feeding is difficult. Due care must be taken to guard against poorly absorbed preparations in malnourished children. Although it may take more than 5 days for the mucosa to regenerate after gastroenteritis, I do not know of any evidence that feeding factors inhibit this process.

Dr. Gracey: The development of intestinal lactase deficiency in certain populations after the age of 2 or 3 years should be referred to as a "prevalent characteristic" rather than a "genetic phenomenon"; this is because of the continuing controversy about its cause. I agree that the evidence points to this being a characteristic of certain racial groups. Incidentally, we have recently documented intestinal lactase deficiency in full-blooded Australian aborigines. I also agree that the evidence is against lactase being an inducible enzyme in humans.

Dr. Mata: I am always fascinated at the limited amount of data that exist regarding phospholipids in human milk as compared to cow's milk. More research must be done on lipid composition, because it might be important for the synthesis of surfactant. Is there any information concerning the content of human milk in certain growth maturation factors, such as urogastrone and DNA-promoting substances, which might be important for correction of immaturities in newborns?

Dr. Nordio: Dr. Barness, do you think that vitamin D supplementation is necessary for all breastfed babies? My impression is that in good environmental conditions, it is unnecessary. Do you think that one should speak of protein requirements only in quantitative terms? In the so-called "adapted formula," is it necessary to increase the taurine content and to correct the casein/whey protein ratio?.

Dr. Barness: Over the past few years, a number of reports have been published concerning rickets in breastfed infants of certain groups of people. The first group is where the child is kept in the house for long periods of time; the second is dark-skinned people who live in temperate climates; the third is a racial group of people where not only the babies but the mothers are kept for long periods of time well covered. With respect to vitamin D, it depends on exposure of the mother and the baby to the sun. I think that as countries become more industrialized, less ultraviolet is going to reach the baby, and more vitamin D will be necessary. A fourth group of children that might become vitamin D deficient are those that are breastfed when the mother is a strict vegetarian. Concerning the other question, taurine and carnitine may be essential factors, especially for low birthweight infants.

Dr. Senterre: I was surprised at your statement that in the United States, eczema is becoming a rare disease because infant formulas are now supplemented with linoleic acid. In Europe, it is just the opposite. Pediatricians are more concerned with eczema in infants fed adapted formulas with high beta-lactoglobulin content. I do not think that eczema is related to polyunsaturated fatty acid deficiency, even though there are biochemical signs of essential fatty acid deficiency in babies fed half-skimmed cow's milk.

Dr. Barness: Perhaps I used the wrong word. The incidence of an exfoliative itching skin lesion has decreased over a period of 25 years in one country, and I think it has been coincident with the wider use of polyunsaturated fatty acids and zinc. Not only beta-lactoglobulin but also bovine albumin may be highly allergenic. I think the future belongs to a different type of formula—if human milk is not going to be available—much less allergenic. Probably the approach will be either by splitting the proteins more or getting something like IGA to decrease absorption.

Dr. Rubino: Please discuss the role of the nonprotein nitrogen, which is so high in concentration in the human milk.

Dr. Barness: Paul Gyorgy and others have stressed the importance of N-acetyl glucosamine and other nonprotein nitrogenous factors. Further study is needed in this exciting area.

Dr. Balakrishnan: Prof. Barness, I understand from your chapter that breastfed children do not need any extra water. Would you say, then, that children fed on artificial formula need water? In Malaysia (tropical country), a large number of mothers interpret thirst as hunger and often introduce solids in early life, i.e., at 2 to 3 months when infants cry of thirst.

Dr. Barness: Published studies indicate that even in hot climates, breastfed infants do not require supplemental water. This is not true for formula-fed infants.

Dr. Waterlow: Regarding the question of water requirements, another factor must be taken into account. A high protein feed causes extra heat production and in a hot climate increases the need for sweating. I have read descriptions of infants dying of hyperpyrexia in the Gulf States when fed high protein formulas.

Dr. Whitehead: The issue of whether breastfed children require extra water to drink is very important where uncontaminated water is difficult to obtain. In many countries of the world, it is the custom to provide babies with extra drinks, either in the form of water itself or as dilute "bush" tea or fruit drinks. Clearly, we cannot answer this question with any scientific exactitude. It would be strange if a baby required the same amount of fluid to drink living in the average British room, which is kept at 18°C, as a baby in the developing world would require, with an ambient temperature varying between 35 and 45°C. This is one further area where we need more scientific information if we are to provide confident advice.

Dr. Zoppi: Several papers recently have been published on the influence of diet on amino acid metabolism. Diets have been considered adequate or not on the basis of blood amino acid levels and on urine amino acid excretion.

Dr. Barness: With a healthy child, this is not an important consideration.

Dr. Giovannini: What is your opinion on the presence of hormones in human milk, especially in relation to the possibility of their passage through the intestinal wall and related possible allergenic reactions?

Dr. Barness: They are very important: eight or 10 have already been found in human milk, including the kinins, prolactin, epidermal growth factors, prostaglandins, and others. Dr. Hamosh indicated that 50% of the fat in human milk is digested by lingual lipase. Dr. Barenbaum recently published a paper in which nonnutritive sucking has been found to increase growth rates in premature infants on the same caloric intake. I do not know if that has anything to do with lingual lipase.

Dr. Anderson: I agree that there is now much interest in lingual lipase and its contribution to fat absorption in patients with pancreatic insufficiency. However, I am not sure that it has been conclusively shown in humans to be responsible for the absorption of more than 50% of dietary fat.

Dr. Abdul Kader: The role of lingual and breast milk lipases on fat digestion in human newborns, as proposed by Margit and Michael Hamosh of Georgetown University Medical Center, Washington, D.C., is thought to be important. Increased fat excretion is encountered in infants fed with formula and expressed breast milk when the oral route is traversed with the feeds going straight to the stomach and jejunum, strongly suggesting the role of lingual lipase. Bechat Alemi, also from the same group (Pediatrics, 1981;68:484), has presented data suggesting the contribution of human milk lipase in the digestion and absorption of dietary fat in preterm infants.

On a different note, I would like to comment on vitamin K. The routine administration of vitamin K to all newborns, as recommended by the American Academy of Pediatrics, has been neglected. This can be dangerous in situations where there are home deliveries attended by nonmedical personnel who cannot administer vitamin K and where these mothers are also encouraged to breastfeed. As a result, we have seen a resurgence of hemorrhagic disease of the newborn. To overcome this problem, perhaps vitamin K could be administered by the oral route, as suggested by some Japanese workers. I would like your comments on this. Also why do formula manufacturers include information on vitamin K content in their products when these are usually based on cow's milk and therefore should contain high amounts of the vitamin?

Dr. Barness: Aballi showed that 1 mg vitamin K given orally would prevent hemorrhagic disease of the newborn. My question is: can it be given early enough? There must be a purpose to the low vitamin K in human milk, perhaps related to bone metabolism.

Nutritional Needs and Assessment of Normal Growth, edited by M. Gracey and F. Falkner. Nestlé Nutrition, Vevey/Raven Press, New York © 1985.

Nutritional Requirements of Low Birthweight Infants

Jacques Senterre and Jacques Rigo

Department of Pediatrics, State University of Liège, Bavière Hospital, B-4020 Liège, Belgium

Because of the rapid rate of anabolic processes and brain growth, no patient faces a more critical need for optimal nutrition than the low birthweight (LBW) infant. Nutritional requirements of these infants, however, remain unclear. Much of the controversy centers on the question: How fast should they grow? The Committee on Nutrition of the American Academy of Pediatrics (1) has stated that: "The optimal diet for the low birthweight infant may be defined as one that supports a rate of growth approximating that of the third trimester of intra-uterine life without imposing stress on the developing metabolic and excretory systems." Employing a factorial method, Ziegler et al. (2) summed the tissue accretion of nutrients with estimates of urinary and dermal losses and the extent of absorption to derive theoretical requirements of nutrients for infants of varying gestational ages. These calculations suggest that human milk and many formulas do not provide sufficient quantities of protein and certain minerals to support intrauterine rates of growth. In contrast, Räihä et al. (3,4) reported that preterm infants fed pooled human milk have less metabolic acidosis, low blood urea nitrogen and ammonia values, and fewer amino acid aberrations than infants fed high-protein formulas. These investigators contend that a growth rate and an accumulation of nutrients more important than those provided by human milk are not necessarily desirable. More recent studies conclude, however, that pooled breast milk is not ideal for LBW infants, since this feeding results in poorer fat absorption, a less desirable nutritional status, and slower weight gain when compared to fresh own-mother's milk or formulas adapted for LBW infants (5–7). In this chapter, we suggest some guidelines concerning the nutritional requirements of LBW infants in the light of results of metabolic balance studies carried out by us in more than 100 preterm infants during the last 10 years.

PROTEIN

There are four major considerations affecting the quantity and quality of protein to be given to LBW infants: (a) requirements for maintenance, (b) requirements for normal growth, (c) development of amino acid metabolism and renal function, and (d) energy intake or, more precisely, available energy for growth.

Protein intake must provide amino acids to replace the nitrogen loss resulting from protein turnover. According to studies by Pencharz et al. (8), about 12 g protein/kg are broken down and resynthesized each day in preterm infants. This protein turnover rate represents 10% of total body proteins and is three to four times greater than that observed in children or young adults. Skeletal muscle protein metabolism accounts for only 10 to 20% of whole body protein turnover in LBW infants, as opposed to 30% in adults. If we assume that the efficiency of the recycling of endogenous amino acids is 97%, this protein turnover rate leads to a nitrogen loss approximating 60 mg/kg body weight per day or 1 mg nitrogen/kcal expended. This calculation meshes with the lowest values of nitrogen urinary excretion measured in LBW infants receiving adequate energy and low protein intakes (9).

Protein requirement for new tissue synthesis can be estimated from chemical analyses of human fetal bodies of different gestational ages (10). Mean accumulation of nitrogen between 26 and 36 weeks of gestation is about 300 mg/kg/day or 2% of the weight gain, which corresponds to about 1.8 g protein/kg/day for a weight gain of 15 g/kg/day (11). The amount of protein to be given to LBW infants to achieve a nitrogen retention similar to that *in utero* depends on digestibility and utilization of the protein intake. In initial studies, we carried out metabolic balances in matched groups of LBW infants fed either banked human milk or various isocaloric formulas with different protein content (whey/casein ratio, 60:40). We observed that the fecal loss of nitrogen decreased with increasing postnatal age but was significantly higher in infants fed human milk than in those fed formulas (9,12). Coefficients of protein net absorption ranged from 81 to 87% with human milk as opposed to 86 to 94% with formulas.

The lower apparent digestibility of human milk proteins is probably due to the poorly degraded IgA immunoglobulins and the rapid transit time. Nevertheless, it may be concluded that even in the most premature infants, net absorption of protein is satisfactory. True digestibility of proteins from the diet is probably higher, since fecal nitrogen is partly of endogenous origin—desquamation of mucosal cells, digestive secretions, and bacterial debris. Urinary excretion of nitrogen was lowest in the LBW infants fed human milk (Table 1). It was related to nitrogen intake in those fed formulas and reached up to fourfold the value observed with human milk when protein intake was almost doubled. Nitrogen retention was about 250 mg/ kg/day in the infants fed human milk or the low-protein formula, but reached only 320 mg/kg/day in those fed the high-protein formula. As a result, the coefficients of net protein utilization (nitrogen retention/nitrogen intake) were inversely related to protein intake. This means that, when protein intake increases excessively, a higher proportion is oxidized and used as a source of energy. These observations are similar to those made in studies performed in young animals. In isocaloric conditions, the response to protein supply is related to the logarithm of the intake;

TABLE 1. *Nitrogen balances in LBW infants[a] fed human milk or isocaloric experimental formulas with various protein contents*

Nitrogen (mg/kg/day)	Human milk	Isocaloric formula		
		1	2	3
Intake	424 ± 32	415 ± 26	528 ± 39	736 ± 69
In feces	76 ± 9	55 ± 10	54 ± 13	60 ± 9
In urine	84 ± 12	115 ± 34	182 ± 41	365 ± 57
Retention	264 ± 33	245 ± 30	292 ± 44	311 ± 68
Absorption (%)	82 ± 4	87 ± 3	90 ± 3	92 ± 1
Retention (%)	62 ± 4	59 ± 7	55 ± 8	42 ± 7

[a] n = 20 in each group.

if nitrogen intake increases excessively, the increase in nitrogen retention tends to be small.

The key point in protein utilization is in fact the amount of energy available for growth (13). This amount depends on caloric intake, gut absorption, and energy expenditure. In LBW infants fed isocaloric diets, available energy varies mainly according to the importance of the steatorrhea. To investigate to what extent absorbed energy influenced nitrogen retention in our infants, we measured the net calorie supply by taking into account the fecal loss of fat. Figure 1 shows that there was a positive linear relationship between nitrogen retention and absorbed calories in all groups. However, the slope of the regression lines was sharper in the group of infants receiving a high protein intake. This means that a low calorie supply limits nitrogen retention, whereas at high caloric intakes, nitrogen retention is conditioned by protein intake.

In the light of these data, we carried out metabolic balance studies in preterm infants fed either human milk enriched in protein and energy with a semielemental diet (Alfaré, Nestlé), a human milk formula made of lyophilized bank human milk, or a LBW infant formula (Alprem, Nestlé). As shown in Table 2, nitrogen retentions similar to *in utero* accumulation rates were obtained with the three milks. Urinary excretions of nitrogen were only slightly higher than with human milk or the low-protein formula (see Table 1), and the coefficients of net protein utilization were satisfactory (14–16).

It is well demonstrated that too high an intake of protein may lead to a hazardous accumulation of amino acids, urea, and ammonia in LBW infants because of the immaturity of several enzymatic pathways and a low glomerular filtration rate. We previously reported the factors influencing the serum amino acid concentration in 163 LBW infants fed either parenterally or orally with human milk or adapted formulas (17–20). We observed that threonine, sulfur, and aromatic amino acid metabolism is impaired, whereas that of branched chain amino acids is enhanced in preterm infants. Low lysine concentration even with high protein intake suggests also that the lysine requirement is high or that the lysine content of formulas is not entirely available because of a Maillard reaction during heat processing.

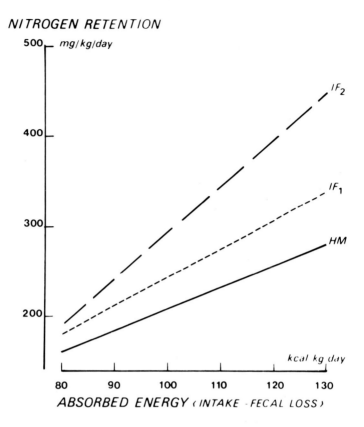

FIG. 1. Relationship between nitrogen retention and amount of absorbed energy in LBW infants fed human milk (HM) or infant formulas (IF$_1$, IF$_2$) providing 2.5 ± 0.2, 3.0 ± 0.3, and 4.3 ± 0.3 g protein/kg/day, respectively. (From refs. 9, 12, and 14.)

From these studies on protein and amino acid metabolism, we suggest that, provided energy intake is adequate, optimal protein intake for orally fed LBW infants is about 3.2 g (500 mg nitrogen)/kg body weight/day. Essential amino acids (9,14–20) should constitute 53% of nitrogen intake.

CARBOHYDRATES

It is well known that brush border lactase activity develops later and is lower than maltase activity during fetal life (21); significant pancreatic alpha-amylase activity appears only several months after birth (22). The question arises: To what extent are LBW infants able to digest lactose and glucose polymers? Boellner et al. (23) observed a flat response curve with a delayed and lower peak of blood glucose in oral lactose tolerance tests in preterm infants during the first week of life. These results suggest that intestinal hydrolysis of lactose is relatively impaired in LBW infants during the early neonatal period. After 10 days of age, however,

TABLE 2. *Nitrogen balances in LBW infants fed human milk (HM) supplemented with whey hydrolysate (WH), a human milk formula, or LBW infant formulas*

Nitrogen (mg/kg/day)	HM–WH[a] n = 20	HM formula[b] n = 13	LBW formula[c]	
			n = 14	n = 20
Intake	602 ± 40	553 ± 43	542 ± 33	594 ± 30
In feces	78 ± 15	105 ± 17	67 ± 20	45 ± 18
In urine	172 ± 23	132 ± 26	119 ± 30	161 ± 33
Retention	360 ± 52	317 ± 42	356 ± 30	388 ± 37
Absorption (%)	87 ± 5	81 ± 4	88 ± 4	92 ± 3
Retention (%)	60 ± 6	57 ± 5	66 ± 6	65 ± 5

[a]Pooled pasteurized human milk supplemented with 2 g/dl semielemental diet powder (Alfaré, Nestlé, Switzerland).
[b]Pooled pasteurized human milk supplemented with lyophilized skimmed milk, medium-chain triglyceride, and linoleate.
[c]LBW infant formulas: *n* = 14, Pregallia, Gallia, France; *n* = 20, Alprem, Nestlé, Switzerland.

oral lactose, maltose, and sucrose tolerance tests were shown to give similar rises in blood glucose in preterm infants with a mean birthweight of 1.5 kg (24).

Atkinson et al. (5) carried out metabolic balance studies in very LBW (VLBW) infants fed either own-mother's milk or an infant formula and found net absorption of lactose ranging from 97 to 99% at the end of the first and second week of life. Metabolic balance studies, however, do not provide a true index of lactose absorption, since gut flora can metabolize lactose reaching the colon. MacLean and Fink (25) performed sequential studies of breath hydrogen excretion in response to lactose feeding in LBW infants of 29 to 38 weeks gestation. They reported that all infants were excreting large amounts of hydrogen during the first 7 weeks of life. Using the 5-hr mean hydrogen excretion, they estimated that 66% or more of ingested lactose was fermented in the colon.

Recent studies by Stevenson et al. (26), however, suggest that hydrogen production by LBW infants is not necessarily related to carbohydrate tolerance but reflects chiefly the composition of colonic flora. Cicco et al. (27) investigated the ability of LBW infants to digest glucose polymers and observed a similar glycemic response to maltodextrins or lactose oral tolerance tests in 2- to 3-week-old preterm infants; plasma insulin response, however, was significantly lower after glucose polymers feeding. These authors suggested that this could be due to a lower secretion of gastric inhibitory polypeptides.

Using a calorimetric bomb, Kien et al. (28) measured fecal energy derived from carbohydrates in two groups of VLBW infants fed a formula differing only in carbohydrate composition: 100% lactose or 50% lactose and 50% glucose polymers. The authors calculated that the coefficients of absorption of carbohydrates were similar and about 95% in both groups. Our metabolic balance studies carried out in LBW infants fed a formula providing 3.6 g/kg/day pregelatinized cornstarch showed that starch absorption ranged between 80 and 97% (29). The good absorption of glucose polymers despite the lack of pancreatic alpha-amylase is probably due to the activity of salivary amylase and brush border glucoamylase, which have been shown to be well developed at birth (30).

In conclusion, the prematurely born infant has a reduced capacity to hydrolyze lactose only during the first days of life. The neonate is well equipped to deal with hydrolysis of sucrose, maltose, and glucose oligosaccharides. In contrast, starch digestion is limited. From a practical point of view, lactose, which has beneficial effects on absorption of minerals and composition of gut flora, must be the main source of carbohydrate in the diet of LBW infants. Maltodextrins, which have a low osmotic activity, are suitable for increasing carbohydrate intake when desired.

FAT

Fat malabsorption is common in LBW infants (31). The results of fat balance studies carried out in preterm infants fed various milks are shown in Fig. 2. In all groups, fat absorption improves with the increase of gestational age. Fat from pooled pasteurized human milk is no better absorbed than fat from most infant formulas. In contrast, fat from LBW infant formulas containing 40% medium chain triglycerides (Alprem,Nestlé) is well absorbed, whereas cow's milk fat is absorbed poorly.

Gas liquid chromatography of fatty acids in milk and stools showed that, whatever the milk, the longer the chain length of saturated fatty acids, the lower the coefficient of absorption; unsaturated fatty acids, such as oleic and linoleic acids, are better absorbed than their saturated homolog, stearic acid (Fig. 3). Watkins (32) has shown that the bile acid pool and the synthesis rate are much lower in preterm infants than in full-term babies or adults. As a result, bile salt concentration in duodenal fluid in LBW infants is often below the critical micellar concentration; this could explain the poor absorption of long chain saturated fatty acids.

Another factor of fat malabsorption in LBW infants is the low activity of pancreatic lipase resulting in impaired duodenal hydrolysis of triglycerides (33). Using thin layer chromatography, we observed that about 50% of fecal fat is neutral lipids.

Fat absorption in LBW infants can be improved first by using raw instead of pasteurized human milk. Indeed, fresh human milk contains an active bile salt-stimulated lipase, which can contribute up to half the total lipase and esterase activity in the duodenum of preterm infants (34). Moreover, it has been shown that intraluminal concentration and pool size of bile salts are higher in preterm infants fed fresh human milk than in those fed formula (35). The practical advantage of feeding non-heat-treated human milk has been clearly demonstrated by Williamson et al. (36). These investigators showed that fat absorption is much better when preterm infants are fed raw human milk as compared to pasteurized or boiled human milk. The addition of raw breast milk to formula or pooled pasteurized human milk can also improve fat absorption (37). The particular structure of the triglycerides of breast milk (palmitic acid mainly esterified in the 2 position of the

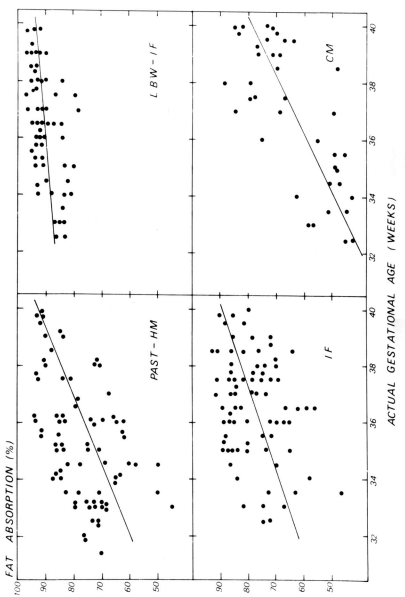

FIG. 2. Percentage of fat absorption according to actual gestational age in LBW infants fed pasteurized pooled human milk (PAST-HM), infant formulas (IF), preterm formulas with 40% medium chain triglycerides (LBW-IF), or a cow's milk formula with 100% butter fat (CM). (From refs. 12,15,16, and 31.)

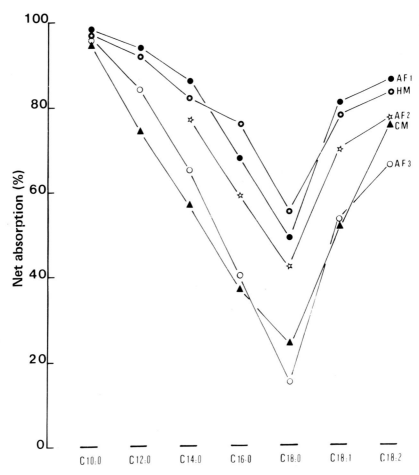

FIG. 3. Net absorption of various fatty acids in LBW infants fed pasteurized pooled human milk (HM), various adapted formulas (AF1, AF2, AF3) or a cow's milk formula (CM). (From refs. 12,15, and 31.)

glycerol molecule) seems of less importance. Indeed, in contrast to pancreatic lipase, breast milk lipase hydrolyzes all three ester bonds in the triglycerides. In addition, it has been shown that 2-monopalmitate is not necessarily better absorbed than palmitic acid if duodenal concentration of bile salts is low (38).

In conclusion, fat malabsorption may lead to a significant fecal loss of energy in LBW infants. Steatorrhea can be minimized by the use of fresh breast milk or formulas containing medium chain triglycerides.

ENERGY

As previously reported, in order to appreciate the outcome of absorbed energy, metabolic balance studies and indirect calorimetry measurements were carried out in two groups of VLBW infants fed either banked human milk or a LBW infant formula (39). Energy intake varied from 100 to 130 kcal/kg/day. In all infants, about 50% of energy absorbed was stored for growth and 50% was utilized for energy expenditure and energy cost of growth. As shown in Fig. 4, in both groups, 80% of absorbed nitrogen was used for new tissue synthesis. About 75% of carbohydrate intake was oxidized and 25% stored, probably as fat. It was the inverse for fat: 35% was oxidized and 65% was stored. There was no difference in fat utilization despite the fact that 40% of fat in the formula were medium chain triglycerides. The LBW infants fed human milk had lower weight gain than those fed the formula. In both groups, however, energy stored was about 3 kcal/g weight gain, and energy cost of growth was estimated at 1 kcal/g weight gain. In both groups, protein deposition represented 10 to 12% of weight gain, as during fetal life. In contrast, fat deposition was about twice as much as *in utero*. Adipose tissue biopsies showed that this elevated fat deposition in preterm infants is associated with an increased cellularity and a lower lipid content of adipose cells when compared to full-term babies at birth (40). Insulin response to diet could play a role in this important accumulation of fat and multiplication of adipose cells during postnatal life.

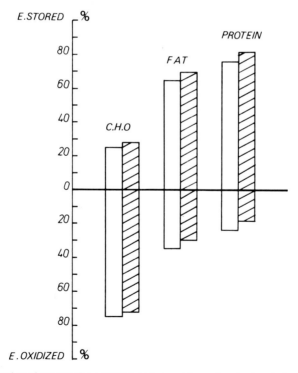

FIG. 4. Proportion of energy (E.) oxidized and stored from absorbed carbohydrates (C.H.O.), fat, and proteins in VLBW infants fed pooled human milk *(open columns)* or a preterm formula *(hatched columns)*. (From ref. 39.)

MINERALS

It has been known for many years that preterm infants fed human milk or formulas may develop signs of osteopenia or overt rickets. The pathogenesis of the skeletal lesions is often multifactorial. Inadequate calcium and/or phosphorus and poor vitamin D status have all been implicated (41).

From chemical analysis of human fetuses it can be calculated that the mean accumulations of calcium, phosphorus, and magnesium during the last trimester of gestation are about 130, 75, and 3.5 mg/kg/day, respectively (11). Human milk and most standard infant formulas do not contain enough calcium and phosphorus to allow preterm infants to accumulate these minerals at the intrauterine rate, even if all the calcium were absorbed and retained. In fact, calcium absorption is affected by a number of factors, such as lactose intake, quantity and quality of fat in the diet, amount of calcium and phosphorus in the milk, intestinal secretion of endogenous calcium, gestational and postnatal age, and vitamin D intake and metabolism (42).

Our metabolic balance studies carried out in LBW infants fed banked human milk show that net intestinal absorption of calcium is in the range of 50 to 70%, whereas that of phosphorus is about 90% (42). Because of the low calcium and phosphorus intake, however, preterm infants fed human milk retain only 20 to 25 mg calcium and phosphorus per kilogram body weight per day, which corresponds to 20% of the calcium and 30% of the phosphorus intrauterine accumulation rate (Table 3). In addition, they may present a phosphorus depletion syndrome characterized by hypophosphatemia, hypercalciuria, and no urinary excretion of phosphorus (43). The shortage of phosphorus is sometimes associated with signs of bone demineralization and high serum levels of alkaline phosphatase (44). In full-term babies, the low phosphorus intake from breast milk is sufficient to meet the requirements of growth, although even in those babies, the addition of phosphorus has been shown to improve calcium and phosphorus retention (45). In preterm infants, the low intake of phosphorus cannot meet the demand due to the rapid growth of skeletal and soft tissues and hypophosphatemia occurs more commonly

TABLE 3. *Calcium balance in LBW infants fed human milk, an infant formula, or a preterm formula*

Calcium (mg/kg/day)	Human milk[a] (n = 8)	Infant formula[b] (n = 19)	Preterm formula[c] (n = 10)
Intake	58 ± 11	81 ± 9	108 ± 12
In feces	25 ± 13	55 ± 12	45 ± 12
In urine	11 ± 6	2 ± 1	2 ± 1
Retention	23 ± 10	24 ± 8	61 ± 15
Absorption (%)	58 ± 19	32 ± 13	59 ± 10

[a]Pooled pasteurized human milk.
[b]Nan, Nestlé, Switzerland.
[c]Alprem, Nestlé, Switzerland.

as a result. Resolution of rickets and hypercalciuria with resultant increase in calcium retention (43) and bone mineral content has been observed in preterm infants fed human milk who were supplemented with phosphate alone (43,44) or with both calcium and phosphorus (46).

The mineral content of most infant formulas is higher than that of human milk. The percentage of absorption of calcium is generally lower, however, so that the amount of calcium retained is not necessarily much higher than with human milk (42,47). Unlike calcium, phosphorus is always well absorbed, net absorption ranging from 80 to 94% (42) (Table 4). In formula-fed infants, in contrast to breastfed infants, urinary excretion of calcium is usually low, whereas that of phosphorus is high (42). Because of the poor calcium absorption, the good absorption of phosphorus, and the low glomerular filtration rate, hyperphosphatemia may develop, causing hypocalcemia.

Supplementation of infant formulas with calcium salts and LBW infant formulas with a high mineral content are generally associated with an improvement of calcium retention (6,7,48). It has been claimed that oral calcium supplements, such as calcium lactate, can result in a calcium retention similar to the intrauterine rate (48); the interpretation of the balance data, however, is difficult, since phosphorus retention was not affected by calcium supplementation, and the apparent calcium/phosphorus retention ratio was at least 5:1. This strongly suggests that sedimentation of calcium salts had occurred in the bottle, so that infants received less calcium than was thought. Increasing calcium and phosphorus intake probably results in an improvement in retention of these elements, since sequential measurements of bone mineral density have demonstrated better bone mineralization in preterm infants fed formulas or human milk supplemented with calcium and phosphorus (46,49). It is not clear whether it is necessary to accumulate minerals at the same rate as *in utero*, however, since decreasing density and remodeling of bone occur in term infants after birth and may be a physiological event. In fact, there is evidence that in preterm infants, formulas containing 70 mg/dl calcium are sufficient to prevent bone diseases (50).

TABLE 4. *Phosphorus balance in LBW infants fed human milk, an infant formula, or a preterm formula*

Phosphorus (mg/kg/day)	Human milk	Infant formula	Preterm formula
Intake	28 ± 5	66 ± 8	68 ± 11
In feces	3 ± 1	4 ± 3	8 ± 2
In urine	1 ± 1	33 ± 10	16 ± 3
Retention	24 ± 5	29 ± 7	44 ± 7
Absorption (%)	89 ± 2	94 ± 5	89 ± 4

[a]Pooled, pasteurized human milk, *n* = 8.
[b]Nan, Nestlé, Switzerland.
[c]Alprem, Nestlé, Switzerland.

On the other hand, high intakes of minerals are not without risk in preterm infants. Too high an intake of phosphorus may lead to hyperphosphatemia, which blocks the production of 1,25-dihydroxy vitamin D [1,25(OH)$_2$-D] and results in hypocalcemia. Too high an intake of calcium has been associated with fat bolus obstruction (51) and lactobezoar formation (52) in the gastrointestinal tract. In addition, high calcium intake may impede fat absorption (12,42,48,53), and high calcium retention may induce metabolic acidosis since calcification of the skeleton is a source of net acid (54).

While delayed bone mineralization in LBW infants is related to inadequate mineral intakes, the role of vitamin D metabolites on the regulation of calcium and phosphorus absorption and their direct and indirect effects on skeletal development cannot be ignored. Our studies clearly demonstrate that absorption and activation of vitamin D is operative in preterm infants after 30 weeks of gestation (42,55,56). There is a close relationship between the maternal and fetal pools of 25-hydroxy vitamin D (25-OHD). In some European countries, there is no systematic vitamin D supplementation, and most of those preterm infants born during winter or spring have low levels of 25-OHD at birth, which reflects a state of relative vitamin D deficiency of the mothers. Daily administration of 2,000 IU vitamin D$_3$ increases the 25-OHD levels from birth; within 3 days, they are brought to levels observed in North America when seasonally adjusted norms are taken as reference (44,55, 56,59). Administration of vitamin D$_3$ also results in an increase of the circulating concentrations of 1,25(OH)$_2$D which, by 48 hr of age, are well above the range observed in adolescents (Fig. 5). This suggests that activation of vitamin D is mature in premature babies, but the substrate concentration is probably a limiting factor in the synthesis of 1,25(OH)$_2$D in LBW infant with a poor vitamin D status at birth. In those infants, the recommended daily allowance (400 IU) for term infants seems to be insufficient for adequate calcium homeostasis and bone mineralization.

CONCLUSIONS

Optimal nutrition for LBW infants remains a matter of considerable debate. Although it may not be necessary for the nutritional management of these infants, it has been recommended to provide them with energy, protein, and minerals in amounts that will allow accretion of nutrients at rates that would occur *in utero* during the third trimester of gestation.

In practice, when breast milk is available, LBW infants should be given preferably own-mother's milk. Raw instead of heat-treated human milk should be used, because it contains antiinfective factors and an active bile salt-stimulated lipase, which improves fat absorption. In growing VLBW infants, human milk should be supplemented with phosphorus, for instance, with 0.3 ml/dl of 1 M solution of disodium or dipotassium phosphate (9 mg P) in order to prevent or correct a phosphorus depletion syndrome. When LBW infants fed human milk are not growing satisfactorily, human milk can be supplemented with proteins (either

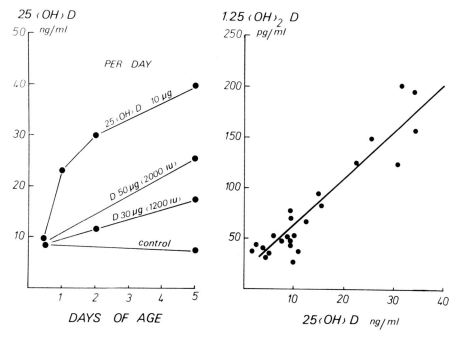

FIG. 5. Serum levels of 25-OHD according to the intake of vitamin D in LBW infants and relationship between 1,25(OH)₂D and 25-OHD serum levels at 5 days of age. (From refs. 42,55, and 56.)

human milk protein or whey hydrolysate). Energy can be added as maltodextrins, and calcium salts can be increased after adaptation of phosphorus content. In LBW infants fed artificially, advisable intakes are 170 to 200 ml of fluid, 110 to 130 kcal, and 3.0 to 3.4 g protein per kg body weight per day. Lactose should account for at least 50% of carbohydrates. Medium chain triglycerides up to 40% of total lipids will ensure good fat absorption. About 120 mg calcium and 70 mg phosphorus appear sufficient for tissue growth and satisfactory bone mineralization, provided vitamin D status is adequate. Whatever the diet, however, it should be noted that postnatal growth seems to differ from fetal growth, especially with respect to fat deposition.

REFERENCES

1. American Academy of Pediatrics. Committee on Nutrition. Nutritional needs of low-birth-weight infants. Pediatrics 1977;60:519–30.
2. Ziegler EE, Biga RL, Fomon SJ. Nutritional requirements of the premature infant. In: Suskind RM, ed. Textbook of pediatric nutrition. New York: Raven Press, 1981:29–39.
3. Räiha NCR, Heinonen K, Rassin DK, Gaull GE. Milk protein quantity and quality in low-birth-weight infants. I. Metabolic responses and effects on growth. Pediatrics 1976;57:659–74.
4. Rassin DK, Gaull GE, Heinonen K, Räihä NCR. Milk protein quantity and quality in low-birth-weight infants. II. Effects on selected aliphatic aminoacids in plasma and urine. Pediatrics 1977;59:407–22.
5. Atkinson SA, Bryan MH, Anderson GH. Human milk feeding in premature infants: protein, fat, and carbohydrate balances in the first two weeks of life. J Pediatr 1981;99:617–24.

6. Atkinson SA, Radde IC, Anderson GH. Macromineral balances in premature infants fed their own mother's milk or formula. J Pediatr 1983;102:99–106.
7. Shenai JP, Reynolds JW, Babson SG. Nutritional balance studies in very-low-birthweight infants: Enhanced nutrient retention rates by an experimental formula. Pediatrics 1980;66:233–8.
8. Pencharz PB, Masson M, Desgranges F, Papageorgiou A. Total-body protein turnover in human premature neonates: Effects of birth weight, intra-uterine nutritional status and diet. Clin Sci 1981;61:207–15.
9. Senterre J. Nitrogen balances and protein requirements of preterm infants. In: Visser HKA, ed. Nutrition and metabolism of the fetus and infant. The Hague: Martinus Nijhoff Publishers, 1979:195–212.
10. Widdowson EM, Dickerson JWT. Chemical composition of the body. In: Comar CL, Bromer F, eds. Mineral metabolism. Vol 2. Part A. New York: Academic Press, 1961:chapter 17.
11. Shaw JCL. Parenteral nutrition in the management of the sick low birthweight infant. Pediatr Clin N Am 1973;20:333–58.
12. Senterre J. L'alimentation optimale du prématuré. [Thesis]. Liège, Belgium: Vaillant-Carmanne, 1976:165 p.
13. Young VR. Protein-energy interrelationships in the newborn: a brief consideration of some basic aspects. In: Lebenthal E, ed. Textbook of gastroenterology and nutrition in infancy. New York: Raven Press, 1981:257–63.
14. Senterre J, Rigo J. Protein requirements of low birthweight infants. In: Monset-Couchard M, Minkowski A, eds. Physiological and biochemical basis for perinatal medicine. Basel: Karger, 1981:125–32.
15. Senterre J. Nitrogen, fat and mineral balance studies in low-birth-weight infants fed banked human milk or an experimental formula. In: Stern L, ed. Intensive care in the newborn. IV. New York: Masson, 1983:89–95.
16. Senterre J, Voyer M, Putet G, Rigo J. Nitrogen, fat and mineral balance studies in preterm infants fed bank human milk, a human milk formula, or a low birthweight infant formula. In: Baum JO, ed. Human milk processing, fractionation, and the nutrition of the low birth-weight baby. New York: Raven Press, 1983:102–11. (Nestlé Nutrition Workshop Series; vol 3).
17. Rigo J, Senterre J. Is taurine essential for the neonates? Biol Neonate 1977;32:73–6.
18. Rigo J, Senterre J. Optimal threonine intake for preterm infants fed on oral or parenteral nutrition. J Parent Enteral Nutr 1980;4:15–7.
19. Rigo J, Senterre J. Amino acid requirements in preterm infants on oral or parenteral nutrition. In: Wesdorp RIC, Soeters PB, eds. Clinical nutrition '81. Edinburgh: Churchill Livingstone, 1982:71–7.
20. Rigo J, Senterre J. Parenteral nutrition in the very-low-birth-weight infant. In: Kretchmer N, Minkowski A, eds. Infant adaptation of the gastrointestinal tract and nutrition. New York: Raven Press, 1983:191–207. (Nestlé Nutrition Workshop Series; vol 3).
21. Auricchio S, Rubino M, Mürset G. Intestinal glycosidase activities in the human embryo, fetus and newborn. Pediatrics 1965;35:944–54.
22. Zoppi G, Andreotti G, Pajno-Ferrara F, Njac DM, Gaburro D. Exocrine pancreas function in premature and full term neonates. Pediatr Res 1972;6:880–6.
23. Boellner SW, Beard AG, Panos TC. Impairment of intestinal hydrolysis of lactose in newborn infants. Pediatrics 1965;36:542–50.
24. Jarret EC, Holman GH. Lactose absorption in the premature infant. Arch Dis Child 1966;41:525–7.
25. MacLean WC Jr, Fink BB. Lactose malabsorption by premature infants: magnitude and clinical significance. J Pediatr 1980;97:383–8.
26. Stevenson OK, Shahin SM, Ostrander CR, et al. Breath hydrogen in preterm infants: correlation with changes in bacterial colonization of the gastrointestinal tract. J Pediatr 1982;101:607–10.
27. Cicco R, Holzman IR, Brown DR, Becker DJ. Glucose polymer tolerance in premature infants. Pediatrics 1981;67:498–501.
28. Kien CL, Summers JG, Stetina JS, Heimler R, Gransz JP. A method for assessing carbohydrate energy absorption and its application to premature infants. Am J Clin Nutr 1982;36:910–16.
29. Senterre J. Net absorption of starch in low birthweight infants. Acta Paediatr Scand 1980;69:653–7.
30. Lebenthal E, Lee PC. Glucoamylase and dissacharidase activities in normal subjects and in patients with mucosal injury of the small intestine. J Pediatr 1980;97:389–93.

31. Senterre J. Fat absorption in the premature infant. In: Arneil GG, Metcoff J, eds. Nutrition. Borough Green, UK: Butterworth, 1984:43–51. (BIMR Pediatrics; vol 3).
32. Watkins JB. Bile acid metabolism and fat absorption in newborn infants. Pediatr Clin N Am 1974;21:501–11.
33. Lebenthal E, Lee PC. Development of functional response in human exocrine pancreas. Pediatrics 1980;66:556–60.
34. Hernell O, Bläckberg L, Fredrikzon B, Olivecrona T. Bile salt stimulated lipase in human milk and lipid digestion during the neonatal period. In: Lebenthal E, ed. Textbook of gastroenterology and nutrition in infancy. New York: Raven Press, 1981:465–71.
35. Watkins JB, Järvenjää AL, Szczepanik Van-Leeuwen P, et al. Feeding the low birth weight infant: effects of taurine, cholesterol and human milk on bile acid kinetics. Gastroenterology 1983;85:793–800.
36. Williamson S, Funicane E, Ellis H, Gamsu RH. Effect of heat treatment of human milk on absorption of nitrogen, fat, sodium, calcium and phosphorus by preterm infants. Arch Dis Child 1978;53:555–63.
37. Alemi B, Hamosh M, Scanlon JW, Salzman-Mann C, Hamosh P. Fat digestion in very low-birth-weight infants: effect of addition of human milk to low-birth-weight formula. Pediatrics 1981;68:484–9.
38. Hernell O, Bläckberg L. Digestion of human milk lipids: physiologic significance of sn-2 mono-acylglycerol hydrolysis by bile salt-stimulated lipase. Pediatr Res 1982;16:882–5.
39. Putet G, Senterre J. Nutrient deposit in low birth weight infants. In: Kretchmer N., Minkowski A, eds. Infant adaptation of the gastrointestinal tract. New York: Raven Press, 1983:171–89. (Nestlé Nutrition Workshop Series; vol 3).
40. Bonnet FP, Senterre J, Heuskin A. Influence of nutrition on the growth and the lipid composition of the subcutaneous gluteal fat in premature and light-for-date infants. In: Bonnet FP, ed. Adipose tissue in childhood. Boca Raton, Florida: CRC Press, 1981:97–102.
41. Atkinson SA. Calcium and phosphorus requirements of low-birth-weight infants: a nutritional and endocrinological perspective. Nutr Rev 1983;41:69–71.
42. Senterre J, Salle B. Calcium and phosphorus economy of the preterm infant and its interaction with vitamin D and its metabolites. Acta Paediatr Scand 1982;(suppl)296:85–92.
43. Senterre J, Putet G, Salle B, Rigo J. Effects of vitamin D and phosphorus supplementation on calcium retention in preterm infants fed banked human milk J Pediatr 1983;103:305–7.
44. Sagy M, Bierenbaum E, Balin A, Orda S, Barzilay Z, Brish M. Phosphate-depletion syndrome in a premature infant fed human milk. J Pediatr 1980;96:683–5.
45. Widdowson EM, McCance RA, Harrison GE, Sutton A. Effect of giving phosphate supplements to breast-fed babies on absorption and excretion of calcium, strontium, magnesium and phosphorus. Lancet 1963;2:1250.
46. Greer FR, Steichen JJ, Tsang RC. Calcium and phosphate-supplements in breast milk-related rickets. Results in a very-low-birth-weight infant. Am J Dis Child 1982;136:581–3.
47. Shaw JCL. Evidence for defective skeletal mineralization in low birth-weight infants. The absorption of calcium and fat. Pediatrics 1976;57:16–25.
48. Day GM, Chance GW, Radde IC, Reilly BJ, Park E, Sheepers J. Growth and mineral metabolism in very low birthweight infants. II. Effects of calcium supplementation on growth and divalent cations. Pediatr Res 1975;9:568–75.
49. Greer FR, Steichen JJ, Tsang RC. Effects of increased calcium, phosphorus and vitamin D intake on bone mineralization in very low-birth-weight infants fed formulas with polycose and medium-chain triglycerides. J Pediatr 1982;100:951–5.
50. Gross SJ. Growth and biochemical response of preterm infants fed human milk or modified infant formula. N Engl J Med 1983;308:237–41.
51. Brooke OG, Gentner PR, Harzer G, Spitz L. Milk fat bolus obstruction in a preterm infant. Acta Paediatr Scand 1982;71:691–2.
52. Schreiner RL, Lemons JA, Gresham EL. A new complication of nutritional management of the low-birth-weight infant. Pediatrics 1979;63:683–5.
53. Katz L, Hamilton JR. Fat absorption in infants of birth weight less than 1,300 gm. J Pediatr 1974;85:608–14.
54. Kildeberg P, Engel K, Winters RW. Balance of net acid in growing infants. Endogenous and transintestinal aspects. Acta Paediatr Scand 1962;58:321–29.

55. Glorieux FH, Salle BL, Delvin EE, David L. Vitamin D metabolism in preterm infants: Serum calcitriol values during the first five days of life. J Pediatr 1981;99:640–43.
56. Salle BL, Glorieux FH, Delvin EE, David LS, Meunier G. Vitamin D metabolism in preterm infants. Acta Paediatr Scand 1983;72:203–6.

DISCUSSION

Dr. Barness: What is the vitamin D requirement of prematurely born or LBW infants?

Dr. Senterre: The requirement may be different, for instance, in the United States and in Belgium. In the United States, the preterm baby has a good vitamin D status at birth, which is of course related to the vitamin D status of the mother. Under those conditions, it seems sufficient to give, from birth on, 10 µg/day vitamin D for maintaining adequate 25-OHD and 1,25(OH)$_2$D plasma levels. In Belgium, however, most preterm infants have a very low level of 25-OHD at birth, and it is necessary to give them at least from 30 to 60 µg/day vitamin D to achieve adequate plasma levels of vitamin D metabolites and good calcium absorption. In premature infants, it has been shown that the 1,25(OH)$_2$D plasma level is highly dependent on the 25-OHD level.

Dr. Marini: We are more interested now in studying growth in preterm babies during the first 2 weeks of life, because this is the most vulnerable time. Please comment.

Dr. Senterre: I do not completely agree. Of course, to stop growth in the first 2 weeks of life is probably not without any risk, but I think we must balance the risks. Indeed, it is practically impossible to have a VLBW infant growing after a few days, because that implies giving a high intake of fluid, protein, and calories. This will result in metabolic stresses, such as hyperglycemia, hyperaminoacidemia, and water retention, which are also deleterious. The problem is a bit different in small-for-date (SFD) infants, because those babies are more mature and they can generally tolerate earlier an energy intake that promotes rapid catch-up growth.

Dr. Marini: Did you find any difference between appropriate-for-gestational age (AGA) and SFD babies?

Dr. Senterre: Our balance studies were carried out in AGA preterm infants, but we have some data on SFD infants. In those infants, the intestinal absorption is impeded, like in preterm infants, probably because intrauterine malnutrition is associated with reduced intestinal function. However, by giving them a supplement of carbohydrates to compensate for fat malabsorption, it is relatively easy to bring them into positive nitrogen balance.

Dr. Abdul Kader: I have a question with respect to medium chain triglyceride (MCT) content. Why do you use 40% MCT instead of a higher or lower content? Have you looked at the rate of calcium absorption and nitrogen retention with increasing or decreasing concentrations of MCT in the diet?

Dr. Senterre: We have used commercially available formulas, which contain about 40% MCT. I think this is a good figure. It has been shown that 80% MCT instead of 40% improves slightly fat and calcium absorption and nitrogen retention in preterm infants. However, the difference is small, and we must take into account the fact that MCTs are artificial fats that are usually oxidized.

Dr. Waterlow: In your chapter, you showed that children were gaining at about 20 g/kg/day, and the energy available for growth after deducting heat production was about 60 kcal/kg. Therefore, you have an energy cost of growth of 3 kcal/kg, which is low by comparison with other figures, suggesting that the infants are storing relatively more lean tissue than fat. The first question is whether this is borne out by your actual figures. Second, if the preterm infant needs about 3.3 g protein/kg and 125 kcal, this is a mixture with a protein-energy ratio of roughly 0.1, which cannot be achieved by human milk.

Dr. Senterre: In our study, the premature infants fed human milk gained about 15 g/kg/day and stored about 45 kcal/kg/day; those fed the formula gained about 20 g/kg/day and stored about 60 kcal/kg/day. Thus in both groups, about 3 kcal were stored per gram of weight gain. The composition of weight gain was similar in both groups: about 11% of protein and 25% of fat. This means that, compared to fetuses of similar gestational age, protein deposition, in percentage, was a bit lower, whereas fat deposition was almost twice as high. Energy cost of protein and fat deposition was estimated by calculating the increase in energy expenditure according to the weight gain. It accounts for about 0.7 kcal/g weight gain with human milk and 1.4 kcal with the formula. Thus it seems that the utilization of energy available for growth is more efficient with human milk.

Dr. Lechtig: Another way of estimating nutrient intake efficiency is relating weight gain per month to total energy intake during the same period. This would allow us to make comparisons with other stages in the life cycle, for example, with the fetal period. Is this information available?

Dr. Senterre: In our studies, weight gain indeed was related to total energy intake or, more precisely, to the amount of energy absorbed. When energy absorbed varied from 85 to 100 and to 115 kcal/kg/day, weight gains were 13, 16, and 20 g/kg/day, respectively. In that range of energy absorbed, we observed that about half the calories were oxidized and half were stored. With higher energy intakes, it may be more difficult to maintain such a good utilization of energy supply.

Dr. Zoppi: In my opinion, during the first months of life, infants need at least 3 g/kg/day protein. If an infant is fed formula, whey protein should be added, which may be allergenic.

Dr. Senterre: It is a problem. Preterm infants are theoretically more at risk of protein intolerance because of the higher permeability of the gut. In my clinical experience, however, I have rarely seen an allergy to cow's milk protein in preterm infants. It is possible that the immunological functions are more immature. However, it has been shown that antigenic properties of cow's milk-based formulas may vary according to the technical processing. There is a place for more research in this field. When I supplement human milk with protein, I use preferably a milk powder made of whey protein hydrolysate without antigenic properties. For instance, I had good results by adding 2% of a semielemental diet (Alfaré, Nestlé) to pooled pasteurized human milk.

Dr. Yips: What is the optimal amount of glucose polymers that can be added to breast milk?

Dr. Senterre: First, I do not think there is a need to supplement human milk with energy alone because human milk has a low protein content and there is a risk of developing signs of protein deficiency. When there is a supplement of protein, glucose polymers, such as maltodextrins, can be added in order to increase the energy content. These are well absorbed, despite the lack of pancreatic amylase. This probably is due to the presence of amylase in the human milk and in the saliva, and most important to the activity of the brush border glucoamylase. We did not observe any trouble in preterm infants receiving up to 14 g maltodextrins/kg/day. In contrast, starch tolerance is much more limited: 2 to 3 g/kg/day.

Nutritional Needs and Assessment of Normal Growth, edited by M. Gracey and F. Falkner. Nestlé Nutrition, Vevey/Raven Press, New York © 1985.

Energy and Protein Intakes of Exclusively Breastfed Infants During the First Four Months of Life

Nancy F. Butte and Cutberto Garza

Children's Nutrition Research Center, Department of Pediatrics, Baylor College of Medicine, Texas Children's Hospital, Houston, Texas 77030

If the breastfed infant is to be upheld as the reference standard for infant feeding, more complete information is needed on nutrient intakes from human milk and on the applicability of this "model" to nonbreastfed infants. Available data suggest that the nutrient requirements of the breastfed infant are not synonymous with those of the formula-fed infant. Qualitative and quantitative differences in composition and nutrient bioavailability of human milk and formula may influence nutrient utilization. Human milk with digestive, protective, inductive, and carrier functions may enhance the use of nutrients through mechanisms unavailable to formula-fed infants. Growth performance has been used as the basis of comparison between feeding regimens, as well as a criterion of nutritional adequacy. Reliance on growth performance ignores the fact that under conditions of dietary inadequacies, adaptive mechanisms may preserve growth at the cost of other physiological functions. Moreover, differences in the patterns of growth may exist between formula- and breastfed infants. For lack of better methodologies, however, growth continues to be the hallmark for overall nutritional assessment of infants.

A critical review of the literature indicates that the number of studies that document the milk intakes of healthy, exclusively breastfed infants is limited (Table 1). Even fewer investigations have determined the 24-hr ingestion of specific nutrients. Because of the diurnal patterns and wide individual variability in milk composition, representative 24-hr determinations of milk quantity and quality are necessary.

In the classic study by Wallgren (1), 363 Swedish infants were studied during the first 6 months of life. Breast milk consumption increased slowly but steadily during the first 3 months and then plateaued. Energy intake estimated from an assumed milk energy density of 70 kcal/dl ranged from 101 kcal/kg/day at 1 month to 72 kcal/kg/day at 6 months. Growth was reported to progress satisfactorily. Similar milk volumes were reported by another Swedish investigator some 30 years later (9). He also demonstrated that protein nitrogen intake decreased from 1.4 g/day (0 to 0.5 month) to 0.8 g/day (3.5 to 6.5 months).

TABLE 1. *Human milk intake and energy intake of exclusively breastfed infants (mean)*

Reference	N	Human milk intake (g/day) Age (days)						Energy intake (kcal/kg/day) Age (days)						Methodology
		30	60	90	120	150	180	30	60	90	120	150	180	
Wallgren (1)	363													Two 24-hr test-weighing (TW)
														Assumed 70 kcal/dl
Tarjan et al. (2) Males	42	645	750	798	821	—	817	101	103	94	87	—	72	One 24-hr TW
Females	50	576	704	733	747	—	740							One 24-hr TW
Lonnerdal et al. (3)		1,029	1,263	—	1,492	1,213								Four 24-hr TW
Whitehead and Paul (4)		724	752			756								
Males	27		791	820	829	790	922		104	97	91	89	87	Assumed 69 kcal/dl
Females	20		677	742	775	814	838		101	94	93	90	88	
Chandra (5)	36		601	626	793	856	925							One 24-hr TW
Picciano et al. (6)	26	606												Three 24-hr TW
Rattigan et al. (7)	13	1,187		1,238			1,164	233						Two 24-hr TW (mother)
														Assumed 70 kcal/dl
Dewey and Lonnerdal (8)	20	673	756	782	810	805	896	118	109	97	96	87	90	Two 24-hr TW
														Macronutrient analysis
														Conversion by Atwater

Breast milk intake and growth rates of 48 infants were monitored for 6 months in the Cambridge study (4). Breast milk consumption was similar to previous studies, and mean weights were above the National Center for Health Statistics (NCHS) 50th percentile for the first 4 months and thereafter displayed a slight tendency to fall below the 50th percentile.

Chandra (5) found that the average intakes of human milk consumed by Canadian infants ranged from 793 to 925 g/day at 4 to 6 months. Picciano et al. (6) reported milk intakes in the lower 600 g/day range. Most recently, Dewey and Lonnerdal (8) provided data on the milk and energy intakes of 20 infants followed longitudinally for the first 6 months of life. Milk intakes were within the range of previous work; energy intakes were similar to estimates in the Cambridge study (4) but higher than those cited by Wallgren (1).

From the foregoing studies, it appears that milk production rates of well-nourished women range from 600 to 900 g/day during the first 6 months of lactation. Two studies take exception to this range (2,7). Exceptionally high milk outputs have been reported for Hungarian and Australian women. Whether these outputs are representative of their respective populations is uncertain. Furthermore, one would expect greater weight gains of the recipient infants than those reported.

Human milk alone can support infant growth adequately for the first 4 to 6 months of life (10). It is evident that significant differences between individuals for milk requirements exist, but the determinants of these requirements remain elusive. Conflicting findings in regard to the influence of infant size, sex, and growth rate on milk intakes reemphasize the complexity of the growing organism and its needs. Few studies actually have determined the energy and protein intakes of breastfed infants, although nutrient concentration would be expected to influence the milk requirement.

In recognition of the need for a comprehensive study to document energy and protein intakes of breastfed infants in relationship to growth, a prospective, longitudinal study was designed. This investigation will be published elsewhere in its entirety (11). Salient results, however, are presented here with a discussion of the implications of these findings for energy and protein requirements during infancy.

MATERIALS AND METHODS

Human milk intake and growth performance of 45 exclusively breastfed infants were monitored over the first 4 months of life. Since the intent of this investigation was to document intake and resultant growth of normal infants, study participation was limited to healthy, term, and appropriate-size-for-gestational age infants. The mean birthweight of the 45 infants was 3.58 ± 0.45 kg (range, 2.56–4.57 kg). The mean gestational age according to the Dubowitz Scale was 39.2 ± 1.8 weeks (range, 37–42 weeks). There were 27 males and 18 females.

The mothers, who were responsible for execution of most of the study procedures, were mature (mean age, 28.0 ± 3.1 years), well-educated (mean level of education attained, 15.4 ± 1.8 years) women from the middle-upper socioeconomic stratum of Houston, Texas.

The study design entailed the determination of breast milk intake by the test-weighing procedure, sampling of milk for compositional studies, and monitoring of infant growth at monthly intervals. The actual times of observation were 35 ± 5, 64 ± 3, 91 ± 4, and 119 ± 6 days postpartum.

Human Milk Intake

The amount of breast milk ingested over a 24-hr period was determined by weighing the infant before and after each feeding. The mothers were instructed in the use of an automatic, electronic balance (Sartorius 3804 MP). The mothers were asked to change the infant's diaper before each feeding, not to change the infant's clothing during a feeding, not to alter the frequency or duration of their usual lactation pattern, and to record any losses of milk, urine, and feces not retained on or about the infants. The accuracy of the test-weighing procedure was evaluated on a formula-fed infant. The mean difference in milk intakes calculated from weighing the infant and weighing the bottle before and after nine successive feedings was 3.2 ± 3.1 g. The difference observed in infant weight before and after a feed always was less than that recorded for the bottle, as would be expected because of insensible water losses during a feed.

Milk Sampling

Breast milk was collected for compositional studies within 3 days after the test-weighing procedure. Mothers were instructed not to alter their usual feeding routine. At each feeding over a 24-hr period, the infant was offered one breast, and the contralateral breast was emptied of its entire contents with the use of an Egnell electrical breast pump (Cary, Illinois). Breasts were alternated for feeding and pumping with successive feeds. If necessary, infants were supplemented with human milk that had been collected and frozen in advance.

Milk samples were refrigerated in sterile, acid-washed polypropylene bottles for a maximum of 24 hr and transported on ice to the laboratory, where levels were measured and 24-hr pooled samples composed.

Biochemical Analysis

The heats of combustion of the milks were determined in an adiabatic bomb calorimeter (Parr) (12). A weighed amount of milk (approximately 0.2 g) was combusted with a known amount of mineral oil. Nitrogen was analyzed by the Kjeldahl method before and after trichloroacetic acid (10% 1:1 volume) precipitation of protein; protein nitrogen (PN) was determined on the solubilized precipitant, and nonprotein nitrogen (NPN) was estimated from the difference between total nitrogen (TN) and PN (9). The PN was converted to protein by the factor 6.25. Infant nutrient intakes were calculated from the 24-hr milk intakes and milk compositional data.

Anthropometry

Infant weight was recorded on the electronic balance before feeding. Infant length was measured on a recumbent infant board. Growth performance was evaluated against the NCHS reference standards (13).

Statistical Analysis

Data were entered into Scientific Information Retrieval (SIR) Data Base Management System (14). Data records were interfaced with Minitab and analyzed by regression and Pearson correlation coefficient (15). Trends over time were tested by fitting polynomials to individuals. The data on intake and growth were analyzed according to sex; however, the high variability in the data obscured detection of statistically significant differences between the sexes.

RESULTS

Human Milk Intake

Human milk intakes averaged 733 ± 89 g/day and were constant throughout the first 4 months of life (Table 2). The variability (coefficient of variation) in milk intake observed in this study was $17 \pm 1\%$ among infants of the same age. Feeding frequency declined slightly from 8.3 ± 1.9 to 6.7 ± 1.8 feedings/day over the study period. The linear regression describing milk intake (Y) (g/kg/day) against age (X) (days) was $Y = 171.69 - 0.553X$. The second degree polynomial term for age

TABLE 2. *Energy and protein intakes of exclusively breastfed infants during the first 4 months of life*

	Age (months)			
Intake	1 ($n = 37$)	2 ($n = 40$)	3 ($n = 37$)	4 ($n = 41$)
Human milk[a]				
g/day	751 ± 130	725 ± 131	723 ± 114	740 ± 128
g/kg/day	159 ± 24	129 ± 19	117 ± 20	111 ± 17
Energy				
kcal/g	0.68 ± 0.08	0.64 ± 0.08	0.62 ± 0.09	0.64 ± 0.10
kcal/day	520 ± 131	468 ± 115	458 ± 124	477 ± 111
kcal/kg/day	110 ± 24	83 ± 19	74 ± 20	71 ± 17
Protein				
mg/g	10.1 ± 1.5	8.9 ± 1.1	8.4 ± 0.9	8.2 ± 1.1
g/day	7.6 ± 1.7	6.5 ± 1.7	6.1 ± 1.3	6.1 ± 1.4
g/kg/day	1.6 ± 0.3	1.1 ± 0.2	1.0 ± 0.2	0.9 ± 0.2

[a]At the onset of the study, milk intake was estimated by deuterium dilution, a technique that later was determined to be inaccurate (16). For this reason, data are missing at 17 time points during the first 3 months. Values are mean $\pm$ SD.

was significant $(p<0.03)$. The quadratic equation defined was $Y = 199.08 - 1.48X + 0.0066X^2$.

The energy content of the milk displayed a significant decrease over time $(p<0.001)$. Mean energy intake was 476 ± 90 kcal/day. Although the absolute amount of energy ingested did not vary over time, energy intake relative to body weight decreased rapidly $(p<0.001)$. The linear regression of energy intake (kcal/kg/day) on age (days) was $Y = 118.95 - 0.44X$. The quadratic equation $(Y = 146.95 - 140X + 0.01X^2)$ was statistically significant $(p<0.01)$.

Because the protein concentration in the milk declined over time, the absolute amount of protein ingested by these infants decreased $(p<0.001)$. Therefore, as body weight increased, protein intake on a body weight basis declined $(p<0.001)$. The NPN, representing 27% of TN, was equal to 0.56 ± 0.28, 0.52 ± 0.20, 0.50 ± 0.13, and 0.48 ± 0.14 mg/g at the 4 respective months. The linear regression describing protein intake (Y) (g/kg/day) against age (X) in days was $Y = 1.71 - 0.0073X$. The quadratic equation was $Y = 2.14 - 0.0218X + .0010X^2$ $(p<0.001)$.

Growth analysis of these breastfed infants is detailed in Table 3. Mean weights were consistently greater than those of the NCHS study population $(p<0.01)$. Infant lengths, although not significantly different at birth, were significantly greater than the NCHS sample at the 4 successive months $(p<0.02)$. The weight-for-age percentile decreased after the first month at a rate of 2.6 percentiles per month $(p<0.01)$. Excluding birth measurements, length-for-age percentile remained stationary throughout the study, and weight-for-length percentile declined slightly $(p<0.01)$.

At birth, 7% and at 1 month, 2% of the infants fell below the 10th weight-for-age percentile; thereafter, none of the infants were below the 10th percentile ranking. On the upper end, 19% of the infants were above the 90th percentile at birth and 14% at 4 months. The remainder of the infants tended to aggregate within the 50th to 90th percentiles.

Infant weight was correlated with milk intake (g/day) at months 1 $(p<0.10)$, 2 $(p<0.01)$, and 4 $(p<0.02)$; however, infant weight explained only 16% of the variability in intake. Milk intake (g/day) was associated with the rates of weight gain (g/day) at months 1 $(p<0.10)$, 2 $(p<0.001)$, and 4 $(p<0.001)$. Milk intake accounted for 10, 30, and 28% of the variability, respectively, in the rate of weight gain at these 3 months. The variables energy and protein concentration did not account for any more of the variability seen in growth rate by multiple regression analysis. Thus the amount of milk, and not the concentration of its constituents, exerted the greatest impact on growth rates.

DISCUSSION

Milk Intake

The milk intakes of these infants were consistent with previous reports in the literature of exclusively breastfed infants reared under privileged conditions (1,4–

TABLE 3. Infant growth and NCHS percentile rankings during the first 4 months of life[a]

Age (months)	N	Weight (kg)	Length (cm)	Weight gain (g/day)	Weight gain (g/kg/day)	Length accretion (cm/month)	Weight-for-age (percentile)	Length-for-age (percentile)	Weight-for-length (percentile)
0	45	3.58 ± 0.45	50.9 ± 2.5	37.3 ± 12.4	10.6 ± 3.8	4.6 ± 2.1	65 ± 28	53 ± 34	46 ± 24
1	45	4.76 ± 0.52	55.7 ± 2.3	32.3 ± 13.8	6.9 ± 3.0	3.7 ± 1.6	71 ± 23	61 ± 30	62 ± 25
2	44	5.62 ± 0.67	59.0 ± 2.6	22.4 ± 7.6	4.0 ± 1.4	2.8 ± 1.3	73 ± 22	62 ± 29	62 ± 26
3	42	6.30 ± 0.30	61.8 ± 2.4	18.3 ± 8.1	2.9 ± 1.3	2.5 ± 1.7	70 ± 22	63 ± 26	57 ± 23
4	41	6.78 ± 0.80	63.7 ± 2.4				64 ± 26	59 ± 26	52 ± 26

[a] Values are mean ± SD.

6,8,9). Typical milk yields ranged from 600 to 900 g/day through the first 4 months of life. A plateau in intake was observed in the present study, contrary to other reports (1,4,5,8) of a gradual, steady increase in intake. The attrition rate in these longitudinal studies may have biased subject selection in favor of the high milk producers, thus resulting in a pattern of increasing milk production. Regression analysis revealed a significant curvilinear relationship between milk intake per kilogram body weight and age. Similar relationships were demonstrated for energy and protein intakes. The decrease in protein and energy requirements is consistent with the deceleration in growth velocity and the relatively inactive state of these infants.

Energy Intakes

Energy intakes of breastfed infants have been measured in only one previous study (8); others have estimated daily energy intakes by assigning an assumed caloric value to human milk (1,4,7). A certain degree of uncertainty is involved in this approach because the energy content of human milk is known to vary substantially throughout the day and among women. A representative 24-hr milk sample is required to reflect infant intake until alternative sampling schemes have been verified.

The energy intakes reported by Dewey and Lonnerdal (8) were higher than those recorded in the present study. Energy intakes per kilogram body weight ranged from 107 kcal/kg/day at 1 month to approximately 85 kcal/kg/day at 5 to 6 months. The macronutrient content of one midmorning milk sample was analyzed and converted to energy by application of the Atwater factors. Unusually high milk fat levels apparently resulted in high energy densities that averaged approximately 0.77 kcal/g.

Whitehead and Paul (4) applied an assumed energy content of 0.69 kcal/g to his milk intake data and predicted the energy requirement to grow along the 50th percentile of the NCHS weight standard. The mean estimations were 102,96,92,90, and 88 kcal/kg/day at months 2 to 6, respectively. These predicted energy intakes were 23 to 30% greater than those observed in the present study.

The energy concentrations of the milk at months 2 to 4 (0.64, 0.62, and 0.64 kcal/g, respectively) were slightly below expected norms. Incomplete expression of milk from the breast could account for the lower values in this study. A positive association was observed between the energy content of the milk and the volume of the aliquot expressed for analysis. However, application of the norm (0.67 kcal/g) to the recorded milk intakes would augment energy intakes by 4 to 6% only.

The gross energy intakes reported here were notably less than most voluntary intakes recorded for formula-fed infants (17–26) (Table 4). Mean metabolizable energy intakes of formula-fed infants decreased from approximately 115 kcal/kg/day at 1 month to 100 kcal/kg/day at 4 months of age. It should be noted that in most of these studies, infants were supplemented with solids or juices. Exceptionally low energy intakes recently have been reported in a Canadian study (30). In the

TABLE 4. *Energy intake of infants fed formula with supplementation of solids*

Reference	N	1–30	31–60	61–90	91–120	121–150	151–180	Methodology
		Infant age (days)[a]						
Beal (17)	26	118	130	119	110	104		Dietary history
Fomon (27)	60	133	127	117	106	100		Metabolic study 85% formula, 15% pooled human milk
Rueda-Williamson and Rose (25)	67			124	117	114		Dietary history
Rose and Mayer (24)	31					105		Dietary history
Beal (18)	28	105	111	105	102	97	95	Interview 24-hr dietary recall
Fomon et al. (28)	32							Weighed intake of formula and strained foods; study conducted at home
Males (133 kcal/dl)	9	138	123	114	99			
Males (67 kcal/dl)	13	112	116	103	98			
Females (67 kcal/dl)	10	101	100	95	93			
Fomon et al. (21)	154							
Males (67 kcal/dl)	69	116	115	101	95			Fomon (28)
Females (67 kcal/dl)	85	110	106	96	92			
Malansky et al. (23)								
Males	66		139			118		Dietary
Females	61		130			126		questionnaire
Ferris (19)	268							
Males		109	120	120	101	108	103	Dietary history
Females		111	116	100	114	101	96	
Yeung et al. (29)	770	120		102		96	93	Dietary record (4 days)
Vobecky et al. (30)	556							
Males		104	92	81	73	74	76	24-hr Dietary
Females		104	99	96	78	78	81	recall

[a]Values are kcal/kg/day.

studies conducted by Fomon and co-workers (20,21,28), formula intake was ascertained by weighing; intake in the other studies was determined by various forms of dietary history and recall. Despite the difficulties inherent in dietary methodologies, the recorded energy intakes of formula-fed infants were quite consistent. Thus by 4 months of age, the breastfed infants in this study consumed approximately 30% fewer calories than formula-fed infants.

Despite the lower nutrient intakes, the growth performance of this group of exclusively breastfed infants compared favorably with NCHS reference standards. There was a slight downward trend in weight-for-age percentiles, particularly evident in the fourth month. None of the infants, however, displayed clinically significant deviations from expected growth projectiles defined at birth.

The efficiency of energy utilization for growth has been examined carefully in formula-fed infants (22); however, incongruous age groupings preclude direct comparison with the present study. The ratios of weight gain (g) per 100 kcal in the formula-fed infants were 7.0(28–41 days), 6.2 (42–55 days), 5.1 (56–83 days), and

4.1 (84–111 days). In the breastfeeding study, ratios were 7.5 (35 days), 7.0 (64 days), 5.2 (91 days), and 3.8 (119 days). In general, the ratios were higher among the breastfed infants, which seems to indicate a higher degree of energy efficiency for growth. If the reported intakes of formula- and breastfed infants are correct, energy utilization differs between the two groups of infants.

Energy balance in the growing newborn may be summarized as: E (intake) $= E$ (growth) $+ E$ (excretion) $+ E$ (expenditure) (7). If breastfed infants attain comparable growth on lower energy intakes, then their excretory losses and/or energy expenditure must be less than formula-fed infants. Excretory losses via urine and feces have been estimated from balance studies (31). The caloric losses in urine were insignificant (1% of gross intake), and fecal losses ($\sim$7% of intake) were equivalent in infants fed human milk or a proprietary preparation based on dried cow's milk, with either lactose or sucrose added. Comparative tests that examine the equivalence of nutrients available from human versus cow's milk formula ideally should use fresh human milk. Otherwise, the effects of human milk processing, i.e., freezing, pasteurization, and storage, on composition and nutrient availability must be ascertained before valid comparisons can be made.

The component of energy expenditure would appear most amenable to adaptive changes. Energy expenditure may be partitioned into needs for maintenance, diet-induced thermogenesis (DIT), activity, and the synthetic cost of growth. Needs for maintenance and the thermic effect of food constitute obligatory energy expenditure. The synthetic cost of growth will vary according to the composition of the tissue being synthesized and so, in this sense, may be adaptive. Activity and DIT are facultative and responsive to changes in energy intake.

Metabolic rates have been shown to be depressed in malnourished infants (32). The infants (ages 4–24 months) studied were, on the average, 52% of expected weight-for-age and 72% of expected weight-for-height. Their mean reduction in resting metabolic rate was 27%. This seemed to represent a reduction in oxygen consumption per unit of metabolically active tissue based on total body potassium measurements and not a reduction due simply to alterations in body composition. Under ordinary nutritional circumstances, one would expect little variance in basal metabolism among infants unless body composition and/or tissue turnover rates were dramatically different.

Energy expenditure due to the thermic effect of food and physical activity has been measured for several hours postprandially in premature infants fed cow's or human milk. The increment above basal was 8.8 kcal/kg/day in the breastfed infant and 15.3 kcal/kg/day in the formula-fed infant (33). The difference was attributed partially to the higher protein and energy intake of the formula-fed infant.

Due to methodological constraints, few investigators have attempted to quantify the contribution of activity to total energy expenditure of infants. Murlin et al. (34) and Rose and Mayer (24) estimated that 27% of total energy expenditure was accounted for by activity, whereas Spady et al. (35) estimated that an additional 10 kcal/kg/day was required for activity. It is known that adults and older children respond to energy restriction by curtailing discretionary energy expenditure. Although activity comprises a comparatively small proportion of the total energy expenditure of infants, activity patterns and muscle tone may be altered in response to changes in dietary intake.

The DIT is an adaptive mechanism by which the body can conserve or expend energy. Brown adipose tissue (BAT), a major site of DIT, is present in the newborn (36). Animal studies have shown that BAT has the capacity to grow and regress according to the need for thermogenesis. This BAT is active in the newborn and may be susceptible to dietary influences, although studies have not been done in this age group. Thyroid hormones and catecholamines may be important mediators of this adaptive response.

For discussion purposes, the factorial approach has been applied to calculate theoretical energy requirements of infants in this study (Table 5). The energy required for maintenance was calculated from Levine-Marples' regression equation (37) derived from Benedict-Talbot's values (40). The mean energy requirement for maintenance of these infants would be 52 kcal/kg/day. In order to obtain subject cooperation, Benedict quieted his infants with a small meal prior to testing. Therefore, the metabolic rates measured under prevailing experimental conditions included not only the energy needed to maintain homeostasis but also energy expended for tissue synthesis, minimal voluntary muscular activity, and the postprandial increment of feeding.

The energy requirement for growth comprises the energy used for tissue synthesis and the energy inherent in the synthesized tissues. The energy cost of growth has been estimated from energy balance studies of infants undergoing accelerated growth, i.e., premature infants or infants recovering from malnutrition (35,38,39). The total energy cost of growth from these studies would be 4.4 kcal/g. This total is divided into 3.4 kcal/g for the energy content of the tissue and 1.0 kcal/g for tissue synthesis. The latter was included in the estimate for maintenance; an additional 16 kcal/kg/day would be required to cover the mean rate of weight gain of 27 g/day. The energy allowance for activity varies but can be estimated at two levels, 10 and 30 kcal/kg/day.

The total theoretical energy requirements of these infants in terms of metabolizable and gross energy are presented in Table 5. The observed intakes of the breastfed infants in this study did not deviate significantly from theoretical estimates at the lower activity level; however, discrepancies were apparent at the higher activity level.

Despite lower energy intakes, the breastfed infants displayed growth rates comparable to those cited for formula-fed infants. Infants may respond to varying energy levels by alterations in DIT, activity, and body composition. The thermic effect of food also may contribute to differences in energy expenditure. The significance of adjustments in these various components of total energy utilization cannot be determined without further study.

TABLE 5. *Estimated energy requirements of breastfed infants*

Age (months)	Mean weight (kg)	Weight gain (g/day)	Energy requirement (kcal/kg/day) for			Total energy requirement (kcal/kg/day)		Observed mean gross energy intake from breast milk (kcal/kg/day)	Observed mean metabolizable energy intake from formula[e] (kcal/kg/day)
			Maintenance[a]	Growth[b]	Activity[c]	Metabolizable	Gross[d]		
0–1	4.76	37	50	26	10–30	86–106	93–115	110	116
1–2	5.64	32	52	19	10–30	81–101	88–110	83	112
2–3	6.32	22	53	12	10–30	75–95	82–103	74	100
3–4	6.78	18	54	9	10–30	73–93	79–101	71	96

[a]Levine and Marples (37).
[b]3.39 kcal/g gained (35,38,39).
[c]Spady et al. (35), Murlin et al. (34), and Rose and Mayer (24).
[d]Metabolizable energy = 92% gross energy intake (31).
[e]From ref. 22.

Protein Intakes

The factorial approach as applied to protein requirements of infants assesses the maintenance losses of nitrogen together with the amounts laid down during growth. The maintenance requirement replaces obligatory urinary, fecal, integumental, and miscellaneous nitrogen losses. The requirement for growth entails the deposition of nitrogen in new tissues and chemical maturation (the increase in nitrogen concentration in the tissue).

Maintenance losses determined for infants on low protein diets vary. Barness et al. (41) and Kaye et al. (42) estimated that 120 mg N/kg/day and 100 to 110 mg N/kg/day, respectively, were required to maintain nitrogen equilibrium. The total maintenance nitrogen losses determined by Fomon et al. (28) were 57 mg N/kg/day (37 mg/kg/day in urine and 20 mg/kg/day in feces). Integumental losses have been approximated at 5 mg N/kg/day. The nitrogen requirement for growth based on the increment in body weight and body nitrogen content has been estimated to be 140 mg N/kg/day for infants 0 to 6 months (43). Based on available data, the minimum nitrogen requirement ranges from 202 to 265 mg/kg/day by the factorial approach. The factorial approach is problematic, however, because the efficiency of nitrogen utilization is dependent on the level of protein intake. Therefore, net nitrogen losses determined on protein-free or low-protein diets are not representative of adequate diets.

Because of the uncertainties of nitrogen losses and increments during growth, an empirical approach to protein requirements during infancy has been taken (44, 45). Requirements have been based on the observed nitrogen intakes of healthy infants growing normally (46). Nitrogen intakes recorded for infants receiving cow's milk formula (1.03% protein) were 282 ± 46 mg/kg/day (0–3 months) and 236 ± 30mg/kg/day (3–6 months).

Fomon and May (47) demonstrated that 240 mg N/kg/day from human or cow's milk or soy-based formula supported similar nitrogen retentions and normal growth. These intakes probably do not represent the minimum requirement for growth, since they were determined by infant appetite and the composition of the formula.

Protein requirements of the breastfed infants in this study are estimated in Table 6. These theoretical requirements may be compared with the observed intakes in this study. Equivalent protein intakes have been calculated from TN and PN. If all the nitrogen present in human milk were utilizable by the infant, then the theoretical protein requirement would be fulfilled. If NPN is not available to the infant, however, the PN would fall short of estimated needs.

The protein intakes of these breastfed infants were in agreement with observations made on Swedish infants, whose protein intakes were 8.8 g/day (0–0.5 month), 6.9 g/day (0.5–1.5 months), 5.6 g/day (1.5–3.5 months), and 5.0 g/day (3.5–6.5 months) (9). However, intake levels were considerably less than those of formula-fed infants who received 1.1 to 2.1 g protein/100 ml (22).

Fomon (27) demonstrated that nitrogen retention rates increased linearly with rising nitrogen intakes. However, the higher nitrogen intakes were not associated

TABLE 6. *Estimated protein requirements of breastfed infants*

| Age (months) | Mean weight (kg) | Weight gain (g/day) | Nitrogen requirements (mg/day) for[a] | | Nitrogen requirement | | Protein requirement | | Observed mean intake (g/kg/day) from breast milk | | Protein equivalent | | Observed mean protein intake from formula (22) (g/kg/day) |
			Maintenance	Growth[b]	g/day	g/kg/day	g/day	g/kg/day	TN	PN	TN	PN	
0–1	4.76	37	571	925	1.50	0.31	9.38	1.97	0.34	0.26	2.12	1.63	1.93
1–2	5.64	32	677	842	1.52	0.27	9.50	1.68	0.25	0.18	1.56	1.13	1.80
2–3	6.32	22	758	660	1.42	0.22	8.88	1.40	0.22	0.16	1.38	1.00	1.69
3–4	6.78	18	814	565	1.38	0.20	8.62	1.27	0.20	0.14	1.25	0.88	1.60

[a]Maintenance: 120 mg/kg/day (47).
[b]Growth: nitrogen content of tissue gained: 25 mg N/g; 26.3 mg N/g; 30 mg N/g; 31.4 mg N/g for four successive months (43).

with increased growth. The apparent nitrogen retention rates would result in body nitrogen contents beyond that expected by chemical maturation. These high nitrogen retentions are, in part, artifacts of the balance technique, which tends to overestimate intake and underestimate losses. Holt and Snyderman (48) contend that the technical errors account for only a small portion of the excessive nitrogen retentions; to date, the fate of the retained nitrogen remains elusive.

Balance studies have demonstrated higher nitrogen, as well as mineral, retention rates in formula-fed infants than in breastfed infants (31,49). Chemical maturation of the fat-free body mass is thought to be achieved by 4 years of age (50). The significance of accelerated chemical maturation in body composition of infants is unknown.

Parallel to the deceleration of growth velocity, protein requirements decrease throughout the first year of life. During the first months of infancy, when growth rates are highest, the protein requirement should be greatest in proportion to the caloric requirement. Human milk conforms to the protein-energy needs of the growing neonate. As seen in this study, the protein/calorie ratio decreased through infancy. The ratios observed in this study were 1.5, 1.4, 1.3, and 1.3 g protein/100 kcal for the 4 successive months.

Fomon and May (47) demonstrated that 1.6 g protein/100 kcal either from cow's milk or soy-based formula supported normal growth and nitrogen retention rates similar to those of breastfed infants (47). The authors concluded that the protein requirement was not greater than 1.6 g protein/100 kcal.

By the fourth month of life, the infants in this study were receiving 1.3 g protein/100 kcal or, in terms of PN, 145 mg PN/kg/day. Because the minimum nitrogen requirement for growth is unknown, it is uncertain if these nitrogen intakes are marginal. Confronted with a limited supply of dietary protein, the breastfed infant may conserve nitrogen by decreasing protein turnover, increasing conservation of endogenous amino acids, altering the composition of newly accrued tissues, and/or utilizing nonprotein sources of nitrogen. Human milk is composed of approximately 27% NPN. Free amino acids and peptides, which represent 10 to 20% NPN, are most likely metabolized (3). The extent to which urea, the major component of NPN, is utilized is unknown. Children on low-protein diets have retained nonspecific nitrogen efficiently (51). Snyderman et al. (52) demonstrated that weight gain could be restored in infants fed low-protein diets by the administration of nonessential nitrogen in the form of glycine or urea. Presumably, gut bacteria hydrolyze urea to ammonia, which may be absorbed by the portal system and thereby be made available for protein synthesis. The utilization of NPN from human milk has not been evaluated.

In conclusion, the levels of protein intake of these breastfed infants supported weight gains comparable to those of formula-fed infants. Whether the composition of the weight gained was equivalent to that of the formula-fed infant was not ascertained, and the long-term consequences of varying protein intakes during infancy are unknown.

These results have a narrow application. Inferences are limited by the favorable living conditions of the middle- and upper-income groups from which the subjects were drawn. There are abundant data, however, indicating that increased nutrient needs are imposed by adverse living conditions. In infant populations, infections probably represent the major challenge. Living conditions that promote an increased risk of infections simultaneously necessitate an increase in the quantity of nutrients needed to cope successfully with this challenge (26). Although the risk of infections is minimized in breastfed children, breastfeeding does not eliminate risk. Mechanisms that account for the increases in nutrient requirements under disadvantaged living conditions are found at each phase of nutrient assimilation: absorption may be impaired, and nutrient metabolism may be altered quantitatively and qualitatively. The rate of metabolism is increased, with resultant higher catabolic losses, and nutrients are directed away from normal processes to respond to the infection or other insults (53).

Two factors are particularly important in the further consideration of the present findings. The first is the effect of infections on nutrient utilization (54,55), and the second is the metabolic response to overt and marginal states of undernutrition. The adverse effects of infections on nutritional status are mediated via anorexia, possible impairment of digestive and absorptive function, and alterations in metabolism (26). There are few reasons to expect that breastfed infants are not susceptible to the same pathophysiologic demands. The magnitude of the response to these challenges, however, has not been measured in infants, although increases in energy expenditure, protein needs, and other nutrient requirements would be expected.

The adaptations in nutrient utilization made by undernourished adults and children undergoing nutritional repletion are well documented (56). An increased level of efficiency is maintained until repletion is achieved. Periods of convalescence also are characterized by increased voluntary intakes. Rates of milk production in response to the increased demands of the breastfed infant during periods of convalescence have not been described. Also, it is possible that the nutrients in breast milk are used more efficiently during the period following infection. The increase in efficiency, however, may be minimal given the high level of metabolic efficiency characteristic of the healthy breastfed infant.

Understanding the responses made by breastfed infants to such normal stresses is central to determining the nutrient needs of less advantaged populations. Without these data, it will not be possible to assess optimal periods of exclusive breastfeeding, to identify the best foods to complement human milk in the diet of the infant, and to evaluate the full benefits of human milk.

SUMMARY

The energy and protein intakes of 45 exclusively breastfed infants were documented during the first 4 months of life and found to be substantially less than those reported for formula-fed infants. Despite lower intakes, the breastfed infants gained weight at rates similar to formula-fed infants, which indicates a more efficient utilization of energy and nitrogen for growth. A better understanding of the adaptive mechanisms by which infants adjust to a given plane of nutrition is required in order to interpret the functional significance of the present findings.

ACKNOWLEDGMENTS

This work is a publication of the USDA/ARS, Children's Nutrition Research Center in the Department of Pediatrics at Baylor College of Medicine and Texas Children's Hospital.

REFERENCES

1. Wallgren A. Breast milk consumption of healthy, full-term infants. Acta Paediatr Scand 1945;32:778–90.
2. Tarjan R, Kramer K, Szoke K, Lindner K, Szarvas T, Divorschak E. The effect of different factors on the composition of human milk. II. The composition of human milk during lactation. Nutr Diet 1965;7:136-54.
3. Lonnerdal B, Forsum E, Hambraeus L. The protein content of human milk. I. A transversal study of Swedish normal material. Nutr Rep Int 1976;13:125-34.
4. Whitehead RG, Paul AA. Infant growth and human milk requirements. Lancet 1981;2:161-3.
5. Chandra RK Breast-feeding, growth, and morbidity. Nutr Res 1981;1:25-31.
6. Picciano MF, Calkins EJ, Garrick JR, Deering RH. Milk and mineral intakes of breast-fed infants. Acta Paediatr Scand 1981;70:189-94.
7. Rattigan S, Ghisalberti AV, Hartmann PE. Breast milk production in Australian women. Br J Med 1981;45:243-9.
8. Dewey KG, Lonnerdal B. Nutrition, growth, and fatness of breast-fed infants from one to six months [Abstract]. Fed Proc 1982;41:352.
9. Lonnerdal B, Forsum E, Hambraeus L. A longitudinal study of the protein, nitrogen, and lactose contents of human milk from Swedish well-nourished mothers. Am J Clin Nutr 1976;29:1127-33.
10. Committee on Nutrition, American Academy of Pediatrics. On the feeding of supplemental foods to infants. Pediatrics 1980;65:1178-81.
11. Butte NF, Garza C, Smith EO, Nichols BL. Human milk intake and growth performance of exclusively breast-fed infants. J Pediatr 1983;104:187–195.
12. Miller DS, Payne PR. A ballistic bomb calorimeter. Br J Nutr 1959;13:501-8.
13. National Center for Health Statistics. NCHS growth curves for children, birth–18 years. 1977; DHEW publication no. (PHS)78-1650.
14. Robinson BN, Anderson GD, Cohen E, Gazdzik WF, Karpel LC, Miller AH, Stein JR. Scientific information retrieval. User's manual version 2, 1980.
15. Ryan TR, Joiner BC, Ryan BF. Minitab version 81.1, 1981.
16. Butte NF, Garza C, Smith EO, Nichols BL. Evaluation of the deuterium dilution technique against the test-weighing procedure for the determination of breast milk intake. Am J Clin Nutr 1983;37:996-1003.
17. Beal VA. Nutritional intake of children I. Calories, carbohydrate, fat, and protein. J Nutr 1953;50:223-34.
18. Beal VA. Breast- and formula-feeding of infants. J Am Diet Assoc 1969;55:31-7.
19. Ferris AG, Vilhjalmsdottir LB, Beal VA, Pellett PL. Diets in the first six months of infants in western Massachusetts. J Am Diet Assoc 1978;72:155-63.
20. Fomon SJ, Owen GM, Thomas LN. Milk or formula volume ingested by infants fed ad libitum. Am J Dis Child 1964;108:601-4.
21. Fomon SJ, Filer LM, Thomas LN, Rogers RR, Prolisch AM. Relationship between formula concentration and rate of growth of normal infants. J Nutr 1969;98:241-54.
22. Fomon SJ, Thomas LN, Filer LN, Ziegler EE, Leonard MT. Food consumption and growth of normal infants fed milk-based formulas. Acta Paediatr Scand 1971;(suppl 223):1-36.
23. Maslansky E, Cowell C, Carol R, Berman S, Grossi M. Survey of infant feeding practices. Am J Public Health 1974;64:780-5.

24. Rose HE, Mayer J. Activity, calorie intake, fat storage, and the energy balance of infants. Pediatrics 1968;41:18-29.
25. Rueda-Williamson R, Rose HE. Growth and nutrition of infants: influence of diet and other factors on growth. Pediatrics 1962;30:639-53.
26. Scrimshaw NS, Garza C, Young VR. Human protein requirements: effects of infection and caloric deficiencies. In: Shimazono N, ed. Influences of environmental and host factors on nutritional requirements. Tokyo: Japanese Malnutrition Panel of United States–Japan Cooperative Medical Science Program, 1975:3-24.
27. Fomon SJ. Nitrogen balance studies with normal full-term infants receiving high intakes of protein. Comparisons with previous studies employing lower intakes of protein. Pediatrics 1961;28:347-61.
28. Fomon SJ, DeMaeyer EM, Owen GM. Urinary and fecal excretion of endogenous nitrogen by infants and children. J Nutr 1965;85:235-46.
29. Yeung DL, Hall J, Leung M. Adequacy of energy intake of infants. J Can Diet Assoc 1980;41:48-52.
30. Vobecky JS, Vobecky J, Demers PP, Shapcott D, Blanchard R, Black R. Food and nutrient intake of infants in the first fifteen months. Nutr Rep 1980;22;571-80.
31. Southgate DAT, Barrett IM. The intake and excretion of calorific constituents of milk by babies. Br J Nutr 1966;20:363-72.
32. Brooke OG, Cocks T, March Y. Resting metabolic rate in malnourished babies in relation to total body potassium. Acta Paediatr Scand 1974;63:817-25.
33. Mestyan J, Jarai I, Rekete M. The total energy expenditure and its components in premature infants maintained under different nursing and environmental conditions. Pediatr Res 1968;2:161-71.
34. Murlin JR, Conklin R, Marsh E. Energy metabolism of normal newborn babies with special reference to the influence of food and crying. Am J Dis Child 1925;29:1-28.
35. Spady DW, Payne PR, Picou D, Waterlow JC. Energy balance during recovery from malnutrition. Am J Clin Nutr 1976;29:1073-88.
36. Himms-Hagen J. Nonshivering thermogenesis, brown adipose tissue, and obesity. In: Beers RJ Jr, Bassett EG, eds. Nutritional factors: modulating effects on metabolic processes. New York: Raven Press, 1981:85-9.
37. Levine SZ, Marples E. The respiratory metabolism in infancy and in childhood XII. A biometric study of basal metabolism in normal infants. Am J Dis Child 1931;41:1332.
38. Brooke OG, Alvear J, Arnold M. Energy retention, energy expenditure, and growth in healthy immature infants. Pediatr Res 1979;13:215-20.
39. Sauer PJJ, Pearse RG, Dane HJ, Visser HKA. The energy cost of growth estimated from simultaneous direct and indirect calorimetry in infants of less than 2500 g. In: Visser HKA, ed. Nutrition and metabolism of the fetus and infant. The Hague: Martinus Nijhoff, 1979:93-107.
40. Benedict FG, Talbot FB. Metabolism and growth from birth to puberty, 1921; publication 302. Carnegie Institution of Washington.
41. Barness LA, Baker P, Guilbert P, Torres RE, Gyorgy P. Nitrogen metabolism of infants fed human and cow's milk. J Pediatr 1957;51:29-39.
42. Kaye R, Caughey RH, McCrory WW. Nitrogen balances on low nitrogen intakes in infants and the effects of gelatin supplementation with and without vitamin B_{12} and aureomycin. Pediatrics 1954;14:305-13.
43. Waterlow JC, Thomson AM. Observations on the adequacy of breast-feeding. Lancet 1979;2:238-42.
44. Committee on Dietary Allowances, Food and Nutrition Board. Recommended dietary allowances. Washington, DC: National Academy of Sciences, 1980.
45. FAO/WHO. Energy and protein requirements. WHO technical report series no. 522. Geneva, 1973. (Report series no. 52).
46. Fomon SJ. Comparative study of adequacy of protein from human milk and cow's milk in promoting nitrogen retention by normal full-term infants. Pediatrics 1960;60:51-61.
47. Fomon SJ, May CD. Metabolic studies of normal full-term infants fed a prepared formula providing intermediate amounts of protein. Pediatrics 1958;22:1134-47.
48. Holt LE, Snyderman SE. Protein and amino acid requirements of infants and children. Nutr Abstr Rev 1965;35:1-13.
49. Slater, JE. Retentions of nitrogen and minerals by babies 1 week old. Br J Nutr 1961;15:83-97.

50. Moulton CR. Age and chemical development in mammals. J Biol Chem 1923;57:79-97.
51. Read WWC, McLaren DS, Tchalian M, Nassar S. Studies with ^{15}N-labeled ammonia and urea in the malnourished child. J Clin Invest 1969;48:1143-9.
52. Snyderman SE, Holt LE, Dancis J, Roitman S, Boyer A, Bales ME. "Unessential" nitrogen: a limiting factor for human growth. J Nutr 1962;78:57-72.
53. Beisel WR. Nonspecific host factors—a review. In: Suskind R, ed. Malnutrition and the immune response. New York: Raven Press, 1977:341-74.
54. Beisel WR, Sawyer WD, Ryll ED, Crozier D. Metabolic effects of intracellular infections in man. Ann Intern Med 1967;67:744-79.
55. Beisel WR, Pekarek RS, Qu, BO, Wannemacher RW Jr. The impact of infectious disease on trace-element metabolism of the host. In: Haebstra WG, et al. Trace element metabolism in animals. Baltimore: University Park Press, 1974:217-40.
56. Chan H, Waterlow JC. The protein requirements of infants at the age of about 1 year. Br J Nutr 1966;20:775-82.

DISCUSSION

Dr. Zoppi: Dr. Butte, does the protein/energy ratio change during the first months of life?

Dr. Butte: It decreased over the first 4 months from 1.5 to 1.3 g protein/100 kcal.

Dr. Zoppi: We have observed 76 normal full-term infants from birth to the fourth month of life; 36 were breastfed *ad libitum*, the others were fed *ad libitum* four different (conventional and "adapted") formulas containing different amounts of energy, protein, fat, and carbohydrate. The control of volume intake functioned well only in infants fed human milk. The others showed either a high blood urea nitrogen or high levels of insulin and parathormone. It is concluded that it is possible to feed *ad libitum* only breastfed infants, and the composition of adapted formulas should be revised.

Dr. Samsudin: Dr. Butte, what is the relationship between maternal energy intake and milk production?

Dr. Butte: There was a positive correlation between maternal energy intake and milk production; this factor, however, accounted only for 13% of the variability in milk output.

Dr. Waterlow: We have been struggling for nearly 2 years to produce a new report for FAO/WHO on energy and protein requirements. Obviously, much of the data presented here is highly relevant. The age of 4 months is a critical one; in developing countries, it is common to see growth beginning to falter at that age or even earlier (Waterlow JC, Ashworth A, Griffiths M. Faltering in infant growth in less developed countries. Lancet 1980;ii:1176-8). Second, in both developed and less developed countries it is common for complementary feeding to start at about this age. Let us accept that most mothers, if they are healthy, can breastfeed their babies adequately for around 4 months. After that, if there is no limitation of food supply, the baby's appetite is probably the best guide. If, however, there is a limitation, then we need to know how much food the baby needs and of what kind if its growth is not to be impaired.

I am not concerned if a child grows along the 25th percentile rather than the 50th, because, after all, the NCHS reference is a description of the growth of American children, and no one claims that it is an optimum. The 25th percentile is probably just as good as the 50th, for all we know, but the 5th percentile probably is not. Therefore, I ask the question: What level of energy intake would be safe to prevent children's growth falling below the 5th percentile?

I am happy with the figure of 85 to 90 kcal/kg, which Whitehead produced as the average requirement at about 6 months, because it fits with other data. For example, the studies of Torún at INCAP showed, admittedly in slightly older children, that when the energy intake was reduced from 100 to 90 kcal/kg, there was no difference in growth, nitrogen balance, or physical activity, but when it was dropped to 80 kcal/kg, the children became less active (Report on the Informal Gathering of Experts to review the Collaborative Research Programme on Protein Requirements and Energy Intake. ESN/MISC/80/P3. FAO, Rome, 1980).

I think we can accept Whitehead's figures, but I have difficulty in accepting the value of 70 kcal/kg that Dr. Butte discusses. It does not seem to fit with what we know about the physiology of energy metabolism. I question the figure of 50 kcal/kg as representing the maintenance requirements; it approximates the basal or resting metabolic rate in children fasted for several hours [Karlberg P. Determination of standard energy metabolism (basal metabolism) in normal infants. Acta Paediatr Scand 1952;41,(suppl 89)]. The maintenance requirement has to allow for the thermic effect of food as well as a minimal level of physical activity. It is usually taken as 1.5 times the basal metabolic rate (FAO/WHO. Energy and protein requirements. WHO technical report series no. 522. WHO, Geneva, 1973). On top of that, there must be a substantial allowance for growth at this age. I do not see how all this can be fitted into 70 kcal/kg; yet the growth velocities appear to be satisfactory. Therefore, there is a problem in interpreting these studies. If we put the energy requirement at this age as low as 70 kcal/kg, practically no children in the world should be malnourished, except perhaps because of the effect of infection. Is that a sensible position to take?

Dr. Butte: We were quite surprised at the low intakes, but as we completed more and more infants, it was quite consistent. I do suspect, although we did not follow the infants beyond 4 months, that many would have been supplemented at 4 months onward. Several of the mothers called and asked what they should supplement with at that time. It is possible that energy requirements were at their lowest in accordance with decelerated growth velocity and relative inactivity. With an increase in activity as the infants began to crawl and such, one would have expected energy requirements to increase. I would like to emphasize that these infants were reared under very protective environmental conditions. I would be reluctant to apply 70 kcal/kg/day as the recommended level of energy intake for infants reared under less favorable environmental conditions or for formula-fed infants. I do not know if the discrepancy in energy intake between formula- and breastfed infants is as large as I am stating; since we did not study formula-fed infants, I can rely only on the literature. Recent studies indicate lower energy intakes among formula-fed infants, but we still need to explain the discrepancy between Fomon's reported energy intakes and related growth rates and our observations.

Dr. Whitehead: Clearly, the quality of data currently available to us is not as good as we would like it to be, but I would suggest that it indicates that intakes of around 92 to 93 kcal/kg/day at 4 months down to about 90 kcal/kg/day at 6 months is certainly adequate for the average child, whether he be bottle-fed or mixed-fed. Indeed, data for breastfed children would indicate such a value as being unnecessarily high.

Perhaps I could also clarify my attitudes toward the use of growth charts. I do not think it matters if an *individual* child grows steadily along either the 5th or 95th percentile. This just indicates that he is naturally small or big. What does matter is switching from one percentile to the next. This is where the use of existing growth charts for determining lactational inadequacy becomes important. Our data indicate that now children are being breastfed for longer and are being given solids later, their pattern of growth is not the same shape as it was in the 1950's and 1960's when our existing growth charts were compiled. The danger is that mothers are led to believe that their babies' growth is starting to falter before this is indeed the case.

Dr. Waterlow: One comment, which is perhaps more suitable for tomorrow, is that I plead for velocity standards, rather than percentiles. If 20 g/day at 4 or 5 months is a reasonable weight gain, we know from Fomon's data (Fomon SJ. Infant nutrition, 2nd ed. Philadelphia: W.B. Saunders, 1974) that the standard deviation of that velocity is very high; I do not think one can call it faltering until the velocity falls down to, say, 2SD below the mean. One can detect the change in velocity much more quickly than a change in attained weight.

Dr. Falkner: Dr. Butte, in your comparison with the NCHS standards, in the age group concerned, those in fact were children given in the Fell's longitudinal study. How many of them were breastfed?

Dr. Butte: Information was available on 75% of the infants. About 17% were exclusively breastfed for 3 months; very few infants were breastfed beyond that.

Dr. DeMaeyer: It may be of interest to report on some of the data collected during the WHO collaborative study on the volume and quality of breast milk. The study was conducted over the last 4 years in six countries: two industrialized countries, Sweden and Hungary, and four developing ones: Nigeria, Guatemala, Zaïre, and the Philippines. The study was cross-sectional, and data were collected for as long as breastfeeding was continued. In Hungary and in Sweden, where the population is homogenous from the socioeconomic point of view, only one group of population was selected for the study. In the developing countries, where there are socioeconomic differences between the different classes, three groups were selected: an urban well-to-do, an urban poor, and a rural poor. It was assumed that because of the socioeconomic differences, there would also be differences in the nutritional status of the different groups; that was confirmed by some of the parameters that were measured. In Sweden, the volume of milk increased over the first month and then remained fairly stable for the next 5 months; the average volume was about 800 ml/day. In Hungary, the volume was about 680 ml. In the developing countries, it was between 550 and 650 ml, except in one group in Zaïre, which was extremely malnourished and where the volume was about 300 ml.

It is interesting to note that within certain limits, the nutritional status of the groups did not influence the volume of milk that was taken by the child; it was only when very severe stages of malnutrition were reached that an influence on the volume of breast milk was observed. Differences in nutritional status did not seem to influence the length of breast-feeding, and even in the very severely malnourished group in Zaïre, the length of lactation was still 24 months, and at 24 months the women were still secreting significant amounts of milk.

Concerning the energy value of breast milk, in Sweden, the values were extremely high, ranging between 73 and 83 kcal/100 ml. In Hungary, they were between 60 and 65, and in the developing countries between 56 and 65; there was no statistically significant difference between the developing countries and Hungary. In all these populations, supplementation started relatively early; from the second or third month on, the mother was already giving a supplement, which might be a purée containing some energy.

It was possible to calculate the energy intakes for Guatemala and for Hungary; these were not statistically different. At 1 month of age, the energy intake was ranging between 82 and 90 kcal/kg, at 3 months, between 75 and 80, and at 4 months, between 70 and 80. These were values calculated taking into account the breast milk intake plus any supplement that may have been taken.

Nutritional Needs and Assessment of Normal Growth, edited by M. Gracey and F. Falkner. Nestlé Nutrition, Vevey/Raven Press, New York © 1985.

Human Lactation, Infant Feeding, and Growth: Secular Trends

R. G. Whitehead and A. A. Paul

Medical Research Council Dunn Nutrition Unit, Cambridge CB4 1XJ, United Kingdom; and Keneba, The Gambia

This chapter discusses food intakes, principally of dietary energy, in infants fed in various ways: exclusively from the breast, with breast milk plus supplementary or complementary foods, and by artificial feeding. Changing attitudes toward infant feeding are emphasized, and it is shown that as in many other age groups in industrialized countries, the amounts of food consumed during infancy and the early preschool period are probably lower now than in the past, a fact that is influencing growth.

CHANGES IN ATTITUDES TOWARD BREASTFEEDING

Until 10 years ago, the incidence of breastfeeding in the Western world was falling off rapidly, and few women were breastfeeding their babies beyond 2 to 3 months. The changing situation in the United Kingdom is illustrated in Fig. 1, in which Wharton (1) has summarized the results of two national surveys carried out by the Office of Population Census and Surveys (OPCS) in the years 1975 and 1980 (2,3). In 1975, only 30% of mothers claimed to be breastfeeding at 3 months; 5 years later, however, this figure was above 50%. There has also been a corresponding shift in the timing of the introduction of solids, such as commercial cereals.

As Fig. 2 demonstrates, however, the acceptance of breastfeeding is highly polarized, depending on social class. In Cambridge, United Kingdom, Whichelow and King (4) showed in 1978 that among social grade I wives, those of professional workers, the incidence of breastfeeding was high; this was far from the case with the wives of unskilled manual workers (social grade V). These class differences are an important complicating factor in any attempt to relate diet to growth, as we know that social class is also statistically related to the size of children (5). To what extent these anthropometric variations are due to genetic factors or to dietary and other environmental factors is not known, but there is clearly a danger of undesirable biases being introduced into any simple analysis.

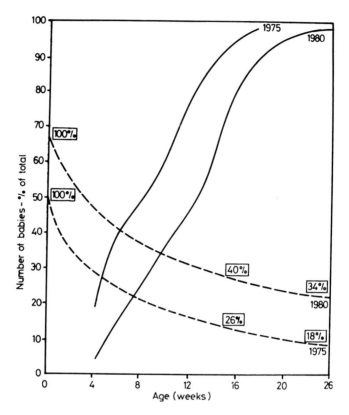

FIG. 1. Proportion of babies in England and Wales being breastfed (---) and receiving solid foods (—) during the first 6 months of life in 1975 and 1980; percentage of those who started breast feeding, 100%. [Abstracted from OPCS surveys (2,3) by Wharton (1).]

ENERGY INTAKE OF EXCLUSIVELY BREASTFED BABIES

There are few truly reliable data on the milk intake of babies who are solely breastfed, certainly after 2 months of age. It is now generally accepted by investigators who study human lactation that even when a mother claims to be exclusively feeding her child at the breast, careful questioning frequently reveals that small amounts of other foods, particularly fluids, are in fact also being given. Many mothers regard only another form of milk as "real food" when their babies are small and, unless pressed, tend to dismiss other small but nevertheless nutritionally significant items. This represented a major technical complication to be overcome in our Cambridge study on lactation (6).

The frequent consumption of additional types of food other than breast milk becomes readily apparent when the deuterium oxide (dose to the mother) method (7) for measuring the breast milk intake of young babies is used. This method measures body water turnover as affected by both sources of food. In a study carried out in the suburban township of Bakau in The Gambia, for example,

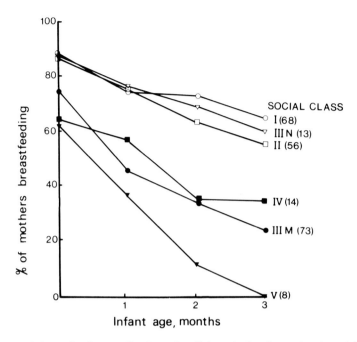

FIG. 2. Decline in breastfeeding over first 3 months of infancy in six cohorts of mothers delivered at Mill Road Maternity Hospital, Cambridge, in 1978, according to social class. Number of mothers shown in parenthesis. [Based on data of Whichelow and King (4).]

measurements of breast milk intake were initially carried out using the more simple dose to the child method (8). The investigator, Dr. Rowland *(private communication)*, had been assured by the mothers of a group of particularly well growing children that they never gave their babies water or other sources of food before 6 months. The amounts of breast milk the children were apparently consuming appeared particularly high (mean, 1,191 ml/day), but when the dose to the mother method was introduced to check the data, significantly lower values (although still comparatively large by international standards) were obtained. Typically, 200 to 300 ml water was being consumed by the babies from one source or another, in addition to breast milk.

Table 1 shows the most complete set of data claimed to be from solely breastfed children (9). The data are now almost 50 years old, but Table 2 provides similar values from a more recent study performed in Cambridge (6). In the latter study, it is apparent that even though all the mothers breastfed their babies for more than 4 months, only a minority continued to do so exclusively after 3 to 4 months, despite being committed to this form of feeding.

The progressive selection of babies in the Swedish study is more difficult to follow. The data were a mixture of cross-sectional and prospective information and exclude any subject who was suspected of not consuming the quantity of milk

TABLE 1. *Intakes of exclusively breastfed Swedish infants collected in the 1930s[a]*

Age group (months)	N	Mean body wt (kg)	Mean milk consumption (ml/day)
Girls			
1	65	4.08	576
2	70	4.83	704
3	43	5.59	733
4	46	6.32	747
6	26	7.56	740
Boys			
1	58	4.35	645
2	72	5.08	750
3	49	5.93	798
4	42	6.72	821
6	33	8.02	817

[a]From ref. 9.

TABLE 2. *Milk intakes of fully and partly breastfed babies in Cambridge[a]*

Month	Fully breastfed (ml/day)			Partly breastfed (ml/day)		
	N	Mean	SD	N	Mean	SD
Boys						
1–2	27	791	116	1	648	—
2–3	23	820	187	5	833	123
3–4	18	829	168	10	787	172
4–5	5	790	113	20	699	204
5–6	1	922	—	25	587	188
6–7	0	—	—	21	484	181
7–8	0	—	—	18	342	203
Girls						
1–2	20	677	87	0	—	—
2–3	17	742	119	2	601	—
3–4	14	775	138	6	664	258
4–5	6	814	113	11	662	267
5–6	4	838	88	15	500	194
6–7	1	854	—	15	481	246
7–8	1	786	—	11	329	242

[a]From ref. 6.

"corresponding to or less than his requirement." In the later stages, when the number of subjects had fallen off, additional babies were sought to fill in the gap in information. Both sets of data have frequently been used to illustrate the normal pattern of milk output and intake up to 6 months in exclusively breastfed children, but this is misleading. In practice, both sets of data represent a progressively selected subsection of the mother-infant population. Thus two potential biases are introduced. There is a specific selection of women who have no problem in maintaining or increasing their milk output well into the second trimester of lactation, and individual babies are selected who might be metabolically more efficient than the average child and thus have lower than average energy and nutrient requirements.

Another investigator who has studied exclusively breastfed babies between 3 and 8 months is Chandra from Newfoundland (10). In Fig. 3, the energy intakes from

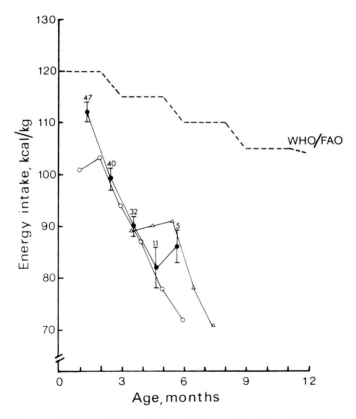

FIG. 3. Total energy intake per kilogram body weight in exclusively breastfed infants compared to WHO/FAO 1973 estimated requirements (11). *Open circles*, Wallgren (9) (*n* = 304 at 1 month falling to 180 at 6 months); *triangles*, Chandra (10) (*n* = 32 at 3–4 months falling to 24 at 7–8 months); *solid circles*, Whitehead and Paul (6). Cambridge infants, mean and SEM with number of subjects.

breast milk for exclusively breastfed children in Sweden, the United Kingdom, and Newfoundland are expressed on a per kilogram body weight basis. Also provided for purposes of comparison are the well-known 1973 WHO/FAO (11) estimated mean physiological requirement values. It is apparent that by 3 to 6 months, the energy intakes of the breastfed children are dramatically lower.

Table 3 provides a more general list of breast milk intakes of children from the industrialized countries of the world, regardless of whether or not they are exclusively fed from the breast; Table 4 covers the developing countries. While average values from the latter areas do tend to be lower, it is remarkable how well these mothers are able to perform when one considers their level of nutrition.

INTAKES OF FORMULA-FED CHILDREN

A discussion of the energy and nutrient intakes of formula-fed children, in contrast to those who are exclusively breastfed, is complicated by the fact that the attitudes of both the medical profession and mothers toward infant feeding and what constitutes a desirable baby shape and size have been changing dramatically over the past 10 to 15 years. While the data in Tables 1, 2, 3, and 4 indicate that there has been little trend with time in the quantities of breast milk consumed by babies of different ages, the same cannot be said for babies who are formula-fed. Some idea of the magnitude of the change can be deduced from a comparison of Figs. 4 and 5. Figure 4 shows data collected in the United States from 1946 to 1967 (12,13): energy intakes, expressed per kilogram body weight, are similar to the 1973 FAO/WHO theoretical requirements. Figure 5 illustrates much more recent information from two detailed and large studies carried out in Canada (14,15). While there must always be some doubt attached to the absolute accuracy in measurements of food intake, especially in such young babies, the data indicate a profound change. The fall in energy intake with age during the first half of infancy in the Canadian sets of data is much more like that encountered with breastfed babies. During the second half of infancy in both Canadian studies, however, there were indications of an upward trend once more in energy intakes per kilogram; this is discussed in a subsequent section of this chapter.

It is unfortunate that there are so few recent data on the precise intake of formula-fed children; understandably, interest has mostly concentrated on the nutritional adequacy of lactation. With the trend in Cambridge being so firmly toward breastfeeding (4), it has proved extremely difficult to find children to study who start life being bottle-fed, especially if one is to avoid the problem of social class bias discussed earlier, which makes a true comparison between the breast- and bottle-fed child so difficult. Acknowledging this shortcoming, Fig. 6 illustrates data on nine Cambridge bottle-fed babies whom we have recently studied. It will be noted that the intake is significantly lower than the 1973 FAO/WHO estimated requirement but not as low as found in the Canadian study of Vobecky et al. (14) although similar to that of Yeung and co-workers (15).

Perhaps it is not surprising that downward trends in the energy intakes of young babies who are artificially fed have been taking place, since similar trends have

TABLE 3. *Milk output of well-nourished mothers from industrialized societies*

		Month of lactation (ml/day)											
		1		2		3		4		5		6	
Reference	Country	Mean	Range	Mean	Range	Mean	Range	Mean	Range	Mean	Range	Mean	Range
Wallgren (9)[a]	Sweden	610	416–839	727	508–964	766	497–1,029	784	577–1,065	—	—	778	510–1,123
Lonnerdal et al. (58)	Sweden	724	490–958[d]	752	575–929	—	—	—	—	756	476–1,036[a]	—	—
Hofvander et al. (59)[a]	Sweden	656	360–860	773	575–985	776	600–930	—	—	—	—	—	—
Whitehead and Paul (6)[b]	UK	740	480–1,059	785	380–1,235	784	280–1,114	717	210–1,091	588	183–1,020	493	135–906
Chandra (10)[a]	Canada	—	—	—	—	793	651–935[a]	856	658–1,054[a]	925	701–1,149	872	602–1,124[a]
Rattigan et al. (60)[c]	Australia	1,187	799–1,611	1,238	862–1,543	—	—	—	—	—	—	1,128	608–1,610
Pao et al. (61)[b]	USA	569	398–989	—	—	523	242–1,000	—	—	—	—	436	147–786
Picciano et al. (62)[a]	USA	606	336–876[a]	601	355–847[a]	626	392–860[a]	—	—	—	—	—	—

[a]Exclusively breastfed.
[b]Includes mixed feeding.
[c]Data obtained by weighing the mother, not the child.
[d]Ranges calculated from mean ± 2 SD.

TABLE 4. *Milk output of women from the developing world*

Reference	Country	Month of lactation (ml/day)															
		1		2		3		4		5		6		7–9		9–12	
		Mean	Range	Mean	Range	Mean	Range	Mean	Range	Mean	Range	Mean	Range	Mean	Range	Mean	Range
Holemans et al. (63)	Zaire	436	—	405		380		417		415			—	323		—	—
Hennart and Vis (64)	Zaire	517	250–780	—		605	390–920					525	180–1,080	580	210–950	582	270–850
Van Steenbergen et al. (65)	Kenya		—	675	271–1,079[a]					555	189–921[a]			487	153–821[a]		—
Martinez and Chavez (66)	Mexico		—	577	433–842		—	537	455–663		—	561	432–850		—	462	337–670
Prentice (67; unpublished)	The Gambia		—	677	525–1,055		—		—	617	355–885		—	595	435–744	542	210–730

[a]Ranges calculated from mean ± 2 SD.

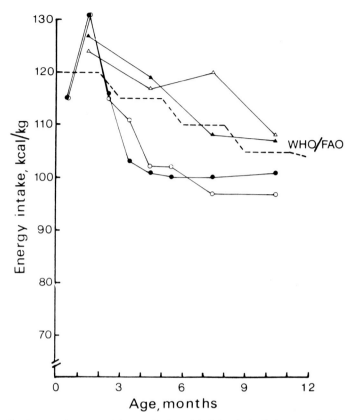

FIG. 4. Total energy intake per kilogram body weight in bottle-fed infants studied between 1946 and 1967 in comparison to WHO/FAO estimated requirements (11). *Solid circles*, boys (*n* = 33 at 1 month, rising to 49 by 1 year); *open circles*, girls studied longitudinally by Beal (12) (*n* = 23 at 1 month rising to 44 by 1 year); *solid triangles*, boys (*n* = 41 at 0–3 months rising to 79 at 9–12 months); *open triangles*, girls from the cross-sectional study of Fryer et al. (13) (*n* = 76 at 0–3 months rising to 59 at 9–12 months.)

been reported at virtually all other crucial stages of life. Figure 7, for example, shows a recent analysis (16) we have made on the comparative energy intakes of older children, before and after 1955. The striking difference is at puberty in both girls and boys. Many causes have been attributed to these differences in intake, but we favor two as the most important: (a) a lower level of activity, and (b) the current fashion of being as slim as possible. Of even greater relevance to the topic under discussion are the apparent trends in food intake of mothers during pregnancy and lactation shown in Table 5: whereas pregnant and lactating mothers in the industrialized world in the 1960s may have been consuming amounts of dietary energy close to the international RDAs, today's values are considerably lower.

Whatever the causes of these trends might have been, there can be little doubt that from puberty onward, present-day potential mothers have a different personal

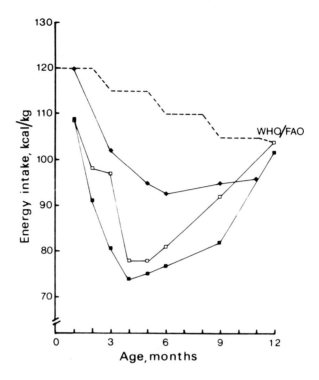

FIG. 5. Total energy intake per kilogram body weight in two recent longitudinal studies of bottle-fed infants in Canada in comparison to WHO/FAO estimated requirements (11). *Solid triangles,* boys and girls from Yeung et al. (15) (*n* = 163 at 1 month rising to 308 at 10 months); *solid squares,* boys and *open squares,* girls from Vobecky et al. (14) (*n* = cohort of 556 infants).

attitude toward diet and, understandably therefore, toward how they would like their babies to look. The bottle-fed baby is now much less likely to be over-encouraged to feed after he has indicated he is satisfied. Mothers in Cambridge have clearly been influenced by the almost certainly fallacious argument that adipocyte hyperplasia in early childhood results in adult obesity (17). The scare about overconcentrated baby foods and hypernatraemia (18) has likely been an additional contributory factor. The redesigned milk powder scoops also make "heaping" much less likely, and mothers now receive strict instructions about adding the exact amount of milk powder to the water. The milk formulations themselves have also been changed (19,20), and most manufacturers initially had reports of the "new foods" not being as satisfying for the baby as the older ones (21,22), again indicating that the babies might have been receiving less net food per feed than before.

HOW MUCH FOOD DO MIXED-FED BABIES RECEIVE?

The concept of long-term mixed, breast-complementary feeding, so usual in rural areas of the developing world, is much less common in such countries as the

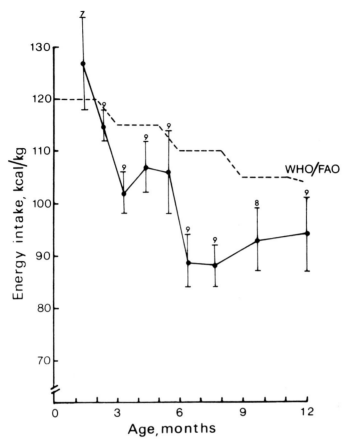

FIG. 6. Total energy intake per kilogram body weight (mean and SEM) in 9 bottle-fed infants (6 girls and 3 boys) in Cambridge in comparison to WHO/FAO estimated requirements (11).

United Kingdom. While in The Gambia, rural mothers usually initiate the weaning process at 4 months, they carry on breastfeeding, irrespective of the amount of milk they are able to produce, invariably up to 18 to 24 months (23). Milk output is maintained at remarkably satisfactory levels, almost certainly because the mothers practice complementary feeding rather than substituting for a given breastfeed. In the United Kingdom, when a mother decides it is time for her child to receive something other than breast milk, it is frequently supplementary—not complementary—feeding that is introduced; as shown in Fig. 8, this has a dramatic effect on milk output. Initially, for the first 3 months, there is remarkably little difference between the Cambridge and Gambian women. From 4 months onward, however, the net output of milk in the former mothers falls away dramatically, until by 7 to 8 months, weaning has virtually been completed (24). In fairness to the Cambridge mothers, however, it should be pointed out that even this 4 months weaning period is a relatively long one for an industrialized country.

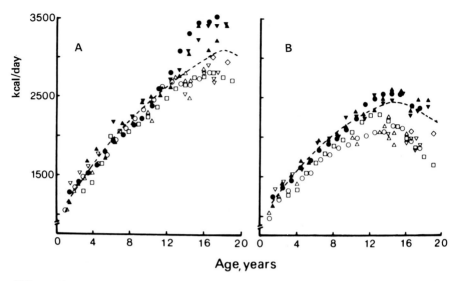

FIG. 7. Energy intakes (kcal/day) of boys **(A)** and girls **(B)** studied between 1930 and 1955 *(solid symbols)* compared to more recent studies (1956–1978, *open symbols*) (16) in relation to WHO/FAO (---) 1973 recommendations (11). Symbols are for the countries, with references, as follows: *open circles*, USA (12); *open downward triangles*, USA (13,79,80); *open upward triangles*, UK (31,72,81–83); *open diamonds*, Australia (84); *open squares*, Australia (85); *solid downward triangles*, USA (86); *solid circles*, USA (87); *solid upward triangles*, UK (88).

Thus in interpreting data on mixed-fed children, it should be recognized that little information is available for healthy Western women who utilize the most desirable method of combining the two ways of feeding. It is readily apparent that women view the introduction of weaning foods as something quite separate from breastfeeding and not part of an integrated process. Now that we have relearned from the women of the developing world that the great majority of women should have no major biological difficulty in starting breastfeeding, perhaps we can also accept the normality of breast- plus complementary feeding after 3 to 4 months and that there is no reason why, once this has started, it should lead to a rapid diminution in lactational capacity.

As with bottle-feeding, it is unfortunate that the literature contains little quantitative data in which the intake of both breast milk and other foods has been simultaneously measured until the time that the child has been fully weaned. Solutions to many of the controversial issues that have plagued pediatric health workers and the infant food industry in recent years require information in this important area. Figure 9 shows the data collected in Cambridge on this subject (6). It is important to note that, as when being solely breastfed, children were not achieving the 1973 WHO/FAO (11) assumed physiological requirement, the same was true after the supplement was introduced. Indeed, during the initial phase of weaning from 3 to 5 months, there was little difference in total energy intake, regardless of whether individual babies were fully or only partially breastfed. The

TABLE 5. *Energy intakes of pregnant and lactating women
from industrialized countries*

Reference	Country	Energy intake[a] (kcal/day)
Pregnancy		
Thomson (68)	UK	2,503
English and Hitchcock (69)	Australia	2,090
Lunell et al. (70)	Sweden	2,154
Smithells et al. (71)	UK	1,957
Darke et al. (72)	UK	2,152
Whitehead et al. (73)	UK	1,980
Lactation		
English and Hitchcock (69)	Australia	2,460
Thomson et al. (74)	UK	2,716
Naismith and Ritchie (75)	UK	2,930
Whichelow (76)	UK	2,728
Abrahamsson and Hofvander (77)	Sweden	2,280
Sims (78)	USA	2,124
Whitehead et al. (73)	UK	2,295
Rattigan et al. (60)	Australia	2,306
Stuff et al. (73a)	USA	2,028

[a] Note than the RDA (WHO/FAO, 1973) for moderately active women during pregnancy is 2,550 kcal/day during the second and third trimesters and 2,750 kcal/day during the first 6 months of lactation.

lack of any sharp upward inflection in intake once other foods were made available is indicative that the seemingly low dietary energy intakes of the breastfed child do reflect true physiological requirements.

Our attempts to estimate energy intakes in mixed-fed babies which are compatible with normal rates of growth on the basis of these dietary data have been reported previously (6,25). Briefly, the total energy intake per day (breast milk plus other food) was related to infant body size at successive months of infancy, as well as to velocity of growth, using multiple regression analysis, with the anthropometric measures as the two independent variables. As shown in Table 6, significant relationships were found at all ages up to 8 months. From the characteristics of the regression equations, it was possible to calculate the energy intake compatible with the growth of a child following the National Center for Health Statistics (NCHS) 50th percentile as well as the corresponding amounts of milk that would have been necessary for the child if he had been breastfed throughout all this period. It will be noted that beyond 4 months, these estimated milk volumes are higher than those found in practice for the majority of women (see Tables 3 and 4). The energy data (kilocalories per kilogram body weight) for these mixed-fed babies is also plotted in Fig. 10 using the same format as for the wholly breast- and formula-fed children. Once again, a steeper fall in energy requirements per kilogram is indicated than with the 1973 WHO/FAO values between 1 and 6 months.

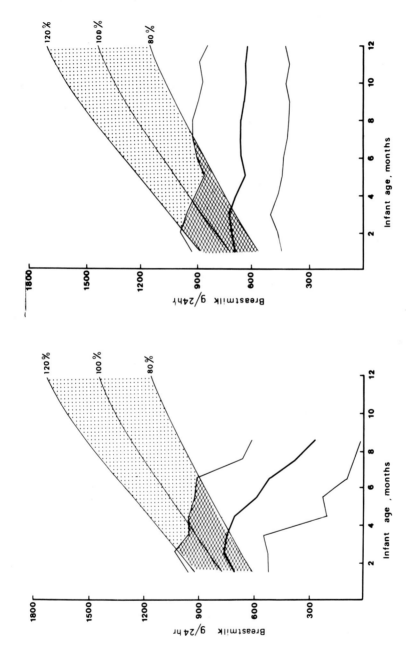

FIG. 8. Measured breast-milk intakes of Cambridge **(left)** and Gambian **(right)** infants. Values are means and ranges. *Hatched area*, intakes overlap with the DHSS estimated requirements (89) calculated with a range for infants 20% above and below standard body weights (24).

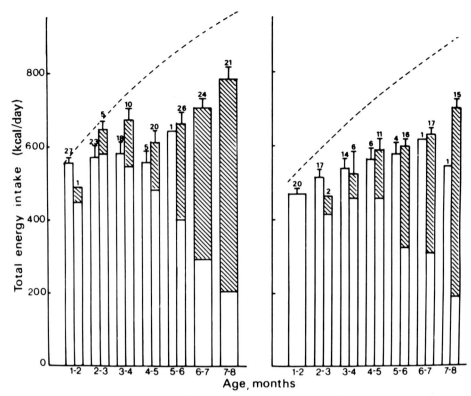

FIG. 9. Breast milk and complementary food energy intake (kcal/day) of Cambridge boys **(left)** and girls **(right)** relative to WHO/FAO (---) estimated requirements (11). *Shaded area*, nonbreast milk energy. Values are means + SEM (6).

FOOD INTAKES IN LATE INFANCY

The data in Fig. 10 indicate that after falling relatively steeply, requirements per kilogram level by 6 months tend to rise again. This was also seen in the case of the recent Canadian studies on artificially fed children (Fig. 5). The fact that there might be such a rise would be expected if intakes were to return to values of around 100 kcal/kg by 1 year. Although dietary data between 6 and 12 months are not so plentiful as in the first half of infancy, several studies have been carried out between 1 and 2 years indicating that intakes had been around this value at 1 year.

Our own literature analysis of the average energy intakes of infants at progressive monthly intervals during infancy has also been discussed before (25,26) and thus needs only to be described in summary. Based on the data shown in Fig. 11, we found the statistical best fit for the relationship between energy intake/kilogram and age to be the quadratic curve given in Fig. 12. The total number of child-day datum points in this analysis was 9,046; the number of studies was 12, eight of which were on artifically fed children. Subsequent discussion led to a pruning of

TABLE 6. *Multiple regression correlation coefficients for the relationship between energy intake, body weight, and growth velocity, together with predicted breast milk and energy requirements for children to grow along different percentiles of the NCHS weight standards*

Age (months)	N	R	p	Breast milk needs (ml/day)			Energy (kcal/kg/day)
				5th[a]	50th[a]	95th[a]	50th[a]
Boys							
2	28	0.64	<0.001	590	780	950	104
3	28	0.69	<0.001	630	840	1,020	97
4	28	0.64	<0.001	720	880	1,040	91
5	27	0.60	<0.01	860	950	1,060	89
6	23	0.47	<0.05	860	980	1,100	87
8	20	0.51	<0.05	980	1,130	1,290	89
Girls							
2	20	0.60	<0.01	580	690	820	101
3	20	0.56	<0.02	560	740	930	94
4	20	0.62	<0.01	640	800	980	93
5	20	0.56	<0.02	790	860	930	90
6	19	0.42	0.07	830	910	1,000	88
8	15	0.55	<0.05	990	1,090	1,190	92

[a]NCHS percentiles.

the data in Fig. 11 because of doubts expressed concerning some of the methodologies that had been used to assess the food intake of the babies. The revised quadratic curve, shown in Fig. 13, is essentially similar to that in Fig. 12 except that the minimum is now around 90 rather than 85 kcal/kg. The average monthly energy intakes predicted by both regression equations are shown in Table 7 together with the Cambridge predicted amounts from Fig. 10 and the 1973 WHO/FAO theoretical physiological needs. The data clearly support the concept of rising energy intakes/kilogram body weight in the second half of infancy following a steep fall in the first.

Cross-sectional analysis can be misleading, however, especially in terms of the detailed shape of a complex quadratic relationship: a fall in energy intake from one set of data can conceal a rise in another, leading to apparent lack of change over that time period. Likewise, predictions toward the data limits, e.g., at early or late infancy, can also be inaccurate for similar statistical reasons. It is illuminating to examine exactly what happens to individual babies as they pass through infancy and on into the second year of life.

Tables 8 and 9 show the results for a series of boys and girls who were a subgroup of the original 48 babies we studied who had been breastfed for at least 4 months. They exhibit a number of important features. While an initial steep fall in energy intakes/kilogram body weight was exhibited by all the children, the age when the minimum was achieved varied from child to child. In some children, this was in the fourth month but in others not until 9 to 10 months.

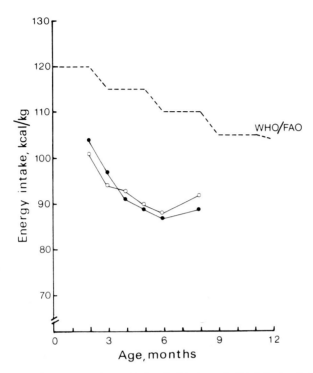

FIG. 10. Predicted energy requirements (kcal/kg) for boys *(solid circles)* and girls *(open circles)* to grow along the 50th percentile of the NCHS weight standard (41) calculated from multiple regression coefficients between energy intake, body weight, and growth velocity in Cambridge breastfed infants (6) in comparison to the WHO/FAO estimated requirements (11).

In Fig. 14, the results have been regrouped according to the month in which the minimum occurred. It now becomes apparent that in the individual, this minimum is a much sharper feature than that indicated by the cross-sectional analysis, and the subsequent rise in energy intake occurs in most children sooner and not so symmetrically. The mean level of energy intake measured at 1 year is also lower than that which has been reported in the past for children of this age. The overall minimum energy intake, when reanalyzed from the grouped data in Tables 8 and 9, is approximately 80 kcal/kg. It is also apparent that the relatively broad base to the cross-sectional quadratic relationship described in Figs. 12 and 13 is probably attributable to the fact that different children achieve their minimum intake at different times during mid-infancy.

It is not apparent why the children have these different characteristics. The most simple explanation would be that the rise in energy intake per kilogram body weight begins when the child starts to receive foods in addition to breast milk, and children receive supplementary foods at different ages. An examination of Tables 8 and 9, however, does not substantiate this conclusion. There is no obvious correlation

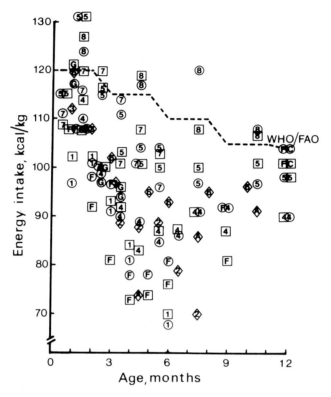

FIG. 11. Energy intakes per kilogram body weight of boys and girls in the first year of life compared with 1973 WHO/FAO estimated requirements (11). Key: *squares*, boys; *circles*, girls; *diamonds*, boys + girls. **1:** Wallgren (9), before 1940, Sweden; **2:** Chandra (10), 1970s, Canada; **3:** Hofvander et al. (59), 1979, Sweden; **4:** Whitehead and Paul (6), 1978–80, UK; **5:** Beal (12), 1946–67, USA; **6:** Yeung et al. (15), 1977–79, Canada; **7:** Ferris et al. (90), 1970s, USA; **8:** Fryer et al. (13), 1965, USA; **A:** Morgan et al. (91), 1973–74, UK; **C:** DHSS (31), 1967–68, UK; **F:** Vobecky et al. (14), 1970s, Canada; **G:** Fomon et al. (32), 1966–70, USA.

between the month when the minimum energy intake occurs and the month when supplementary feeding commences.

We are forced to conclude that a number of factors are involved in determining the U or V shape of the relationship. During early infancy, after 1 to 2 months, the velocity of growth in weight falls rapidly; thus less energy is required for this function. It has also been pointed out that brown fat metabolism probably has an important function in the very young baby in connection with the need to maintain temperature homeostasis (27). Apparently, this activity drops away quickly as the baby grows older; presumably, therefore, he becomes metabolically less wasteful in terms of converting energy intake into tissue. Different children could vary in the way these changes in energy efficiency take place. The most likely explanation for the rise in energy expenditure would be an increase in activity. Unfortunately,

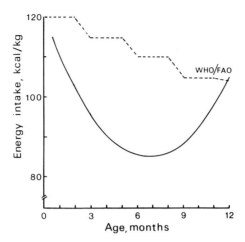

FIG. 12. Quadratic regression line of energy intake per kilogram body weight of boys and girls in the first year of life calculated from the data in Fig. 11, compared to the WHO/FAO requirements (11). Energy = 120 − 10.4 (months) + 0.76 (months)².

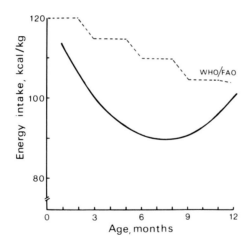

FIG. 13. Revised quadratic regression line of energy intake per kilogram body weight of boys and girls in the first year of life calculated after excluding two studies, **7** (90) and **F** (14), from the data used in Fig. 11. Energy = 123 − 8.9 (months) + 0.59 (months)².

however, data on the energy expenditure of these children were not collected. The children studied were all European and thus were relatively inactive over the initial stages of infancy.

Another explanation for the U shape was given at a recent scientific meeting in Berkeley, California by Professor Ekhard Ziegler of the Department of Pediatrics in the University of Iowa. He pointed out that while the velocity of fat deposition did fall rapidly in infancy from 14.1 g/day at 1 to 2 months down to 4.1 g/day at

TABLE 7. *Mean energy intakes of infants predicted from the two quadratic relationships in comparison with current recommendations and data calculated from the Cambridge study*

Month	Predicted energy intake (kcal/kg)[a]		Cambridge data (kcal/kg)		WHO/FAO (1973) (kcal/kg)
	A	B	Boys	Girls	
0.5	115	118	—	—	120
1	110	114	—	—	120
2	102	107	104	101	120
3	95	101	97	94	115
4	90	96	91	93	115
5	87	93	89	90	115
6	85	91	87	88	110
7	85	90	—	—	110
8	86	90	89	92	110
9	88	91	—	—	105
10	93	93	—	—	105
11	98	97	—	—	105
12	105	102	—	—	104

[a]Quadratic relationships: A. Energy $= 120 - 10.4$ (months) $+ 0.76$ (months)^2 ($R = 0.64$, $p < 0.001$). B. Energy $= 123 - 8.9$ (months) $+ 0.59$ (months)^2 ($R = 0.63$, $p < 0.001$).

5 to 6 months and 1.0 g/day at 1 year, nevertheless, the percentage of fat in the body as a whole increased from 13.7% at birth to a maximum of 25.4% at 6 months and then fell to 22.5% at 12 months (28). These compositional changes, shown in Fig. 15, parallel quite closely the pattern of dietary energy intake expressed on a kilogram body weight basis. It would not be unreasonable to suggest that part of the dip in energy consumption per kilogram might be due to the increase in an essentially metabolically inert component of weight. As shown in Fig. 15, however, the percentage of protein is not greatly affected, mainly because the changes in fat content are paralleled by reciprocal alterations in the percentage of total body water. This would also be metabolically inert; perhaps the most metabolically meaningful baseline we have is the percentage of protein. If this were used, then compositional changes would account for, on the average, less than 10% of the dip in energy intake per kilogram.

With respect to explaining the differences in individual response illustrated in Fig. 14, one can only conclude that there must be a number of factors influencing the precise shape of an individual's response over time to energy intake, including velocity of growth, body composition, metabolic efficiency, and exercise. Despite these complexities, however, the basic conclusions arrived at following the cross-sectional studies (Figs. 12 and 13) are supported by these investigative data collected on individuals.

TABLE 8. Energy intakes of Cambridge baby boys, breastfed to at least 4 months, who were followed prospectively into the early preschool period

Subject no.	Energy intakes (kcal/kg)							Initiation of weaning (month)
	2nd month	Minimum	Month	Subsequent maximum	Month	12–18 months	24 months	
1	113	88	4	102	6	99	75	5
3	109	70	4	109	12	109	85	6
4	117	98	4	108	6	101	87	3
8	93	62	4	92	18	87	73	5
5	131	92	5	106	7	96	101	5
6	84	56	5	97	15	78	71	6
12	116	75	5	94	7	81	—	5
15	106	89	5	108	7	82	83	5
2	108	76	6	99	12	87	81	6
7	125	69	6	108	15	106	88	6
10	111	59	6	103	18	95	75	3
14	106	85	6	117	10	92	88	3
9	129	86	7	111	12	103	93	2
13	117	79	9	94	10	72	104	5
11	122	69	10	78	12	69	50	3
Mean ± SE	113 ± 3	77 ± 3	5.7 ± 0.5	102 ± 3	11.1 ± 1.1	91 ± 3	82 ± 4	4.5 ± 0.4

TABLE 9. *Energy intakes of Cambridge baby girls, breastfed to at least 4 months, who were followed prospectively into the early preschool period*

| Subject no. | 2nd month | Energy intakes (kcal/kg) | | | | | | Initiation of weaning (month) |
		Minimum	Month	Subsequent maximum	Month	12–18 months	24 months	
17	132	94	4	102	5	99	—	7
19	104	77	4	94	8	82	75	5
22	101	67	4	111	6	95	85	3
28	92	64	4	116	15	109	80	6
29	106	84	4	105	8	79	73	5
27	106	83	5	119	8	100	—	4
16	112	76	6	98	8	84	—	5
20	137	80	6	99	15	94	—	5
21	110	75	6	105	10	82	92	4
26	111	73	7	101	8	90	75	3
23	106	80	8	95	15	84	100	4
25	108	81	8	89	10	84	92	7
18	105	69	9	87	10	71	72	10
24	82	72	9	73	12	72	71	5
Mean ± SE	108 ± 4	77 ± 3	6.0 ± 0.5	100 ± 3	9.9 ± 0.9	88 ± 3	82 ± 3	5.2 ± 0.5

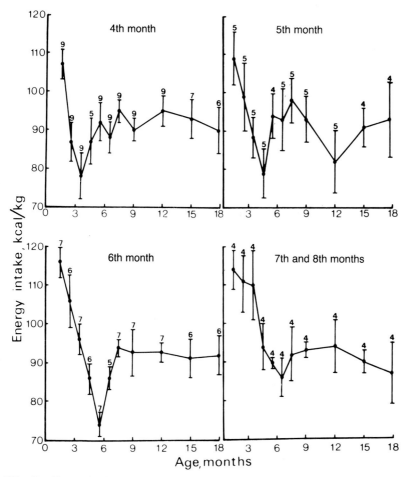

FIG. 14. Energy intake per kilogram body weight of Cambridge breastfed infants grouped according to the month in which the minimum intake occurred. Values are mean + SEM.

ENERGY INTAKE IN THE EARLY PRESCHOOL PERIOD

There is one additional feature in Fig. 14 and Tables 8 and 9 that is important. In the cross-sectional literature analysis (Figs. 12 and 13), the predicted mean intake at around 1 year was 105 kcal/kg; a second statistical analysis covering 1 to 5 years also indicated this to be the mean intake (26). The Cambridge data, however, level off between 9 and 12 months and at a value some 10% lower than this, around 95 kcal/kg. In the second year of life, energy intake per kilogram starts to fall again, reaching as low as 82 to 83 kcal/kg by 2 years, 20% below levels found from the literature 20 or more years ago. It thus seems that the secular trends in energy intake already discussed for puberty, for young female adulthood, during

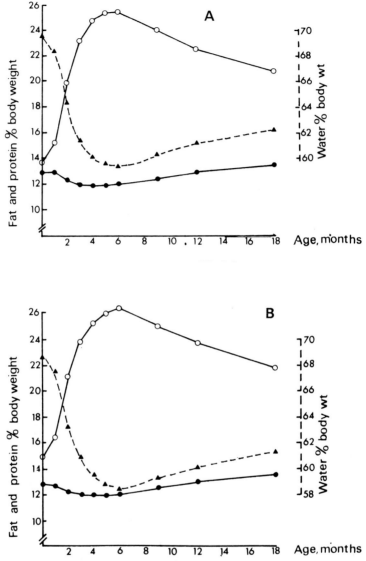

FIG. 15. Body composition of reference infants in the first 18 months of life, as calculated by Fomon et al. (28): **(A)** boys, **(B)** girls, (○) fat, (▲) water, (●) protein.

pregnancy and lactation, and around 4 to 8 months in infancy also occur in the early preschool period. Trends toward lower energy intakes thus seem widespread, and one can only assume that it must be due in part to the current nutritional health emphasis on avoiding obesity. A baby in the United Kingdom is now brought up in a different nutritional environment than a child of a generation ago.

Before leaving this general issue of trends in dietary energy intake, we return to the question of social class differences. In a study of the nutritional intakes of children in Glasgow, McKillop and Durnin (29) reported mean energy intake values of 85 kcal/kg in baby girls from parents of social grade I plus II, aged 0.2 to 1.0 year; in those from social grade V, the corresponding value was 105 kcal/kg. A similar social class bias for energy intakes around 1 year has been reported by a number of other investigators. For example, Black and colleagues (30), working in Newcastle in the north of England, reported that the infants and preschool children of manual workers had intakes 130 kcal/day higher than nonmanual workers after standardizing for body weight, sex, and family size. Similar trends were reported in the United Kingdom Department of Health and Social Security survey of 1967 to 1968 (31); social grade I children between 1½ and 4½ years had mean intakes of 1,286 kcal/day, whereas those of grades IV and V were 1,379 kcal/day. Most of the Cambridge children studied were from white collar families, where the parents were particularly health conscious.

ENERGY INTAKE AND GROWTH

There is good evidence that in very early infancy, a close relationship exists on a month-by-month basis between the size of a baby and the amount of breast milk he takes from his mother. This relationship is established at an early stage. Figure 16 illustrates the amount of milk being consumed at 2 to 3 months relative to the size of the baby at birth in rural African children in The Gambia and in Cambridge babies (24). The precise relationship between body weight, growth velocity, and total energy intake (breast milk plus supplements) during infancy among our Cambridge children has been partly described in Table 6. Initially, high correlation coefficients were obtained (0.6–0.7), but the strength of the relationship tended to deteriorate with time. By 1 to 2 years, typical coefficients were no higher than 0.2 to 0.5.

The relationship between formula milk intake and body weight had previously been studied in detail by Fomon and colleagues (32) in children up to 111 days of age. Between 56 and 111 days, the correlation coefficients were similar to those obtained in Cambridge breastfed babies: 0.61 in boys and 0.48 in girls. As with our breastfed cohort, Fomon and colleagues (32) found that baby boys consumed more than girls, but the difference in gain in weight per unit of energy intake was not statistically significant. They also observed that energy intake per kilogram body weight was significantly higher in young babies (aged 14–27 days) than in older ones (aged 84–111 days). They suggested that this was related to the much more rapid rate of growth in the younger babies. The energy content of Fomon's diets was 67 kcal/100 ml. With boys, the corresponding energy intake values for 50th percentile babies were 121 kcal/kg/day at 14 to 27 days and 96 kcal/kg/day at 84 to 111 days; with the girls, the respective values were 117 and 94 kcal/kg/day. These levels are very similar to those calculated by us for breast- and mixed-fed children at these ages (see Table 6 and Fig. 10).

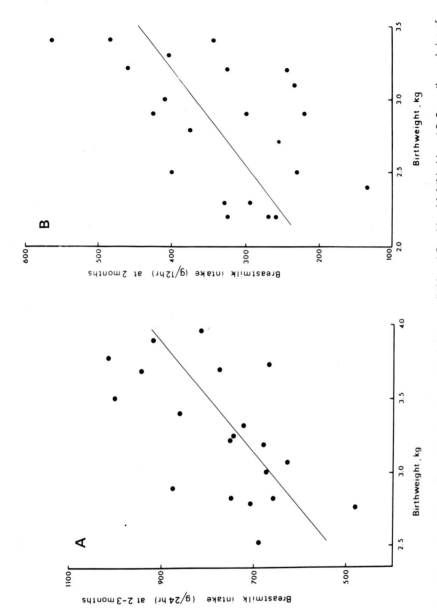

FIG. 16. Relationship between breastmilk intakes of Cambridge (**left**) and Gambian (**right**) babies at 2–3 months and size of the baby at birth. For Cambridge, $r = 0.58$; $p < 0.01$; for The Gambia, $r = 0.56$; $p < 0.01$ (24).

GROWTH OF BOTTLE-FED COMPARED WITH BREASTFED BABIES BEFORE 1972

The relative growth of bottle-fed babies compared with those who are breastfed is a controversial subject. At one time, most workers claimed that the artificially fed baby grows excessively quickly and is fat. The controversy, however, usually can be sorted out if one takes into account the year when the studies were carried out. Before 1972, as already described, infant milk formulas were quite different from what they are now and often were incorrectly prepared. It was also customary to introduce solids, such as cereal preparations, from a very early age. It is not surprising, therefore, that Shukla and colleagues (33), working in Dudley (Worcestershire, United Kingdom) in the late 1960s, found 16.7% of their patients to have infantile obesity and a further 27.7% to be overweight. During the first 3 months of life, the average daily intakes were found to be 136 kcal/kg/day in boys and as high as 149 kcal/kg/day in girls. Forty percent of the babies were offered solids before 4 weeks and 93% before 13 weeks. These values are clearly different from those encountered with present-day babies in Cambridge.

Taitz (34), working in Sheffield at approximately the same time, obtained similar results: 59.6% of his children showed weight gains above the 90th percentile and excess weight gain was more striking in males than females. He placed particular blame on the too early introduction of nonmilk solids. Another report from this era was that of Hooper (35), who worked on the Isle of Wight. He showed that bottle-fed babies gained on average 184 g/week compared with the 156 g/week he observed in breastfed babies. He also claimed that infantile obesity was confined to bottle-fed babies. Somewhat earlier, Stewart and Westrop (36), who studied baby growth in the 1950s in Oxford, found previously bottle-fed babies appreciably heavier at 1 year than their breastfed counterparts, but these authors reported that the latter were somewhat less mature and suggested that these differences might be due to minor degrees of underfeeding among the breastfed babies.

RELATIVE RATES OF GROWTH: THE CURRENT SITUATION

The situation described above would now appear to be a thing of the past, at least in the United Kingdom. As Taitz and Lukmanji (20) reported, recent years have seen a switch from unmodified formulas to modified baby milks. While rates of growth in breastfed babies have remained virtually constant, those of artificially fed infants have been falling. In addition to the use of modified baby milks, changes in attitudes toward the early introduction of solids seem to have been an important factor.

Taitz and Lukmanji (20) studied a fresh cohort of children aged 39 to 47 days in 1976–1977 and found the situation so changed that now breastfed babies were growing significantly faster than those bottle-fed. Bottle-fed boys were growing on an average of 28 g/day, where breastfed boys had a velocity of 30 g/day; the corresponding values for girls were 22.82 and 25.59 g/day. Once again, however, a social class factor complicated the data, in that the babies of white collar workers grew faster than those of blue collar workers whether or not they were breast- or bottle-fed. With boys, for example, breastfed white collar babies grew at an average of 33.62 g/day, while the corresponding bottle-fed children grew only at 29.82 g/ day. With lower class babies, the two values were smaller but essentially identical: 28.05 and 27.95 g/day, respectively. The difference was much more marked in white collar girls, as well, in whom breastfed girls grew at 27.96 g/day while those bottle-fed achieved only 21.95 g/day; the values for babies of manual workers were 23.85 and 23.05 g/day. Taitz and Lukmanji (20) could not explain these class differences but suggested it might be due to the powerful psychological motivation of the upper class mother to breastfeed as effectively as possible.

Evans (37), working in Wales in 1978, also found that infants fed the latest formulations had considerably smaller weight gains than infants who had been studied in the same region several years earlier and who had been fed on unmodified milks and early solids. In Manchester in 1979, D'Souza and Black (38) reported that by 5 to 7 weeks of age, entirely breastfed male babies had gained more weight than entirely bottle-fed babies, the percentage increase in weight from birth being 42 and 32%, respectively, with the breast plus bottle group occupying an intermediate position of 38%. These differences, however, were not observed in female babies.

Saarinen and Siimes (39) compared a large number of children who were either bottle- or breastfed but in whom weaning food had been introduced as a supplement at 3.5 months of age, regardless of the type of feeding. In early infancy, there were only small differences among the groups of infants, but the breastfed ones did gain slightly more weight than those fed cow's milk-based formulas. The authors concluded that their results contradicted the commonly held notion that bottle-feeding always results in greater weight gain and emphasized that the present recommendations for infant feeding in Finland, the protocol they had followed, prevented overnutrition. The main features of this advice were prolonged breastfeeding and the use of proprietary milk formulas at the beginning of weaning, with solid foods being introduced only later.

The fact that the situation described for Europe may not be the same everywhere is emphasized by the recent data of Boulton (40) from Australia; in 1981, this investigator still found that breastfed babies gained weight less rapidly than did those artificially fed. Between birth and 3 months, the mean differences were 186 and 199 g/week; from 3 to 6 months, they were 126 and 144 g/week. Similar differences were found with height growth.

SECULAR TRENDS AND GROWTH STANDARDS

The secular trends in growth described above clearly have significance in terms of the anthropometric standards in common usage. The NCHS standards from birth to 3 years, the current international norm (41), were compiled from data collected at various times starting between 1929 and 1972 by the Fels Research Institute in the United States. It must be assumed that many of the babies and young children would have been bottle-fed at these times on unmodified milk formulas (42). The same is true of the British Tanner standards (43) for weight and height, which were collected prior to 1966, and for the Dutch standards (44), which are also based on pre-1965 data. Anthropometric criteria, particularly monthly incremental weight gains, are increasingly being used in an attempt to answer controversial questions about how long babies can be exclusively breastfed before growth faltering becomes apparent. There must be considerable doubt as to whether standards that were based on bottle-fed children given old type formulas can be used to interpret growth data from breastfed children. Growth data reported by Hitchcock and Owles (45) from Perth, Western Australia, illustrate the worry well. In 1964, the average baby boy at 3 months weighed 6.54 kg; in 1980, when a high incidence of breastfeeding had returned, he weighed only 5.92 kg. At 6 months, the difference was 1,001 g, 8.84 kg, and 7.85 kg. In fact, the authors pointed out that the 1980 weight patterns were more similar to 1933 values when breastfeeding also predominated.

In view of the changing patterns of energy consumption discussed earlier in this chapter, it is not surprising that anthropometric parameters relating to adiposity, such as skinfold thickness measurements, have shown the greatest change over the past 15 years. Figure 17 shows the Tanner triceps standards (46) derived from data collected between 1966 and 1967 in the area of Bakewell in Derbyshire, United Kingdom (47). The 50th percentile values between 6 and 10 months are approximately 11.5 mm in girls and slightly more in boys. Figure 17 also shows data collected after 1975 from Australia (40), Germany (48), the United States (49), and in our own cohort of children from Cambridge. The change is so marked that all the data now cluster close to the original 10th percentile, typical values around 6 months being 8 to 8.5 mm. It is of interest that earlier Tanner skinfold standards based on data collected in the 1950s from Belgium (50) were also lower than the 1975 standards, with mean values nearer the 25th percentile. Again like the Australian growth data, this indicates some growth peaking in the 1960s.

Limb circumference measurements show similar trends. Figure 18 illustrates the WHO standard values for mid-upper arm circumference compiled from data collected by Wolanski (51) together with the values we obtained in our Cambridge children. At all times, both boys and girls had considerably lower mean limb circumferences than the standard; after 12 months, for example, the standard value for boys had been assumed by Jelliffe in the WHO monograph (51) to be 16 cm, whereas our values were all nearer 14.5 cm.

Weight and height growth changes have already been mentioned, and Figs. 19 and 20 show these values for the 15 boys and 14 girls of our total cohort of 48 breastfed babies whom we were able to study for a full 2 years. The children tended to grow relatively more quickly than the standards for the first few months when they were, to all intents and purposes, fully breastfed. From 4 to 6 months, however, the mean growth curves crossed back over the percentile lines until the boys, who in the first 3 months had been near the 75th percentile, ended up in the second year toward the 25th percentile for weight; a similar effect occurred with height

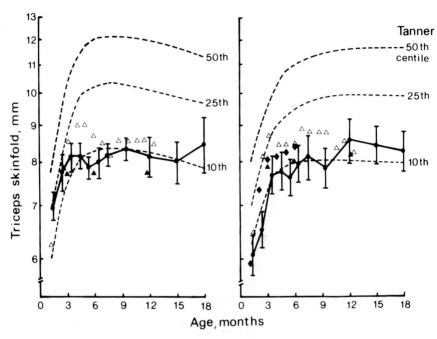

FIG. 17. Triceps skinfold thickness (mean + SEM) of two cohorts of Cambridge breastfed boys (**left**, *n* = 15) and girls (**right**, *n* = 13) compared to the Tanner standards, using a logarithmic scale (46), and to mean values from other recently reported studies of breast- plus bottle-fed infants. Symbols indicate country, year of study, and reference, as follows: *Solid triangles*: Australia, 1976–8 (40); *open triangles*, Germany, 1974–5 (48); *diamonds*, USA, 1970s (49).

(Fig. 20). The girls reacted correspondingly. It is tempting to conclude that the relatively low velocity of growth we found in the latter part of infancy and in the early preschool period reflected the relatively low energy intakes we measured at the same time, as discussed earlier. This pattern of growth after 6 months in children who are breastfed for an extended period appears to be quite common. Whether the low intakes in the early preschool period reflect solely the mother's anxiety about infantile and more long-term obesity or whether the babies had become accustomed to low energy intakes during lactation, which had been programming their more long-term appetite, is not known; this certainly merits further consideration.

Another major investigation showing the same phenomenon is that of Ahn and Maclean in the United States (42) who studied 96 infants of mothers who were members of *La Leche League International*. The average period of exclusive breastfeeding was said to be 7 months. Figure 21 shows the values for male babies together with the NCHS standards. As with the Cambridge children, the babies initially grew faster than the standard, the average reaching the 75th percentile at 3 months. From 4 months onward, however, the average growth curve began to fall back, crossing the 50th percentile at 7 months and reaching the 25th percentile

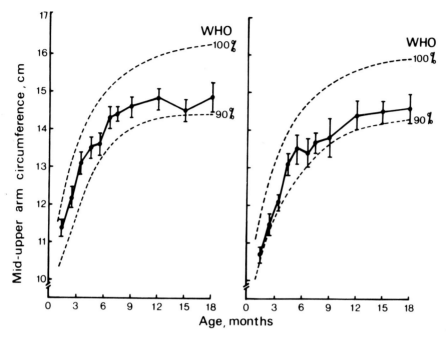

FIG. 18. Mid-upper arm circumference (mean + SEM) of two cohorts of Cambridge breastfed boys (**left,** *n* = 15) and girls (**right,** *n* = 13) compared to the WHO standards compiled from data of Wolanski (51).

at 10 months. The girls responded quantitatively and qualitatively in a similar manner. The authors made no comment on the latter part of the growth curve and concentrated on the period of "good" growth when the babies were exclusively breastfed, although they presumably regarded this subsequent growth performance as adequate.

Another detailed study of the growth of exclusively breastfed babies showing the same pattern is that of Jackson and colleagues (52) in Missouri, which dates from the early 1960s. This, too, shows mean growth curves recrossing the standards, in this case the Iowa standards (53), between 3 and 6 months. More recently, Chandra (10,54) has also reported faltering of growth in exclusively breastfed babies by the age of 4 months in 8% of his children, by 13% at 5 months, a further 22% at 6 months, 9% at 7 months, and 33% at 8 months; however, he did not regard this growth as normal and recommended supplementation after 4 months (10).

Most investigations of children who have been breastfed for extended periods of time have taken place in the developing world. In the rural village of Keneba, The Gambia, we have again reported accelerated rates of weight gain in early infancy, which subsequently fall back after 4 months (55). Such data are more difficult to interpret, however, as the children are in general born small and the initial rise in velocity has usually been interpreted as catch-up growth. The ultimate fall in

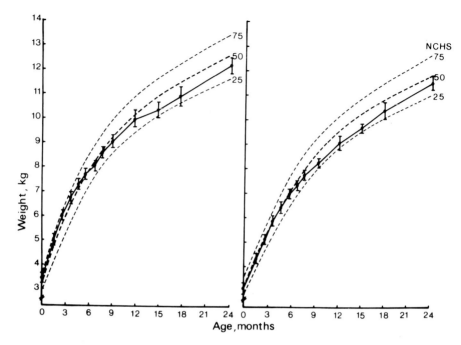

FIG. 19. Body weights (mean + SEM) of two cohorts of Cambridge breastfed boys (**left**, *n* = 15) and girls (**right**, *n* = 14) for the first 2 years of life in relation to the NCHS standards (41).

growth velocity has in turn been assumed to be totally the result of nutritionally and bacteriologically inadequate weaning foods (23). In the light of the above discussion, these explanations could be an oversimplification. The growth data of Lauber and Reinhardt (56) from a much wealthier village in the Ivory Coast are similar, as are recent data from M. G. M. Rowland *(personal communication)* working among relatively well-nourished mothers and children from the urban township of Bakau, The Gambia.

INFANCY: SPECIFIC GROWTH STANDARDS

Compiling good standards for infancy and the early preschool period based on subjects fed according to more up-to-date dietary regimens clearly is important if such standards are to be used for interpreting the nutritional adequacy of breast-feeding. All the growth data reported here for breastfed children are at variance with the precise shape of the NCHS and other national and international growth standards, regardless of the home environment of the baby. Using current standards, we are perhaps in danger of misinterpreting growth data from breastfed babies and of concluding that weight faltering has started before this in fact may be true.

The compilation of new standards should not be undertaken lightly. Studies of growth patterns destined to lead to new growth standards should be coupled with more general investigations into child development and behavior so that we can be

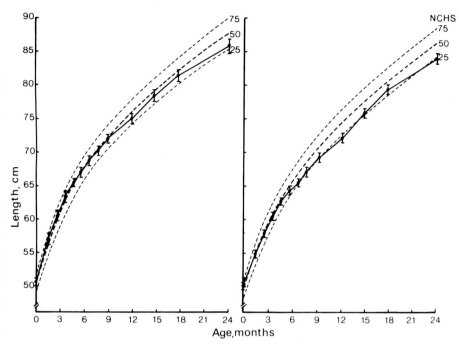

FIG. 20. Length (mean + SEM) of two cohorts of Cambridge breastfed boys (**left**, *n* = 15) and girls (**right**, *n* = 14) for the first 2 years of life in relation to the NCHS standards (41).

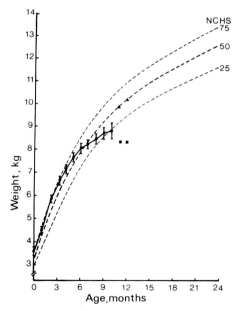

FIG. 21. Body weights (mean + SEM) of exclusively breastfed boys studied by Ahn and MacLean (42) in relation to the NCHS standards (41). Monthly sample size from birth to 10 months: 56; 56; 56; 56; 53; 52; 45; 24; 17; 8; 4. *Triangles* and *squares*, individuals at months 11 and 12.

certain that the more shallow growth seen from 4 to 6 months onward in babies breastfed for an extended period truly can be deemed normal. There are other design considerations that must be taken into account. Existing standards for infancy are based on data collected too infrequently, at best 0, 1, 3, and 6 months: prospective measurements will need to be made on representative populations at the least monthly and preferably weekly if we are to avoid excessive statistical smoothing (57).

CONCLUSION

The purpose of this chapter has been to point out that human lactation, infant feeding, and growth patterns are in a state of gradual change, particularly in the Western world. Not only must this be recognized, but we also need more detailed studies so that we are in a position to advise on what really is the best dietary regimen to produce a pattern of growth that reflects ideal health and well-being.

REFERENCES

1. Wharton BA. A quinquennium in infant feeding. Arch Dis Child 1982;57:895–7.
2. Martin J. Infant feeding 1975: attitudes and practice in England and Wales. London: H.M. Stationery Office, 1978.
3. Martin J, Monk J. Infant feeding 1980. London: Office of Population Censuses and Surveys, 1982.
4. Whichelow MJ, King BE. Breast-feeding and smoking. Arch Dis Child 1979;54:240–1.
5. Rona RJ. Genetic and environmental factors in the control of growth in childhood. Br Med Bull 1981;37:265–72.
6. Whitehead RG, Paul AA. Infant growth and human milk requirements: a fresh approach. Lancet 1981;ii:161–3.
7. Coward WA, Cole TJ, Sawyer MB, Prentice AM. Breast milk intake measurement in mixed-fed infants by administration of deuterium oxide to their mothers. Hum Nutr Clin Nutr 1982;36C:141–8.
8. Coward WA, Whitehead RG, Sawyer MB, Prentice AM, Evans J. New method for measuring milk intake in breast-fed babies. Lancet 1979;ii:13–14.
9. Wallgren A. Breast milk consumption of healthy full-term infants. Acta Paediatr Scand 1944-5;32:778–90.
10. Chandra RK. Breast-feeding, growth and morbidity. Nutr Res 1981;1:25–32.
11. WHO/FAO: Energy and protein requirements. WHO technical report series no 522, 1973. (FAO nutrition meetings report series no 52).
12. Beal VA. Nutritional intake. In: McCammon RW, ed. Human growth and development. Springfield, Illinois: Charles C Thomas, 1970:63–100.
13. Fryer BA, Lamkin GH, Vivian VA, Eppright ES, Fox HM. Diets of pre-school children in the North Central Region. J Am Diet Assoc 1971;59:228–32.
14. Vobecky JS, Vobecky J, Demers PP, Shapcott D, Blanchard R, Black R. Food and nutrient intake of infants in the first fifteen months. Nutr Rep Int 1980;22:571–80.
15. Yeung DL, Hall J, Leung M. Adequacy of energy intake of infants. J Can Diet Assoc 1980;41:48–52.
16. Whitehead RG, Paul AA, Cole TJ. Trends in food energy intakes throughout childhood from one to 18 years. Hum Nutr Appl Nutr 1982;36:57–62.
17. Edelman B, Maller O. Facts and fictions about infantile obesity. Int J Obesity 1982;6:69–81.
18. Department of Health and Social Security: present-day practice in infant feeding. Reports of health and social subjects, no. 9. London: H.M. Stationery Office, 1974.
19. Department of Health and Social Social Security: present-day practice in infant feeding. Reports of health and social subjects, no. 20. London: H.M. Stationery Office, 1980.

20. Taitz LS, Lukmanji Z. Alterations in feeding patterns and rates of weight gain in South Yorkshire infants 1971–1977. Hum Biol 1981;53:313–20.
21. Valman HB. The first year of life. Crying babies. Br Med J 1980;i:1522–5.
22. Wilkinson PW, Davies DP. When and why are babies weaned? Br Med J 1978;i:1682–3.
23. Rowland MGM, Barrell RAE, Whitehead RG. Bacterial contamination in traditional Gambian weaning foods. Lancet 1978;i:136–138.
24. Whitehead RG, Paul AA, Rowland MGM. Lactation in Cambridge and in The Gambia. In: Wharton, BA, ed. Topics in paediatrics 2: nutrition in childhood, Tunbridge Wells: Pitman Medical, 1980:22–3.
25. Whitehead RG, Paul AA, Cole TJ. How much breast milk do babies need? Acta Paediatr Scand 1982;(suppl)299:43–50.
26. Whitehead RG, Paul AA, Cole TJ. A critical analysis of measured food energy intakes during infancy and early childhood in comparison with current international recommendations. J Hum Nutr 1981;35:339–48.
27. Hull D, Smales ORC. Heat production in the new-born. In: Sinclair JC, ed. Temperature regulation and energy metabolism in the new-born, New York: Grune & Stratton, 1978:129–56.
28. Fomon SJ, Haschke F, Ziegler EE, Nelson SE. Body composition of reference children from birth to age 10 years. Am J Clin Nutr 1982;35:169–75.
29. McKillop FM, Durnin JVGA. The energy and nutrient intake of a random sample (305) of infants. Hum Nutr Appl Nutr 1982;36A:405–21.
30. Black AE, Billewicz WZ, Thomson AE. The diets of pre-school children in Newcastle-upon-Tyne 1968-71. Br J Nutr 1976;35:105–13.
31. Department of Health and Social Security: A nutrition survey of pre-school children 1967–8. Reports of health and social subjects, no. 10. London: H.M. Stationery Office, 1975.
32. Fomon SJ, Thomas LN, Filer LJ, Ziegler EE, Leonard MT. Food consumption and growth of normal infants fed milk based formulas. Acta Paediatr Scand 1971(suppl);223:1–36.
33. Shukla A, Forsyth HA, Anderson CM, Marwah SM. Infantile overnutrition in the first year of life: a field study in Dudley, Worcestershire. Br Med J 1972;ii:507–14.
34. Taitz LS. Infantile overnutrition among artifically fed infants in the Sheffield region. Br Med J 1971;i:315–16.
35. Hooper PD. Infant feeding and its relationship to weight gain and illness. The practitioner, 1965;194:391–5.
36. Stewart A, Westrop C. Breast feeding in the Oxford child health survey. Pt. II. Comparison of bottle and breast fed babies. Br Med J 1953;ii:305–8.
37. Evans TJ. Growth and milk intake of normal infants. Arch Dis Child 1978;53:749–51.
38. D'Souza SW, Black P. A study of infant growth in relation to the type of feeding. Early Hum Dev 1979;3/3:245–55.
39. Saarinen UM, Siimes MA. Role of prolonged breast-feeding in infant growth. Acta Paediatr Scand 1979;68:245–50.
40. Boulton J. Nutrition in childhood and its relationships to early somatic growth, body fat, blood pressure and physical fitness. Acta Paediatr Scand 1981(suppl);284:1–85.
41. Hamill PVV. NCHS growth curves for children, birth to 18 years. Hyattsville, Maryland: National Center for Health Statistics, 1977; DHEW publication no. (PHS) 78-1650.
42. Ahn CH, MacLean WC. Growth of the exclusively breast-fed infant. Am J Clin Nutr 1980;33:183–92.
43. Tanner JM, Whitehouse RH, Takaishi M. Standards from birth to maturity for height, weight, height-velocity and weight velocity: British children 1965. Arch Dis Child 1965;41:613–35.
44. Van Wieringen JC, Wafelbakker F, Verbrugge HP, de Haas JH. Growth diagrams 1965 Netherlands. Netherlands Institute for Preventative Medicine TNO, Leiden. Groningen: Wolters-Noordhoff Publishing, 1971.
45. Hitchcock NE, Owles AN. Australian growth studies: the Perth study. Proc Nutr Soc Aust 1980;5:71–8.
46. Tanner JM, Whitehouse RM. Revised standards for triceps and subscapular skinfolds in British children. Arch Dis Child 1975;50:142–5.
47. Hutchinson-Smith B. Skinfold thickness in infancy in relation to birth weight. Dev Med Child Neurol 1973;15:628–34.
48. Schluter K, Funfack W, Pachaly J, Weber B. Development of subcutaneous fat in infancy. Standards

for tricipital, subscapular and suprailiacal skinfolds in German infants. Eur J Paediatr 1976;123:255–67.

49. Ferris AG, Beal VA, Laus MJ, Hosmer DW. The effect of feeding on fat deposition in early infancy. Pediatrics 1979;64:397–401.

50. Tanner JM, Whitehouse RH. Standards for subcutaneous fat in British children. Br Med J 1962;ii:446–50.

51. Wolanski N. Standards for arm circumference. Quoted in Jelliffe DB. The assessment of the nutritional status of the community. WHO monograph no. 53. Geneva: WHO, 1966.

52. Jackson RL, Westerfeld R, Flynn MA, Kimball ER, Lewis RB. Growth of "well-born" American infants fed human and cow's milk. Pediatrics 1964;33:642–52.

53. Jackson RL, Kelly HG. Growth charts for use in pediatrics practice. J Pediatr 1945;27:215–29.

54. Chandra RK. Physical growth of exclusively breast fed infants. Nutr Res 1982;2:275–6.

55. Whitehead RG. Infant feeding practices and the development of malnutrition in rural Gambia. UNU Food Nutr Bull 1979;1:36–41.

56. Lauber E, Reinhardt M. Studies on the quality of breast milk during 23 months of lactation in a rural community of the Ivory Coast. Am J Clin Nutr 1979;32:1159–73.

57. Whitehead RG, Paul AA. Growth standards for early infancy. Lancet 1981;ii:419–20.

58. Lonnerdal B, Forsum E, Gebre-Medhin M, Hambreus L. Breast milk composition in Ethiopian and Swedish mothers. II Lactose, nitrogen and protein content. Am J Clin Nutr 1976;29:1134–41.

59. Hofvander Y, Hagman U, Hillervik C, Sjölin S. The amount of milk consumed by 1-3 months old breast- or bottle-fed infants. Acta Paediatr Scand 1982;71:953–8.

60. Rattigan S, Ghisalberti AV, Hartmann PE. Breast milk production in Australian women. Br J Nutr 1982;45:243–9.

61. Pao EM, Himes JM, Roche AF. Milk intakes and feeding patterns in breast-fed infants. J Am Diet Assoc 1980;77:540–5.

62. Picciano MF, Calkins EJ, Garrick JR, Deering RH. Milk and mineral intakes of breast-fed babies. Acta Paediatr Scand 1981;70:189–94.

63. Holemans K, Lambrechts A, Martin H. Etude qualitative et quantitative du lait des femmes indigènes du Kwango (Congo Belge). Rev Med Liege 1954;9:714–23.

64. Hennart Ph, Vis HL. Breast-feeding and post partum amenorrhoea in Central Africa. I Milk production in rural areas. J Trop Paediatr 1980;26:177–83.

65. Van Steenbergen WL, Kusin JA, Van Rens MM. Lactation performance of Akamba mothers, Kenya. Breast-feeding behaviour, breast milk yield and composition. J Trop Paediatr 1981;27:155–61.

66. Martinez C, Chavez A. Nutrition and development of infants in poor rural areas. I Consumption of mother's milk by infants. Nutr Rep Int 1971;4:139–49.

67. Prentice AM. Variations in maternal dietary intake, birth weight and breast milk output in The Gambia. In: Whitehead RG, Aebi H, eds. Maternal nutrition during pregnancy and lactation, Berne: Hans Huber, 1980:167–83.

68. Thomson AM. Diet in pregnancy. I. Dietary survey technique and the nutritive value of diets taken by primigravidae. Br J Nutr 1958;12:446–61.

69. English RM, Hitchcock NE. Nutrient intakes during pregnancy, lactation and after the cessation of lactation in a group of Australian women. Br J Nutr 1968;22:615–24.

70. Lunell NO, Persson B, Sterky G. Dietary habits during pregnancy. Acta Obstet Gynecol Scand 1969;48:187–94.

71. Smithells RW, Ankers C, Carver ME, Lennon D, Schorah CJ, Sheppard S. Maternal nutrition in early pregnancy. Br J Nutr 1977;38:497–506.

72. Darke SJ, Disselduff MM, Try GP. Frequency distributions of mean daily intakes of food energy and selected nutrients obtained during nutrition surveys of different groups of people in Great Britain between 1968 and 1971. Br J Nutr 1980;44:243–52.

73. Whitehead RG, Paul AA, Black AE, Wiles SJ. Recommended dietary amounts of energy for pregnancy and lactation in the United Kingdom. UNU Food Nutr Bull 1981(suppl);5:259–64.

73a. Stuff JE, Garza C, Smith EOB, Nichols BL, Montendon CM. A comparison of dietary methods in nutritional studies. Am J Clin Nutr 1983;300–6.

74. Thomson AM, Hytten FE, Billewicz WZ. The energy cost of human lactation. Br J Nutr 1970;24:565–72.

75. Naismith DJ, Ritchie CD. The effect of breast-feeding and artificial feeding on body-weights,

skinfold measurements and food intakes of forty-two primiparous women. Proc Nutr Soc 1975;34:116A–7A.
76. Whichelow MJ. Success and failure of breast-feeding in relation to energy intake. Proc Nutr Soc 1976;35:64A–5A.
77. Abrahamsson L, Hofvander Y. Näringsintaget hos ammande mödrar. Resultat fran 3-dagars Kostregistrering av 25 mödrar i Uppsala. Naringsforskning 1977;21:93–4.
78. Sims LS. Dietary status of lactating women. I. Nutrient intake from food and from supplements. J Am Diet Assoc 1978;73:139–46.
79. Hampton MC, Huenemann RL, Shapiro LR, Mitchell BW. Caloric and nutrient intakes of teenagers. J Am Diet Assoc 1967;50:385–96.
80. Wharton MA. Nutritive intake of adolescents. J Am Diet Assoc 1963;42:306–10.
81. Cook J, Altman DG, Moore DMC, Topp SG, Holland WW, Ellio A. A survey of the nutritional status of school children: relation between nutrient intake and socio-economic factors. Br J Prev Soc Med 1973;27:91–9.
82. Darke SJ, Disselduff MM. A nutrition study of primary school children aged 10-11 years in Bristol, Croydon and Sheffield made in the first three months of 1971. In: Subcommittee on nutritional surveillance 2nd report. DHSS reports on health and social subjects, no. 21. London: H.M. Stationery Office, 1981.
83. Durnin JVGA, Lonergan ME, Good J, Ewan A. A cross-sectional nutritional and anthropometric study, with an interval of 7 years, on 611 young adolescent school children. Br J Nutr 1974;32:169–79.
84. McNaughton JW, Cahn AJ. A study of the food intake and activity of urban adolescents. Br J Nutr 1970;24:331–4.
85. Steel JE, Johnson JM. Nutrient intakes of the subjects of the Melbourne University Child Growth Study. J Diet Assoc Vic 1975;26:18–26.
86. Eppright ES, Sidwell VD, Swanson PP. Nutritive value of the diets of Iowa school children. J Nutr 1954;54:371–88.
87. Burke BS, Reed RB, van den Berg AS, Stuart HC. Caloric and protein intakes of children between 1 and 18 years of age. Pediatrics 1959;24:922–40.
88. Widdowson EM. A study of individual children's diets. Special report series, Medical Research Council, no. 257. London: H.M. Stationery Office, 1947.
89. Department of Health and Social Security. Recommended daily amounts of food energy and nutrients for groups of people in the United Kingdom. Reports on health and social subjects, no. 15. London: H.M. Stationery Office, 1979.
90. Ferris A, Vilhjalmsdottir LB, Beal VA, Pellet PL. Diets in the first six months of infants in western Massachusetts. J Am Diet Assoc 1978;72:115–63.
91. Morgan J, Mumford P, Evans E, Wells JKC. Food intake and anthropometric data on children under 4 years old living in the south of England. Proc Nutr Soc 1975;34:116A–7A.

DISCUSSION

Dr. Lechtig: Please comment on maternal malnutrition and how this might affect milk production. The suckling reflex is said to be important in this regard. Is it possible to measure the strength of suckling? Finally, and for clarification, it seems that with the methodologies presently being used, one is not really measuring breast milk production but breast milk ingestion by the baby. It could be that the baby, by being weakened in some way, might be the cause of apparent lactational inadequacy in some women.

Dr. Whitehead: Your last comment is absolutely correct: few people have measured breast milk production. When one test weighs babies, it is milk ingestion that is being measured. In very early infancy, breast milk production would appear to be considerably more than the baby requires; but as time goes on, production and actual ingestion probably equate much more closely.

You raised an interesting question concerning the strength of suckling required to achieve enough milk. Our view is that initially, the amount of suckling required is probably quite small. As time goes on, however, perhaps by 3 or 4 months, the intensity of suckling might be the limiting factor in determining milk production. Dr. Baum's technique, in which a breast shield is used to measure flow rates of milk, could provide useful information on this topic. In addition to the flow transducer, a pressure transducer could also be introduced into the milk flow line.

We have postulated that the child of an undernourished mother may have to suck much harder to get sufficient milk than the baby of a well-nourished mother. We have suggested that this is the reason for the particularly high plasma levels of the hormone prolactin in lactating mothers from the developing world. Corroborative evidence has also been made available from animal studies.

Finally, concerning the weakened baby, this could influence milk production, but we have not directly studied this phenomenon.

Dr. Barness: Dr. Whitehead, with respect to the caloric density of the formulas used in your studies and in those of Fomon, a paper was published reporting that when the reconstituted formulas were measured by bomb calorimetry, the energy content was 9% more that that recommended on the label by the manufacturers. An earlier study found a variation of something like $\pm 50\%$. In your studies on formula-fed children, was the content based on weighed samples?

Dr. Whitehead: The Fomon work was carried out in a metabolic ward; thus there could be little doubt about the energy content of the formulas fed to the babies. Our Cambridge studies could not be so exact, as they were based on children living in their own homes. The primary basis of our data is the number of scoops used in making up the milk and the volume consumed. The volume of milk left over at the end of each feed was recorded, as was the initial volume. We could not chemically analyze all samples of milk made up, but in the subsample in which this was done, the analytical values came close to the manufacturer's recommendations. Perhaps this was not surprising with the type of Cambridge mothers who were collaborating with us in our studies.

Having said this, I think your question is important, as it emphasizes one of the great weaknesses of nutritional science, i.e., the precise measurement of exactly what people actually are eating in different parts of the world when studied under free-living situations.

Dr. Senterre: I must express some concern about what you appear to be recommending. We know perfectly well that when the energy intake of a baby is reduced, the first thing affected is his activity. It seems dangerous to look only at growth curves and say that if these are acceptable on lower intakes of energy, then the latter must be adequate. We should also take into account such things as the amount of crawling and walking the young baby does.

Dr. Whitehead: I agree completely. In our more formal publication on this subject, we have given a warning that our studies were based predominantly on babies from the Western world who are encouraged to spend most of the time asleep between meals, particularly in the first 6 months of life. We have indicated that where a child's lifestyle is totally different, our data might be erroneous. For example, it is possible that more energy might be required by a baby when he is carried about on his mother's back all day long, as occurs in many countries in Africa.

Nutritional Needs and Assessment of Normal Growth, edited by M. Gracey and F. Falkner. Nestlé Nutrition, Vevey/Raven Press, New York © 1985.

Monitoring Growth

Frank Falkner

School of Public Health, Maternal and Child Health Program, University of California, Berkeley, California 94720; and Department of Pediatrics, University of California, San Francisco, California 94143

From the nutritional point of view, what is needed ideally to monitor growth is methodology that is comparable nation to nation, sample to sample, and within such groups or communities to show the distribution of good or malnutrition, and the degree of the latter. Although perhaps trite, it is necessary to emphasize that nutrition is not biochemistry or caloric intake. The interrelationship of the many factors and disciplines involved makes nutritional science highly complex. It is important to emphasize that a clear-cut methodology as mentioned above is surely out of reach. Contributory methodologies do exist, however, and better ones must be sought. Physiological-biochemical monitoring is not addressed in this chapter.

GROWTH STANDARDS AND NORMS

Before discussing specific measures to monitor growth, a general overview of standards and norms is appropriate.

The most common method of collecting human growth data is the cross-sectional method. Here, individuals are measured once, and mean values of a measure are found for various ages. Age differences usually are calculated by comparing mean values of different age groups or by using all individual measures and computing the regression on age. The majority of the standards used in human biology have been, and are, produced from cross-sectional studies. Such studies are the basis of the provision of standards of many different measures in different populations. They form the foundation of countless tables of norms and charts, grids, and so forth. If measures of dispersion (e.g., percentiles) are added and the samples are reasonably large and representative, then such cross-sectional studies indicate much about growth–mainly as distance data (that is, average measurements attained at various ages).

Cross-sectional studies are comparatively easy to perform and inexpensive, and data are produced quickly. They indeed are a vital part of growth study methodology. The value of simply plotting growth measures for an individual child on charts based on cross-sectional data (1) is encouraged, particularly in developing countries. A cautionary note: In using such standards, the influence of a potential secular trend occurring in the population studied must be evaluated. Thus moderately slower rates of early growth, for example, that are being encountered increasingly in some subpopulations may not in fact be indicating necessarily adverse changes in the child's growth.

When information is needed on change or velocity over time, the cross-sectional study is inappropriate. A longitudinal study method must be used. In such studies, the same individual subjects are measured at specific ages over a period of time.

In the human, longitudinal studies can be undertaken from birth to maturity or to the grave. Clearly, the time factor of the study itself virtually prohibits study of an individual's entire lifespan. Now that more growth indicators may be studied prenatally, it should be emphasized that in studying early childhood development, the time series of the longitudinal study could, and should, begin in fetal life.

The key to the collection of velocity data is continuity. The search usually is for a functional relationship with time, and even if only two points are available on a curve, the slope of that curve may still indicate a great deal. What information is sought will determine the number of points needed and then separation in time. Good velocity data by no means require an overly long period of time.

It is common to think in terms of size achieved at various ages, in terms of an infant growing steadily. The word "steadily" is a deeply embedded misconception. The changes that occur in the growing human can only be studied and understood if growth is regarded as a continuum: hence the study of growth velocity. Clearly, these velocities are by no means steady, and incremental growth varies widely at different ages.

If a measurement is somewhat unstable and capable of negative velocity (such as weight loss), then it may be necessary to make measurements frequently to obtain good incremental data that are helpful in assessing factors or effects in operation. One of the great advantages of using velocity over distance data for specific monitoring purposes is that the problem of adjusting for age is largely removed. The plan to measure growth velocity has led to the comparatively recent availability of velocity growth standards [e.g., Roche and Himes (2)]. The usefulness of this approach is afforded by a need to assess the effect of nutritional intervention on a sample of children. An incremental growth rate is chosen, below which those children not achieving it receive nutritional intervention. The effects of such are evaluated by continuing to record incremental data. Incremental data on those children not receiving intervention are also recorded and become useful as comparative data.

It should be noted that for assessment of growth velocity in the first critical months of life, the Roche-Himes velocity growth standards suffer from the drawback that the time intervals are long. What are needed for this particular period are such standards as those of, for example, Fomon et al. (3); and for comparisons of different samples of individuals, standards presented as tables of means, standard deviations (SDs), and percentiles are useful.

There is an inherent pitfall in this methodology: velocity standard curves are appropriately smoothed, whereas even a healthy individual child's curve over short periods of time may be anything but smooth, encompassing even cessation of growth, followed by catch-up. In the above example, therefore, there is potential for the false positive-negative phenomenon. This must be obviated in setting and observing the criteria for intervention and follow-up.

We need more information from hard data on the extent of variability among healthy children. Does a period of slow growth tend to be followed by a period of more rapid catch-up growth? This is not the place for a discussion on the all-important methodology of the analysis of sequential data, but a valuable reference is that of Goldstein (4).

The debate continues whether to use one set of growth standards for international purposes, or to use national standards derived from a privileged sample of the population under study. National standards, although often impractical to obtain, are an ideal, although use of an elite privileged sample has a potential hazard. Such a sample may be different genetically from, for example, a sample of a less privileged segment of the population.

The world's children appear to follow similar growth patterns, although populations of different ethnic and geographical origins have different adult stature and rates of maturation. Thus, children of all ages vary widely in actual stature and in weight for height. We have no data at present to determine how much variation in size among races would exist (particularly, say, under 5 years of age) if all children lived in optimum conditions. With respect to adult height, there appear to be ethnic differences, susceptible to generational change; such genetic differences may be established in puberty.

This leads to the basic question concerning use of standards: for what purpose does one wish to use them: To screen an individual child for a growth indicator, or to compare one sample of children with another? For the former, if there exists a good national standard of some kind of the population from which the individual comes, that is appropriate. If not, and for the latter, a good representative national sample from another country may be used if there is some agreement as to tolerable degrees of deviation from whatever norm is chosen, for example, National Center for Health Statistics (NCHS) United States standards (5) that have many percentile curves.

The place for international reference values is exemplified by WHO charts (6). These offer a simple and practical approach for health screening by the use of a series of reference values derived from one set of measures. A value range is selected that most closely resembles that of healthy children in the population concerned.

Use of international standards must not imply that any goals or aims are involved. They simply constitute independent points with which to compare individual children or samples of children. There are now a host of growth standards existent in many countries, some good, some poor; it is questionable whether additional ones are necessary. What are needed are new standards based on new and different criteria.

Summarizing points already made, perhaps one of our greatest needs is infancy-specific growth standards (distance and velocity) derived from infants on whom information is available.

PERINATAL GROWTH

There are three basic periods of perinatal growth: (a) intrauterine (prenatal), (b) transitional, and (c) extrauterine (postnatal). A discussion of prenatal growth standards, which are needed, follows. In the transitional period, the first 6 to 12 days of postnatal life are characterized by large variations and fluctuations, and growth follows no standards. After this period, postnatal growth velocity is distinctly faster than in the late prenatal period, so neither can be applied to the other. Separate standards thus are needed to evaluate perinatal growth.

We know comparatively little about the 40-week period of prenatal growth. For somatic assessments of fetal growth, we must rely on measurements made on fetuses expelled early in pregnancy as a result of social abortion or fetal abnormality (see, e.g., ref. 7). Later fetuses either are born too soon or are too small for their gestational age. The creation of fetal growth curves in this fashion, useful though they may be, has one basic, serious fault: the assumption that such fetuses may be considered normal in the sense of growth normality. This hazardous assumption may be justified if the truly prematurely born infant, without any congenital abnormalities, is predicted to continue to grow normally postnatally in exactly the same way as infants born at 40 weeks of gestation.

The outcome for all fetuses is what is important, and acceptable fetal growth curves related to outcome will be welcomed by many disciplines involved in fetal and infant health. With the advent of noninvasive ultrasonography, it is now possible to measure longitudinally, from 12 weeks of gestation, a linear body measurement of fetal growth: femur length (8). A similar linear measure can then be made postnatally for those fetuses born alive—also longitudinally. In fact, the femur length measure cannot be continued (other than by unacceptable radiography). Falkner and Roche (9), however, in a longitudinal study using radiographs that were available at birth, have shown, as would be expected, that femur length is highly correlated with recumbent length and stature. The crux of this method is that curves can be created by fetuses destined to be either full-term (FTI), preterm (PTI), or small-for-gestational-age (SFGAI) infants. Outcome for each then can be measured postnatally; since it is likely to be different for each group, important indications for intervention and prevention could be revealed.

Particularly in monitoring early growth is it important to understand the basic differing postnatal growth patterns of FTI and infants of low birthweight (ILB). It seems that PTI, without congenital malformations and receiving reasonable care, exhibit catch-up growth and by 3 years of age reach the same size as comparable FTI (10). This is not the case for SFGAI. There appears to be a distribution curve of size outcome across those who exhibit sufficient catch-up to achieve the same result as the above-mentioned PTI and those who do not and will remain permanently and irreversibly smaller. This has important implications if it can be shown that fetal malnutrition is a major causation of SFGAI.

Falkner (11) described a pair of monozygous (and thus phenotypically similar) twins born at 39 weeks of gestation. One twin was an ILB weighing half that of his twin. Avoiding a discussion of cause, a summary of outcome for each twin postnatally shows that the smaller twin, albeit "healthy," had a growth pattern exactly consistent with that of a SFGAI whose immediate postnatal catch-up was insufficient and by 16 years of age remained irreversibly and markedly smaller in size across many anthropometric measures. By holding the genetic growth factor the same for both infants–adolescents, the relationship between prenatal growth and postnatal outcome (in this case somatically) is shown to be important for nongenetic factors influencing growth.

Much attention to these aspects of prenatal growth and outcome is needed, together with the ability for prediction. Smallness, per se, may be of little moment, but if associated with, for example, stunting of other biological factors, such as brain development, it becomes, as an indicator, all important (12).

FETAL AND EARLY POSTNATAL SIZE AND MATURATION

The most commonly measured monitor of fetal and infant maturity is birthweight. This measure indicates other factors than maturity, but it is simple to measure reasonably accurately and does play a key role. Gestational age data (time-dependent indicator) are less commonly available, in part due to the difficulty in recording them accurately.

Genetic influences on the variance in fetal growth are thought to comprise approximately 20% maternal, 20% intrinsic fetal, perhaps 5 to 10% paternal, and the rest gathered under the umbrella of "nonnutritional." There is no agreement on how important the maternoplacental-fetal nutrition factor is, and it is interesting to note that before the 32nd week of gestation, fetal weights are similar throughout many countries with great differences in nutritional status. Under severe conditions of maternal malnutrition, it might be expected that any maternal factor regulating fetal growth would act protectively to prevent serious depletion of maternal nutrient and mineral supplies by slowing down fetal growth. Near-normal fetal growth under severe maternal malnutrition would indicate that there are placental and fetal growth-controlling factors that operate normally under these circumstances. These factors may exhibit feedback by entering the maternal circulation and then inhibiting maternal metabolic mechanisms. How is it, then, that especially the nutrition component of poor and adverse environmental conditions is associated with lowered human birthweight? This is largely due to factors causing an abnormal and marked reduction in growth rate after 36 weeks, for the mean birthweights of infants born at 36 weeks in many parts of the world under different circumstances are quite similar.

A mother not achieving her own growth potential, due to malnutrition or other such adverse environmental factors, is likely to have a smaller fetus and newborn infant than had she grown in good circumstances. Clearly, two generations or more may be needed to reverse the results of poor environment on birth size. Mothers of short stature in Guatemala have babies of smaller size than do mothers of medium stature. A food supplement given to both samples of mothers during pregnancy increases the birth size of the smaller mothers' infants more than it does those infants of larger mothers, nearly but not entirely eliminating the difference (13).

The monitoring of weight gain in pregnancy has recently been found to be of greater significance than was realized in relationship to birth size. "Normal values" cannot be ascertained with precision; estimates of average patterns are made and are useful, although in any sample there will be considerable distribution about the mean.

Total maternal weight gain during normal pregnancy averages around 11 kg. Small gains occur in the early weeks; near 12 weeks, weight accrues. Although there is much individual variability, this gain continues until term in virtually linear fashion, averaging 350 to 400 g/week. It is important to realize that, assuming an 11-kg total gain, the maternal component is 6 kg and the fetal component, 5 kg. These components vary in amount and rate during the second and third trimesters. During the second, most of the gain is in the maternal component, with blood volume increases, growth of uterus and breasts, and the all-important storage of fat. The third trimester sees the major weight gain in the fetal component, involving the fetus, placenta, and amniotic fluid. The maternal component is also increased in this period, largely by extracellular fluid increase.

S.M. Garn (*personal communication*), in an analysis of 44,725 pregnancies from the National Collaborative Perinatal Project, summarizes that prepregnancy maternal weight is as good, or better, a predictor of birth size than more complex indices of maternal body mass. Furthermore, there is a far greater effect of pregnancy weight gain on birth weight than there is of prepregnancy weight on birth weight. While there is no maternal age effect on the relationship between prepregnancy weight and birth weight, there is an age effect on the pregnancy weight-gain/ birthweight relationship. Apropos of this, there is clear evidence that birth size differs for the same level of pregnancy weight gain in younger and older women. Analysis of the data indicates also that the fetus of a teenage pregnancy (given good prenatal care) adapts much better than the fetus of an older woman. Monitoring of maternal weight gain in pregnancy in differing environmental conditions and genetic populations is profitable and requires greater attention.

MONITORING POSTNATAL GROWTH AND MATURITY

In order to allow monitoring of growth to contribute as much information as possible, growth measures clearly must be related to concomitant growth factors, for example, dietary, health, and feeding pattern data. Anthropometric measures do not require great skills but, like all measurements, do require reasonable accuracy and appropriate apparatus in order to minimize errors. Single measurements are less useful as monitors than repeated ones over time, as we have already discussed. Here, though, errors are cumulative, and if potential observer-error is added, assessing velocity growth can be difficult if these considerations are not addressed. Anthropometry techniques and apparatus are not necessarily expensive, nor is training difficult. Careful attention to any one of a number of instructional texts is mandatory, particularly in field work (14,15).

There are four key anthropometric measures for growth monitoring that are practical and may be measured in the field: body weight, length-height, head circumference, and mid-upper arm circumference. First, it should be noted that body weight is an unstable and individually variable measurement over time. Body weight decrements frequently occur in health. Catch-up growth occurs; and when studying growth of an individual(s), particularly in the early postnatal months, it is necessary that the incremental periods be short in order that the actual pattern of growth emerges. Under these circumstances, body weight can be a sensitive monitor of growth, if assessed frequently.

During the early days of life, there is a 5 to 10% body weight loss in healthy infants, due largely to diminution of body water content. This normal phenomenon proceeds until the third or fourth day, when weight gain begins; by the tenth day, the birthweight has been regained. As a rough guide, body weight usually doubles between birth and 4 to 5 months and triples by 1 year of age. The general course of growth then is followed. Interpretation of body weight patterns must always be based on the realization that a gain in weight may indicate fat growth, bone and muscle growth, a seasonal effect, catch-up growth, gain in total body water, increased caloric intake, and so forth. Body weight patterns, then, may hide important factors. Ideally, assessments of growth during infancy need some parallel measures of body composition to identify possible adaptations to a wide range of intakes.

Length-stature is a stable and valuable measure of growth. Especially in the field, the thought of measuring length in early life causes distress; yet those who plead for the use of an accurate monitor of linear growth for all ages (particularly in consideration of velocity data) know that simple measuring boards for infants up to 2 years of age are available, easily transported (easier than body weight balances), and provide greatly needed raw data.

Simple monitoring, particularly in the developing world, where lack of skilled personnel is likely, may be done by using two indices: (a) length-height for age and (b) weight for length-height. When age is known, the first index poses no problem, except training and equipment. Length-height at each age is distributed virtually in Gaussian fashion; thus comparisons are simple, provided care is taken to eliminate all possible errors in measurement techniques, instrumentation, and recording sources of error known to cause upset to those who will later analyze results.

Weight-for-height measurement, an index independent of age certainly up to the prepubertal period, is a useful monitor for size, and standards are available. It is questionable, however, whether pooling between ages is acceptable, which involves comparisons of distributions, means, and variances. Is the mean weight of a 6-

year-old's height of 120 cm the same as the mean weight of a 7-year-old of 120 cm? If so, are the 5th and 95th percentile weights of 6-year-olds 115 to 125 cm tall the same as those of 7-year-olds 115 to 120 cm tall? Ages can be pooled legitimately, if these conditions are met.

The addition of the parental size factor for individual children has great use. The genetic factor in human size is, of course, significant, and relating "mid-parent stature"[1] to the growth plots of individual children is valuable, when it can be done (16). Standards for children's heights, allowing for parental height, are available (17). It should be taken into account that genetic potential and relationships with parental size are more fully expressed in the developed world, whereas in the developing world, environmental factors may confuse the issue.

Head circumference is a reasonable indicator of head and brain size, and thus a most important measure. Its velocity curve is different from that of general growth. A period of rapid incremental growth occurs from birth, and then a marked deceleration occurs until the age of approximately 10 years, the size of the skull having reached nearly 90% of its adult size by this age. Thereafter, the increments are minimal until adulthood.

This measurement may also be used to provide an example of the necessity to consider growth patterns within certain age groups or categories of infants and children. Patterns may occur which deviate from normal patterns yet are not, in themselves, indicative of pathologic processes. Particularly in the first 3 years of life, the monitoring of head circumference growth is valuable for determining the outcome of infants who may have been deprived prenatally.

As an indicator of muscle growth, hence mainly the protein nutrition factor, Shakir (18) pioneered the use of mid-upper arm circumference as a nutritional indicator. He pointed out that upper-arm circumference changes little between the ages of 1 and 5 years, and in an age group so vulnerable to malnutrition, an age-constant standard may be used. It is clearly a most convenient measure: a simple apparatus is needed, and error is small in field conditions. Comparisons of groups and individual children with standards indicate various degrees of malnutrition as well as, e.g., weight for height and also may be used on individual children to assess change over time.

There are other somatic indicators that are useful and acceptable for growth monitoring, but the above four are among the most sensitive. It is clear that one must restrict the number, particularly in the field. It should be noted that studying the joint relationships and distributions of such variables, where appropriate, will often lead to more fruitful information than studying just one.

With respect to other measures, body fat may be monitored by measuring subcutaneous fat by skinfold calipers. This is a useful screening measure of nutritional status, although such measures in early postnatal life are difficult and of doubtful significance. We must be careful, however, since these measures may not be a sensitive index of nutritional status or growth among populations with char-

---

[1]The mean of both parents' stature.

acteristically low or high fatness when healthy. For example, contrary to common teaching, the Eskimo infant–child has a relatively low skinfold thickness (19). This value, together with the estimation of total body fat, is similar to that of many groups of European children living in temperate climates. Eskimos protect themselves from the environment by their dwellings and clothing; such microclimates to which individuals must adapt hence may be different from those of their surroundings, and physique may not reflect the effects of the cold.

Body fat has a complex growth pattern of its own and must be taken into account when its growth is being monitored. Fat increases steadily and rapidly for the first (approximately) 9 months of life. A plateau is then reached, and increments will be zero. Soon thereafter, there is a true loss of fat until about 7 years. (Thus any curve depicting fat growth must be able to record negative increments or decrements.) At 7 years, fat is gained once more. In many male children, a growth spurt of fat occurs before the individual's general adolescent growth spurt. When the general body adolescent spurt begins (including muscle and bone mass), this external fat is stretched over the rapidly growing frame. In addition, there is an actual loss of fat, or return to decremental growth, during adolescence.

The female child follows a different pattern: in early childhood, her fat loss is less than that of the male. Hence the average female reaches adulthood with more total fat than the average male. Added to these normal patterns are such interrelated factors as hypercaloric food intake and true obesity. The complexity of fat growth is apparent.

Bone growth is obviously assessed by height measurement and thus follows the general growth curve. Individual bones in a child may grow at widely different rates, however, an important factor influencing final body proportions. Muscle growth is closely similar to the overall pattern of bone growth, but of all the tissues, muscle is the one, especially in the male, that is laid down heavily during the adolescent growth spurt.

Recently, some workers (20) have suggested that measurement of hair growth, particularly in the newborn and early childhood period, is a good and sensitive index of nutritional status. Measurement of root diameters and shaft length were obtained in two studies. This index deserves further evaluation.

MEASURES OF LATER MATURITY

Skeletal maturity is an important indicator of maturational or developmental age, although requiring radiography makes it impractical in, for example, field conditions. Added to this impracticality is the question of radiation, albeit of minute quality, to individuals for other than clinical assessment. Particularly at times of rapid growth, chronologic age is apt to be unhelpful as a marker in an individual child, and maturation of the skeleton (skeletal maturity; "bone age") is often more useful.

Radiographic examination reveals the stage of maturity by the use of standards, comparing, for example, the stage of maturation of several ossification centers

(21). Since in health, 100% of maturity of any maturational indicator is eventually reached by all children, skeletal maturity provides a good common growth scale. Prediction of growth outcome may also be made, to some extent, by its estimation and by relating it to an individual's general growth curve.

Puberty Ratings

Monitoring of prepubescent and puberty status is remarkably simple and non-invasive yet is rarely carried out. Puberty stages in health are consistently correlated with adolescent growth spurt curves and skeletal maturation, hence their usefulness. The stages may be easily assessed according to criteria described by Tanner (22). The stages are determined by a 5-point rating for genital (penile) development in boys and breast development in girls, and a 5-point rating for pubic hair in both sexes. These ratings are particularly useful in monitoring maturation of individual children.

Age of Menarche

This indicator of maturity is also an indicator of the secular trend or shift in growth over time of children and adults and is correlated with some environmental and nutritional factors. Unlike the male, the female has a clearcut point in her development in that studies have recorded its chronologic date and distribution over at least a century. Tanner (22), in an exhaustive review of records and a rework of Norwegian data, recently showed that from the mid-19th century until today, there has been a trend in many different populations where menarche has occurred earlier in age, from, for example, 15.5 years to near 13 years today, or 0.3 years each decade.

In using the age of menarche as a maturity indicator, the following questions show how care is needed in interpretation of this measure: Do environmental factors influence menarcheal age differences between populations? Less privileged girls have their menarche at later ages than more privileged females across all populations studied. Is there a genetic minimum age for menarche? The age of menarche seems to have become level and static in certain populations, and this may be due to a natural phenomenon or to improved environmental factors. Is the relative independence of growth and this maturational indicator genetically based? Tall and well-fed populations do not have the earliest ages of menarche.

In summary, in the 19th century, there was a notable difference in age of menarche between the well-to-do and the poor and, for example, between northern Europe and the Mediterranean. These differences have diminished with the social class difference to zero in some countries. Geographical differences are reduced to some 5 months on the average where it is thought the Mediterranean female child has reached the limit of earliness in age.

REFERENCES

1. Morley D. Paediatric priorities in the developing world. London: Butterworths, 1973.
2. Roche AF, Himes JH. Incremental growth charts. Am J Clin Nutr 1980;33:2041–52.

3. Fomon SJ, Ziegler E, Filer LJ, Andersen TA, Edwards B, Nelson E. Growth and serum chemical values of normal breast-fed infants. Acta Paediatr Scand 1978 (Suppl);273:1–29.
4. Goldstein H. The design and analysis of longitudinal studies. London: Academic Press, 1979.
5. National Center for Health Statistics. Growth charts. Rockville, Maryland: NCHS, 1976. [Monthly Vital Statistics Report, 25 (3):Supp. DHEW publication no. (HRA)76-1120.]
6. World Health Organization. A growth chart for international use in maternal and child health. Geneva: WHO, 1978.
7. Usher R, McLean F. Intrauterine growth of liveborn Caucasian infants at sea level: standards obtained from measurements in 7 dimensions of infants born between 25 and 44 weeks of gestation. J Pediatr 1969;74:901–10.
8. O'Brien GD, Queenan JT. Ultrasound fetal femur length in relation to intrauterine growth retardation. Am J Obstet Gynecol 1982;144:35–9.
9. Falkner F, Roche AR. Lower limb relationship to recumbent length and stature in fetal, neonatal, and early childhood growth. Ann Human Biol (in press).
10. Cruise MO. A longitudinal study of the growth of low birth weight infants. Pediatrics 1973;51: 620–8.
11. Falkner F. Implications for growth in human twins. In: Falkner F and Tanner J, eds. Human growth (vol II). New York: Plenum, 1978:397–413.
12. Falkner F. Maternal nutrition and fetal growth. Am J Clin Nutr 1981;34:769–74.
13. Lechtig A. Maternal nutrition and fetal growth in developing societies. Am J Dis Child 1975;129: 434–7.
14. Cameron N. The methods of auxological anthropometry. In: Falkner F, Tanner J, eds. Human growth (vol. II). New York: Plenum, 1978:35–90.
15. Falkner F. Office measurement of physical growth. Pediatr Clin N Am 1961;8:13–8.
16. Himes JH, Roche AF, Thissen D. Parent specific adjustments for assessment of recumbent length and stature. Monogr Paediatr, vol. 13. Basle: Karger, 1981.
17. Tanner JM, Goldstein H, Whitehouse RH. Standards for children's height at ages 2–9 years, allowing for height of parents. Arch Dis Child 1970;31:372–81.
18. Shakir A. Arm circumference in the surveillance of protein-calorie malnutrition in Baghdad. Am J Clin Nutr 1975;28:661–5.
19. Shephard RJ. Body composition of the Eskimo. Eur J Appl Physiol 1973;32:3–15.
20. Berger HM, King I, Doughty S, Wharton BA. Nutrition, sex, gestational age and hair growth in babies. Arch Dis Child 1978;53:290–4.
21. Tanner JM, Whitehouse RH, Goldstein H. A revised system for estimating skeletal maturity from hand and wrist radiographs, with separate standards for carpals and other bones (TW II system). Paris: International Children's Centre, 1972.
22. Tanner JM. A history of the study of human growth. Cambridge: Cambridge University Press, 1981:286–98.

DISCUSSION

Dr. Whitehead: With respect to the need for specific growth charts during infancy, my own chapter in this volume ended with a plea for their development, particularly now that feeding patterns in the western world have become so different from what they once were. Growth charts are not only required for the assessment of the health of communities of babies, they are increasingly being used to answer questions about lactational inadequacy in the individual mother. Theoretically, it would be important to carry out anthropometric studies among a number of different tribal groupings. The problem, however, is how to avoid complications relating to environmental conditions that are too adverse, as in the developing world.

A great deal of thought is necessary before such new growth surveys are commenced. Clearly, measurements would have to be taken much more frequently than was the case when the existing growth standards were compiled; we have suggested monthly measurements as a minimum. We must also decide which growth parameters need to be measured. As well as weight and height, it would be highly desirable to produce more up-to-date values for such parameters as mid-upper arm circumference and triceps skinfold thickness because of their importance in the developing world. Measurements of head circumference would likewise be valuable. The data would also need to be measured prospectively so that true velocity charts could be compiled.

Dr. Falkner: I agree completely with Dr. Whitehead. For new growth standards of a different kind that would be useful to us, I think we ought to concentrate almost entirely on infancy, where the greatest gap exists.

Dr. Waterlow: Regarding the question of whether we should have one standard or many, I accept the proposition of Habicht et al. (Lancet 1974;1:611) that the growth potential of young children is similar in all ethnic groups. Dr. R. Martorell reported on the heights of 7-year-old boys in Brazil, Costa Rica, Guatemala, Haiti, Jamaica, Nigeria, India, and Hong Kong, which is a wide spread of ethnic groups. In the upper socioeconomic classes, the average heights in all the countries lay between the 25th and 50th NCHS percentiles, whereas in the lower classes, they range from the 10th to below the 5th. As Cravioto has pointed out, the genetically determined relationship between the height of children and height of mothers is seen only in well-to-do societies and disappears when the height of the children is affected by environmental factors. It is a tenable proposition that there are real ethnic differences in adult height and that these differences become apparent during the growth spurt of puberty. My hypothesis is that this is where the genetic factor comes into play.

In relation to catch-up and regression toward the mean; I do not know whether it is valid to draw conclusions from the cross-sectional figures of the NCHS population, but if one compares children starting from birth at the 20th, 50th, and 80th percentiles, the average gain in weight of children growing along those centiles during the first 4 months is smaller in the lighter children and larger in the heavier ones. From 4 to 12 months, however, the gain is identical in the three groups: 3.5 kg. Does this mean that the tendency to regress toward the mean only begins later in infancy?

Finally, while it is almost certainly true that an individual child's growth does not occur along a smooth curve, it is difficult to obtain hard evidence for this. What is the range of deviation around the smoothed curve that you would expect to find?

Dr. Falkner: I do not think that data have been published to answer that question. In the Fells data, the shortest age period in the early months of life is never less than 3 months and then goes into 6-month periods, thus 6-month increments, for plots of an individual child. There is a seasonal effect, it seems. Although even plotting carefully measured lengths or heights, they do not look like Dr. Waterlow's mountains but they do look very irregular; I do not think anyone has estimated the degree of variability.

Dr. Waterlow: Fomon (Fomon SJ. Infant nutrition, 2nd ed. Philadelphia: WB Saunders, 1984) has some 2-weekly measurements of individual children in a reasonably large sample. He shows that if you take the growth in any 2-week period, the coefficient of variation between the individuals is as high as 35%. He has not calculated the intraindividual coefficient of variation from one successive 2-week period to another.

Dr. Falkner: The data would be available for 6-month increments.

Dr. Waterlow: A final point is that from the practical point of view in third world countries, the weight gain velocity is extremely important and sensitive. One of my colleagues was able to show in Nepal, on a sample of less than 20 children, a highly significant difference in monthly weight gains between the pre- and postmonsoon seasons. This tells what is happening in a way that attained weights and heights would never be able to.

Dr. Whitehead: If new standards are compiled, they should be analyzed statistically in a more adequate manner than is the case with the existing ones. One particular point of importance relates to the phenomenon known as regression toward the mean. Children who are born small tend to grow relatively more quickly in early life and those born big relatively slowly. This means that there is a smaller variance by the time children have reached 6 to 12 months than in the first few months of life. These considerations are clearly of practical importance when one is considering the dietary adequacy of individual babies and the assessment of things such as lactational inadequacy.

Dr. Falkner: Perhaps by the age of 1 year, the perinatal factors, such as influences on growth, have lessened and individual children are then getting onto the genetic target curve, which is where the alteration comes.

Dr. Whitehead: I agree; and the next time when changes occur is puberty.

Dr. Falkner: There is good evidence that onset of puberty in healthy children is largely genetically determined.

Dr. Waterlow: Are you supporting the hypothesis that genetic differences could make themselves apparent at puberty? If so, what you have just said seems a bit strange, because the earlier the onset of puberty, the earlier bone maturation will finish and the epiphyses close. On the whole, however, in the groups in which poor growth is environmentally determined, puberty has a somewhat later onset.

Dr. Falkner: "Healthy" is a vague term. I should have said, in samples of children who have good environment and have no evidence of poor nutrition, there seems to be a strong genetic factor in the time of onset of puberty.

Dr. Waterlow: Would these be genetically shorter or taller children? I am confused about puberty.

Dr. Falkner: The timing of the onset of puberty—strongly genetically influenced—is not related to the size of the child.

Dr. Marini: Returning to small-for-gestational age (SGA) infants, it is difficult to have a good prenatal growth curve. In Italy, we have conducted an anthropometric study of newborns, and we found that it was difficult to get a sufficient number below 32 weeks of gestational age. Concerning your ultrasound measurements of femur length, how many pregnancies did you include in your study in order to have a good standard for the population?

Dr. Falkner: Samples derived from approximately 2,000 live births per year in an obstetric service is practical, and subsamples of whatever the percentages in that community are of low birthweight, preterm, and SGA infants. The reason I suggested "consortium" is that, following necessary breakdowns for sex, socioeconomic categories, and so on, the numbers become small; to build up these numbers, cooperative studies are needed, all doing the same thing at the same time.

Dr. Marini: There is another problem: when you talk about not proportionate SGA, usually obstetricians refer to the abdominal circumference in comparison with the head circumference; on the other hand, neonatalogists work on chest circumference. Do you think it would be a good idea to advise people to measure head and chest, or head and abdomen, in order to have a comparison of data?

Dr. Falkner: The short answer is yes. The problem is that for those measurements, there has been little follow-up of the fetuses measured showing their postnatal growth patterns. In starting an ultrasonography study of fetuses, one must guard against the catch-all approach by which many things are measured, "in case" they might be useful.

Dr. Abdul Kader: With regard to this nonhomogenous population of SGA infants, there have been several reports on the use of ultrasonography to identify these groups. One of the studies suggested that if ultrasound was done early enough, it might be able to identify early intrauterine growth retardation. These infants would belong to the hypoplastic group of SGA infants whose catch-up growth is not going to be good. If intrauterine growth retardation occurs after 16 weeks of gestation, however, catch-up growth among the SGA infants born may be sufficient. Therefore, it is difficult to be certain whether there is going to be a period whereby the perinatal influences will be negated and only environmental factors will be affecting growth, because the effects of perinatal factors in certain instances can be permanent despite the environmental influences on future growth and development.

Dr. Falkner: You mentioned the important Chicago study in which the "asymmetrical fetus" was first described. The authors also suggested, as you describe, that the timing of the intrauterine growth failure during pregnancy is probably vital and will perhaps decide whether the smallness is going to be irreversible or can be overcome by catch-up. I think the needed fetal growth curves will reveal the impact factors regarding outcome for the SGA infant. Professor Widdowson's classic study of outcome for rats (an animal born, of course, immature) showed the importance of length and timing of starvation and subsequent unlimited calorie feeding.

Dr. Abdul Kader: It is crucial to determine what is the best measurement to use when assessing fetal growth by ultrasonography. Is it the head circumference or the femoral length, as you suggested, or the abdominal capacity, the crown-rump length, or the chest circumference? This is where general agreement is lacking as to which of these is the most sensitive to discover growth retardation.

Dr. Falkner: It is not completely a question of sensitivity, but of choosing a measurement(s) that can be repeated during the entire pregnancy. Crown-rump can be measured ultrasonically accurately until 20 weeks of age, and then it is almost impossible. I suggested femur length simply because it is a linear measurement that can be measured from 14 weeks until term. I am sure there are others, such as abdominal circumference and chest diameter, but these need assessing and are related to postnatal growth patterns.

Dr. Senterre: Some neonatologists have proposed expressing growth as increment in percentage of initial value in order to narrow the range when comparing different babies.

Dr. Falkner: That is a good idea, indeed, if the sample is reasonably homogeneous.

Dr. Zoppi: As I reported during the discussion following Dr. Butte's paper, we have shown that infants receiving high calorie intakes show higher growth rates and higher levels of insulin. In our opinion, this could be a risk factor.

Dr. Falkner: Disregarding the infant of low birthweight, there does not seem to be any agreement on how much energy actually is required for growth in the human. For example, in the adolescent growth spurt, there would be a need for a large increase in energy intake. Is this correct?

Dr. Waterlow: The evidence is reasonably consistent, from the kind of data Professor Senterre produced on prematures, from malnourished children growing rapidly, and from adults who are either under- or overfed. Obviously, the energy stored varies according to the composition of the tissue gained and will be greater if more fat and less lean is being stored. I think the figures that Professor Senterre gave us fit in well with the other information: if you are storing about 3 or 4 kcal/g tissue gained, which should be a reasonable proportion of fat and lean, and in addition you have to add another 1 kcal/g for the energy cost of the storage, the result is between 4 and 6 kcal/g weight gain, ranging from prematures up to adults. The reason that this big increase in requirements is not seen during the puberty growth spurt is precisely the point that Professor Senterre made; if the weight gain is expressed as a fraction of the existing weight, even in puberty, it is a small fraction, whereas in the premature, it is a large fraction.

Dr. Mata: We were surprised to find, in a long-term study of Costa Rican poor rural peasants, that they were growing well. As a matter of fact, by classifying the children according to the Gomez criteria, only about 2% had second- and third-degree malnutrition. My impression is that there is a great improvement in weights and heights of children in Venezuela, Costa Rica, Panama, and Colombia, a finding that matches well with the declining infant and preschool mortalities. There is a high proportion of low birthweight babies in less developed countries, higher than reported, because many newborns are reported dead when they actually are born alive. Placing a nurse around the clock in Santa Maria Cauqué permitted us to find that 40% of babies are low birthweight, four-fifths small-for-dates. As a country goes into transition, the rate 1:4 changes to 1:1; at the present time, Costa Rica has a rate of 2 preterm babies for 1 small-for-date. Would it not be better to have reference curves set according to fetal maturity (as established at birth) with growth curves for cohorts of children born with specific biological characteristics? Such curves would be more func-tional because children's growth and survival vary as a function of birthweight and of events that occur before birth.

Dr. Falkner: That is an important point. Growth standards derived from human "elite" samples, however, may not be representative of a population.

Dr. Yip: Professor Falkner, you mentioned that one problem in the inter- and intragroup comparison for weight and height is the adjustment for age. In this regard, you highlighted the usefulness of growth velocity because the effect of age is removed. I agree fully; however, it is possible to remove the effect of age even for static parameters. One method is to calculate the standard division score for weight and height. This is particularly useful in assessing growth over time in abnormal children of different ages, for example, children with leukemia. When assessing weight in an individual, it is also possible to take into account, at least to some extent, the effect of age and height together. One method is to calculate an index which is the ratio between weight divided by height of the patient and that of the control (at the 50th percentile) for the same age and sex.

Dr. Falkner: Such indices are often useful, although there are such a large number from which to choose.

Nutritional Needs and Assessment of Normal Growth, edited by M. Gracey and F. Falkner. Nestlé Nutrition, Vevey/Raven Press, New York © 1985.

Studies of Growth of Australian Infants

Michael Gracey and Nancy E. Hitchcock

Gastroenterology and Nutrition Research Unit, Princess Margaret Children's Medical Research Foundation (Inc.), and Department of Child Health, University of Western Australia, Perth, Western Australia 6001

> *While we now possess a fairly accurate and extensive knowledge of the normal curve of growth of certain animals, particularly the white rat and the white mouse, it is a regrettable fact that we are not yet in possession of equally reliable and extensive data concerning the growth of human beings.*
>
> T. BRAILSFORD ROBERTSON, 1916 (1)

There is disagreement about what is normal growth in infancy. This is an important issue because "normal" growth charts are used extensively in clinical pediatrics and in public health work to assess the nutritional status of individuals, groups, communities, and countries. There is also disagreement about the relevance of widely used British and American growth charts to other populations. This applies in Australia where the National Health and Medical Research Council (NHMRC) is currently considering whether to undertake a nationwide study to determine local "standards" or whether international values can be used. In some countries, local and international standards are used, sometimes applied to different sections of the population.

There is also some controversy about the dietary patterns and nutrient intakes required to achieve normal growth in early life. In Australia, one of the most basic tools used by dietitians and nutritionists to assess adequate nutrient intakes is the dietary allowances for use in Australia (2). These are used as reference points for an initial assessment of the adequacy of diets of individuals or groups within the community. They were referred to in our own work, for example, when we claimed that the dietary patterns of aborigines (3) or children of migrants (4) were "inadequate" or "unsatisfactory" when compared with these allowances. They are also used as a basis for designing diets for individuals with a wide variety of problems, including obesity, diabetes, hypertension, and other metabolic disorders, as well as for people receiving institutional foods.

The Australian dietary allowances have been revised several times, the latest revision being in 1971 (2). Many of the recommendations in these Australian allowances were based on interpretations of the FAO/WHO expert group reports (5) on requirements for some nutrients. The values for food energy for infants and for children aged 2 to 11 years were obtained from Australian data on food consumption, which were based on Australian studies by Roche and Cahn (6); the data for 2-year-olds were obtained in 1954. The figures for infants were those summarized by Clements (7). Where no Australian data were available for various age groups, recommendations were extrapolated. It seems obvious that these recommendations, currently in use across Australia, contain serious inaccuracies, particularly for young children, in view of the significant differences in lifestyle, breastfeeding patterns, and eating and drinking habits which prevail today in contrast to those in vogue in the 1940s and 1950s when those data were obtained.

There are very few comprehensive, contemporary, longitudinal studies combining assessment of diet, nutrition, and growth of healthy children in early life. The Perth Growth Study (PGS) was designed with this in mind in order to document normal patterns in a well-defined sample of healthy infants in a well-nourished population. The study began in 1979 with a group of more than 200 apparently healthy infants born in the city of Perth, Australia. At the time of this writing the subjects are aged 4 years, and the study is due to continue until they are 5 years old. This chapter discusses the findings of the PGS up to early 1983 and how these relate to other studies of growth and nutrition in Australian infants. The findings then are compared to recent international literature, with particular reference to the use of growth charts to assess nutrition and growth performance in early life.

EARLIER AUSTRALIAN CHILD GROWTH STUDIES

Historically, studies of growth of Australian infants fall into three periods: (a) before 1920, when overseas data were the only ones available and were used to assess the growth of children in Australia; (b) 1920s to 1970s, when several attempts were made to develop Australian growth standards; and (c) since the late 1970s, when serious consideration has been given to the adoption of international reference values.

Brailsford Robertson (1,8) was the first to publish an Australian infant growth study, done about 1915. This study of more than 150 infants in the state of South Australia led the author to suggest that British charts, widely used in Australia at the time, were inappropriate for Australian conditions. The Australian infants were heavier at birth and their "superiority of bodily dimensions" was maintained in the first year. As the Australian community was then overwhelmingly British in origin, this change in growth in infancy was attributed to improved "climatic, social and economic conditions."

In 1926, Southby (9) described a standard which he considered "representative of the ordinary well developed, local baby" from a study of 2,000 subjects drawn from normal births (excluding twins) in an obstetric hospital, children discharged from a children's hospital, competitors in the "Empire Baby Competitions" of 1924, and competitors in a baby show. Not surprisingly, these children were heavier and grew faster than growth charts in use at that time suggested. Despite the bias inherent in the selection of these subjects, the author proposed the development of a local Australian standard for growth. It should be noted that Southby's study was cross-sectional, and the sexes were not separated. A later study of 700 infants in the state of Victoria by Scantlebury (10) also combined the results for boys and girls.

Clements (11) reported a study in 1933 designed to document normal growth patterns for Australian infants. This was a retrospective analysis of weights recorded every 2 weeks from more than 1,000 infants in baby health care centers in the state of New South Wales. They were selected to be representative of Sydney's population of the time and covered the first 12 months of life. Excluded were (a) inadequate records, (b) premature babies, (c) multiple births, and (d) subjects with illnesses during the year.

This was an outstanding study, for its day, and still provides important information about normal growth in early life. Clements compared his findings to those of earlier Australian and overseas studies; his results were remarkably similar to the earlier Australian reports already mentioned (8,10). Clements' figures were adopted for use in baby health care centers in the state of New South Wales and now provide a valuable reference for more recent studies.

Dale (12) undertook a cross-sectional study from 1936 to 1946. It was the first in Australia to document weight gains in the first 5 years of life. These data were subsequently used in the first Australian growth charts in 1957 (12). The Melbourne University Child Growth Study Unit began a major longitudinal study in the 1950s to assess the dynamics of growth. Their subjects were born between 1951 and 1953, and data were taken quarterly between 2 and 4 years of age and biannually thereafter. The 0- to 2-year period was not studied. This was a comprehensive, multidisciplinary study involving specialists in anatomy, anthropology, child health, dentistry, orthodontics, nutrition, and psychology (13). Particular emphasis was given to patterns of development of skeletal maturity. A later study in Melbourne (14) led the authors to comment:

> The indications appear to be for regular upgrading of the Australian standards and the data gathered must represent wide population groups, thus allowing assessments certainly with comparable birth or generation age and ideally for select population and racial groupings. The necessity for nonreliance on overseas standards needs stressing and also an appreciation of the inherent errors in comparing assessments of different population groups.

We believe these comments represent an unrealistic approach to variations in normal growth in a relatively small, ethnically diverse population like ours. The Melbourne Child Health Study data have not been used in Australian growth charts.

Bell and Lay (15) undertook a study of more than 1,000 subjects in the 1960s in baby health centers in New South Wales; this provides important comparisons with the earlier study by Clements (11). About one-third of subjects from Bell and Lay's study were from country centers. As in Clements' study, the records were examined every 2 weeks in the first 12 months of life. Their findings, which showed accelerated growth velocity (for weight) in comparison with 1933, are shown below in relation to Clements' work and our current PGS. It is of interest to read that the increased weight gains found in 1964 were thought to be due to "a general rise in the standards of living in the lower economic groups with an improved diet and a recession of diseases" when compared to the work of Clements, which was conducted during the great depression. We suspect that the decline of breastfeeding and the popularity of bottle feeding in the 1960s were the important determinants of this trend to more rapid weight gains, which we now consider undesirable.

Jones and Hemphill (16) published the first comprehensive survey of physical measurements of infants and preschool children in New South Wales in 1974. This was a cross-sectional study of height, weight, biacromial diameter, subscapular skinfold thickness, head circumference, and length of 16,000 infants and preschool children attending "virtually all baby health centres" in Sydney in 1971–1972. A large number of preschool kindergartens were also visited. Recognizing the bias inherent in their method of sampling, the authors include former attenders at child health centers as well. Their ethnic origins were roughly grouped as: (a) Australian-born of Australian parents, (b) Australian-born of Southern European parents (e.g., Greece, Italy, Spain), and (c) Australian-born of other European parents. The authors concluded that:

> Height increases steadily with age in the pre-school period, with no very obvious change in the pattern as occurs at puberty. The same applies to weight... there was little difference between the various groups classified by national origin, and only a suggestion that children born in Australia with Southern European parents were heavier than Australians from 3 years of age.

They commented on the paucity of earlier Australian studies, acknowledged that the work of Clements (11) was the best available then, and that there had been "an increase in weight for all ages since then." The data gathered by Jones and Hemphill (16) were used to construct the "Charts and tables of heights, masses and head circumferences of infants and children" (17), which are the current national charts used in Australia.

The Tasmanian child growth surveys done over the past decade have also provided important information about Australian children. These have been compared with other Australian studies, including those of Clements (11) and Bell and Lay (15). While the increased weight gains found by the latter had been interpreted as a healthy trend reflecting improved living standards and diet, the Tasmanian study found more evidence of that trend (18) but attributed it to overweight. There was then increasing concern at the extent of childhood obesity in the Australian community. The Tasmanian experience suggested that the incidence of obesity in Australian children was increasing and, as in Britain (19), may have been due to overfeeding in the first years of life. Court et al. (20) found elevated diastolic blood pressures in more than half their obese children studied in Melbourne. This was considered relevant to the development of coronary heart disease in later life, which is a major problem in Australia and similar Western countries. Godfrey and his colleagues (21) found serum cholesterol levels in children in the Western Australian town of Busselton (see Fig. 1) to be higher than in most reported studies and that a significant proportion of their subjects had hypercholesterolemia.

It was becoming evident that nutritionally related disorders were not uncommon in our society. Lewis, a participant in the Tasmanian child growth surveys, had commented that "few people appear to be interested in nutrition in Australia" (22). At that time, our NHMRC did not classify nutrition as a discipline for research studies.

It was against this background and with these gaps in our knowledge of human nutrition in Australia that the PGS was commenced in 1979 (23). The period from 0 to 2 years seemed most important to study, as little local information was available concerning this crucial period.

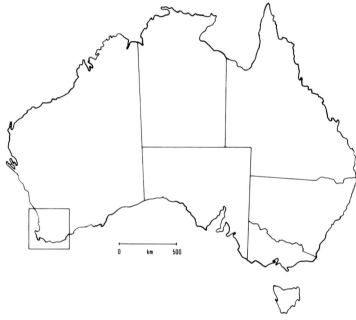

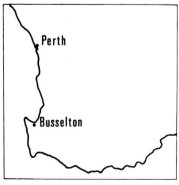

FIG. 1. Map of Australia **(top)** and southwest Australia **(bottom)** showing the locations of Perth and Busselton. (From Hitchcock and Gracey, ref. 3.)

LOCAL CONDITIONS

Australia is an affluent, industrialized nation whose infants and young children should be well nourished. Childhood undernutrition is almost unknown, and the nutritional impact of infectious disease is insignificant, except for vulnerable, disadvantaged groups, which include aborigines, the children of recently arrived migrants, and those from lower socioeconomic classes and unstable families. European settlement began just under 200 years ago, and the current population of 15 million is predominantly European, particularly of British origin. Postwar migration has added substantial numbers of Southern and Eastern Europeans and Southeast Asians in the past 30 years. The population is largely urban, and the largest cities, Sydney, Melbourne, Perth, Adelaide, and Brisbane, are coastally located state capitals containing most of the nation's people.

The PGS reported here is being undertaken in Perth. This city of 900,000 people is the state capital of Western Australia. Although it has only 1.3 million people, it covers 2.4 million square kilometers, the western third of the continent. The climate is typically Mediterranean, with hot, dry summers and wet, mild winters. The food supply is abundant, varied, well organized, and mostly of local origin. Most families shop at large, well-stocked supermarkets, many of which belong to large corporations and all of which are required to meet high standards of food quality and hygiene. In these respects, Australia resembles other Western countries where there have been important changes in food supplies and distribution over the past three to four decades.

Important changes in lifestyle have occurred in Australia and similar countries through the influence of urbanization, automation, and the media. These have probably had significant effects on dietary patterns in the first few years of life, when eating habits are being formed. Another recent trend of relevance to infant nutrition that has emerged in Australia and other industrialized countries is a resurgence of breastfeeding.

THE PERTH GROWTH STUDY

In mid-1979, 104 boys and 101 girls were entered into the PGS. They were selected randomly from metropolitan Midwife Notification of Birth Records kept by the Western Australian Public Health Department. The criteria for selection were that the subjects were: (a) at least second-generation Australian-born, but excluding aborigines; (b) from two-parent families; (c) full-term, single births from uncomplicated pregnancies and deliveries; (d) weighed 2,500 g or more at birth; and (e) living within 12 km of the Perth General Post Office.

These selection criteria were used to choose a sample of manageable size for detailed, long-term dietary and growth studies and to identify them as an apparently "normal" local group. This is important in Australia because of the recently emerging ethnic diversity of our population.

Collection of Data

Birthweight and birth length measurements were available from midwife records. Head circumference at birth, not a routine measurement in all hospitals, was not available in some cases. Measurements of length, body weight, and head circumference of infants have been recorded at 6 weeks of age, and at 3, 6, 9, and 12 months during the first year of life, using standard methods (17).

Information was obtained from the mother by interview, when her infant was 6 weeks of age, concerning the kind and frequency of milk feeding and the kind, amount, and frequency of nonmilk foods consumed by her infant. At all later times, an accurate record of all food and drink consumed by the infant was kept by the mother for 7 consecutive days prior to the day when physical measurements were made. This allowed cross-checking of the record at that time. If the mother was breastfeeding, she recorded the fact and the duration of each feed. Anthropometric and dietary data have been obtained at 3, 6, 9, 12, and 18 months and at 2 and 3 years of age. The study is scheduled to continue until the children are 5 years old.

In addition to anthropometric and dietary data for each infant, information is available from the parents of each child concerning parents' educational achievements and occupations, age, weight, and height of each parent, number of children in the family, and mother's habits of smoking and consuming alcohol during pregnancy and after the infant's birth. Each mother has kept a record in a booklet supplied to her of the major developmental milestones of her infant, and notes about timing of eruption of teeth and any illnesses.

Anthropometric Findings

The mean weights and lengths (up to 24 months) or heights of the subjects from birth to 3 years are shown in Table 1.

TABLE 1. *Weights[a] and lengths[b] or heights[b] of subjects from birth to 3 years*

	Boys			Girls		
Age	n	Weight	Length	n	Weight	Length
Birth	104	3.56 ± 0.04	51.9 ± 0.2	101	3.47 ± 0.04	50.7 ± 0.2
6 weeks	95	4.81 ± 0.06	56.3 ± 0.2	96	4.60 ± 0.05	55.5 ± 0.2
3 months	99	5.92 ± 0.08	60.7 ± 0.2	96	5.61 ± 0.06	59.3 ± 0.2
6 months	95	7.85 ± 0.09	67.5 ± 0.3	94	7.44 ± 0.08	65.9 ± 0.2
9 months	88	9.11 ± 0.10	72.1 ± 0.3	90	8.56 ± 0.09	70.6 ± 0.2
12 months	85	10.01 ± 0.11	75.9 ± 0.3	88	9.50 ± 0.10	74.9 ± 0.2
18 months	80	11.60 ± 0.12	82.7 ± 0.3	79	10.93 ± 0.12	81.7 ± 0.3
24 months	77	12.78 ± 0.15	88.5 ± 0.4	78	12.19 ± 0.14	87.6 ± 0.3
30 months	78	13.77 ± 0.14	92.8 ± 0.4	79	13.27 ± 0.14	91.9 ± 0.3
36 months	76	14.89 ± 0.17	96.9 ± 0.4	76	14.35 ± 0.17	95.9 ± 0.3

[a]Mean values, kg ± SEM.
[b]Mean values, cm ± SEM.

Breastfeeding

Breastfeeding patterns in the first 12 months are shown in Table 2 in relation to social rank using a 4-point local scale (24). The highest (A) includes professionals, e.g., doctors and lawyers; the lowest (D) are unskilled workers. Three-quarters of our sample were from middle-class families (B and C), which reflects the overall distribution of the general Australian population using Congalton's (24) method of assessment of social class.

Most mothers breastfed their babies, particularly those from the upper social ranks. Only 8% of mothers who breastfed their infants gave them complementary feeds. Low-solute (so-called "humanized") formulas[1] were given to most infants who were not breastfed until 6 months of age; after that, these formulas were used less, and cow's milk consumption increased.

Introduction of Nonmilk Food

By 6 weeks of age, 10% of infants were being given some nonmilk foods. The foods given were mainly fruit juice and syrups with vitamin C sweetened with sugar or sorbitol. Cereals and sweet biscuits were used, particularly for formula-fed babies. By 3 months of age, about one-third of infants were having nonmilk food. During the first 6 months, nonmilk foods (or solids) were more prevalent with the formula-fed infants. At 6 months, 8 infants were still being solely breastfed; all the others were being given a variety of foods, but few were given commercially prepared foods, except cereals and fruit syrups. After 6 months, commercially made meats and broths, fruit gels, yogurts, and other desserts were popular (25).

TABLE 2. *Percentage of infants breastfed[a]*

Age	Percentage of total sample	Percentage of each social group[b]			
		A	B	C	D
6 weeks	83	96	97	83	52
3 months (13 weeks)	77	96	90	69	52
6 months (26 weeks)	64	88	80	53	46
9 months (39 weeks)	46	68	58	35	29
1 year (52 weeks)	25	27	39	17	13

[a]From ref. 23.
[b]Highest A → lowest D.

[1]Examples: Lactogen and Nan, Nestlé Company (Australia), Sydney; and SMA, S26, Wyeth Pharmaceuticals Pty. Ltd., Sydney.

Dietary Energy and Nutrient Intakes

Dietary energy and nutrient intakes from foods other than breast milk were calculated from 7-day records of food intake. After detailed instruction, these were kept by the mothers in household measures and checked with her carefully before the calculations were done. The record sheets were manually converted to quantitative metric measures, and calculations were made using a computer program based on "tables of composition of Australian foods" (26) and, where appropriate, on analyses of food supplied by manufacturers. Direct estimates of breast milk consumption were not done in this study. The mean total energy intakes of infants up to 6 months of age were estimated from energy requirements calculated for maintenance and growth (27). These estimates give an acceptable guide to total dietary energy intake up to this age.

At 6 weeks of age, intakes for boys were, on the average, 2,300 kJ/day and for girls 2,135 kJ/day. At 3 months, these rose to 2,570 kJ/day for boys and 2,430 kJ/day for girls. At 6 months, the figures were 3,100 kJ/day and 2,930 kJ/day respectively (28). Dietary energy intakes for subjects not breastfed later were 3,745 ± 95 kJ/day (boys) and 3,620 ± 100 kJ/day (girls) at 9 months and 4,145 ± 108 kJ/day (boys) and 3,975 ± 105 kJ/day (girls) at 12 months of age (28). By 2 years of age, daily dietary energy intakes were 5,350 ± 117 kJ (boys) and 4,850 ± 138 kJ (girls). At 3 years of age, they were 5,740 ± 117 and 5,553 ± 111 kJ, respectively, for boys and girls (29). Intakes of major nutrients from 9 months to 3 years of age are shown in Table 3. Intakes of some minerals and vitamins are shown in Table 4.

Food Consumption Patterns

Apart from estimating the amounts of dietary energy and nutrients consumed by subjects in this study, we have assessed the development of patterns of consumption of dietary components (solids and fluids) in these children. We found that solids were negligible sources of dietary energy at 6 weeks, provided only 2% at 3 months and 22% at 6 months, and, by 9 months of age, provided almost 50%

TABLE 3. *Mean daily intakes of major nutrients*

Age	Protein (g)	Fat (g)	Carbohydrate (g)
Boys			
9 months	33.8 ± 1.2	42.7 ± 1.8	103.4 ± 3.3
12 months	38.5 ± 1.4	42.5 ± 1.6	115.9 ± 3.1
18 months	43.1 ± 1.1	50.5 ± 1.3	142.1 ± 3.7
2 years	43.6 ± 1.3	54.1 ± 1.6	146.9 ± 3.9
3 years	46.3 ± 1.2	57.1 ± 1.4	174.1 ± 4.3
Girls			
9 months	32.8 ± 1.4	39.6 ± 1.5	95.0 ± 2.8
12 months	38.1 ± 1.3	42.4 ± 1.5	103.5 ± 3.4
18 months	39.9 ± 1.4	46.3 ± 1.5	126.0 ± 3.8
2 years	40.9 ± 1.3	50.0 ± 1.5	143.6 ± 4.0
3 years	44.7 ± 1.2	57.2 ± 1.4	163.9 ± 3.6

TABLE 4. *Mean daily intakes of some minerals and vitamins*

Age	Calcium (mg)	Iron[a] (mg)	Thiamine[a] (μg)	Riboflavin[a] (mg)	Niacin[a,b] (mg)	Vitamin C[a] (mg)
Boys						
9 months	790 ± 39	7.0 ± 0.7	786 ± 49	1.6 ± 0.07	6.4 ± 0.6	62.9 ± 6.3
12 months	781 ± 38	5.7 ± 0.3	822 ± 41	1.6 ± 0.07	7.0 ± 0.6	65.8 ± 5.0
18 months	755 ± 31	6.7 ± 0.2	891 ± 30	1.6 ± 0.05	7.8 ± 0.3	73.7 ± 5.6
2 years	722 ± 29	6.6 ± 0.2	819 ± 23	1.4 ± 0.05	7.4 ± 0.3	68.3 ± 5.8
3 years	645 ± 23	7.9 ± 0.2	891 ± 26	1.4 ± 0.05	8.9 ± 0.3	66.1 ± 4.9
Girls						
9 months	838 ± 34	7.5 ± 0.7	691 ± 31	1.7 ± 0.07	6.2 ± 0.5	55.3 ± 4.7
12 months	797 ± 34	5.7 ± 0.4	760 ± 34	1.6 ± 0.05	5.9 ± 0.3	45.8 ± 3.8
18 months	692 ± 33	5.9 ± 0.3	832 ± 30	1.5 ± 0.05	7.5 ± 0.4	68.7 ± 5.7
2 years	615 ± 32	6.1 ± 0.2	789 ± 26	1.3 ± 0.05	7.6 ± 0.3	69.1 ± 6.0
3 years	596 ± 26	7.4 ± 0.3	861 ± 36	1.4 ± 0.05	8.9 ± 0.4	63.5 ± 5.0

[a]This does not include vitamins and minerals from nonfood sources, e.g., medications.
[b]This does not include niacin obtained from dietary tryptophan.

of the dietary energy and more thereafter (25). By 12 months of age, the proportion of dietary energy provided by milk had fallen to 35%; meanwhile, the relative contributions of meat, cheese, and eggs had risen from 10 to 15% and cereals and bread from 11 to 14%.

Daily consumption of cow's milk declined from an average of 490 ml at 1 year, to 350 ml at 2 years, and 300 ml at 3 years of age. The consumption of cheese almost doubled from 7 g/day at 1 year to 12 g/day at 2 to 3 years; the lower levels of calcium consumption were largely due to the drop in milk consumption.

At 1 year of age, two-thirds of the dietary energy came from meat, fish, poultry, eggs, cereals, and milk. By 2 years, this had fallen to 50%. In the second and third years, significantly more dietary energy came from fruit juices, sugars, and sweet biscuits and cakes, which were usually eaten between meals. The habit of adding sugar to cereals was an important reason for increased sugar consumption, but most was due to the consumption of sweetened cordials, carbonated drinks, and confectionery. These trends are reflected in the threefold increase in sugar consumption between 1 and 2 years of age. It is interesting to note that 10% of children at 2 years of age received more than 20% of their total daily food energy from the "sugars" food category.

Sodium intakes were calculated from food records but excluded salt added to food during its preparation at home. Only 56% of mothers added salt to their 1-year-old infant's food (28); this was virtually unchanged for 2-year-olds. By the time their children were 3 years old, however, 72% of mothers were adding salt. The mean sodium intakes at 12 months were 54 (boys) and 52 (girls) mEq; at 2 years, 73 (boys) and 72 (girls) mEq; and at 3 years, 81 (boys) and 79 (girls) mEq (29).

DISCUSSION

The PGS has provided important new information about current feeding practices and the nutrition of Australian infants and young children. These results are relevant to continuing discussion about "growth standards" or "reference values" which are used in growth charts for clinical and public health purposes.

Three-quarters of our subjects are still taking part in the PGS 3 years after it started; we hope that nearly all of these will see the study through to its planned completion when they are 5 years of age. The geography of Perth, its demographic make-up, and the positive image of our Children's Hospital and Research Foundation with our community have helped us retain such a good proportion of participants. Being the only Children's Hospital for more than 2,000 km in what is sometimes described as the most isolated capital in the Western world has been to our advantage. We also have encouraged continued participation by sending all children specially made cards on their birthdays and by reminding mothers by mail about forthcoming interviews and the 7-day food record periods. We also offer bus fares to and from the hospital. Interviews and physical measurements are done in the large, bright, and colorful demonstration kitchen of our hospital's dietetics department. We have assiduously avoided influencing the mother's and family's attitudes to food and nutrition throughout the study. When medical or personal problems have arisen, we have been ready to arrange whatever assistance was required. Most of the dropouts from the study have been because families have moved away. Three mothers returned to fulltime work and decided to withdraw from the study; seven families were unable to be recontacted; several were "unable to cope." Overall, these dropouts have had no significant effect on the socioeconomic distribution of the group.

It could be argued that the PGS sample may not be representative of the wider Australian community. This prompted us to obtain a larger sample of infants born at the same time as PGS subjects, but from the wider community, to determine whether the findings from the Perth study reflect current trends in our community. We obtained relevant information from 704 subjects (365 boys and 339 girls) born between January 1 and June 30, 1979, who had attended 12 metropolitan and six country child health centers (Geraldton, Bunbury, Busselton, Collie, Northam, and Pinjarra). These were within 400 km of Perth and were chosen to represent all socioeconomic groups. The results of this study have been reported elsewhere (30).

The trends in infant feeding and growth in this sample were similar to the PGS results. Using multiple regression analysis with age, social class, and duration of breastfeeding as independent variables, data from the PGS and the wider study adequately fitted a single regression equation; i.e., patterns were similar in each. Just over one-third of infants in both studies were having solids by 3 months. These tended to be introduced earlier in formula-fed infants. Weights of infants in the four social groups were not significantly different at birth. By 12 months of age, however, infants from the lowest socioeconomic group (D) were significantly heavier than those from the highest group (A). This may be because breastfeeding was practiced least by mothers in group D. This is supported by the finding that the child health center study showed an association between social class and breast-feeding, and breastfeeding and weight gain (30). As far as can be ascertained, findings from the PGS give a reasonable indication of what is happening in our community at the present time.

Breastfeeding

At 6 weeks, 83% of mothers in our study were breastfeeding; by 6 months, 64% were still breastfeeding; and at 12 months, 25% of infants were still breastfed to some extent (31). This confirms an apparently widespread trend back to breast-feeding in Australia and other industrialized countries (32–35). In the mid-1960s to early 1970s, only about one-quarter of mothers in the United States and Canada breastfed (36,37). Although there has been some increase in breastfeeding rates since then, most mothers breastfeed for only short periods. Solid foods were introduced to our PGS subjects later than they would have been in Australia a decade ago and to breastfed babies later than to formula-fed infants (25). This is similar to the situation in Canada, where the median age of introduction of solids to breastfed infants is 3 months and to bottle-fed infants, 1 month (37).

Nutrient Intakes in the First 12 Months

The trend back to breastfeeding found in this study was accompanied by signif-icant changes in nutrient intake patterns in these infants. Protein intakes were much less in the first 6 months of life than in earlier studies of predominantly artificially fed infants. For example, the mean daily protein intake of infants aged 6 months in 1965 (38) was 36 g, compared to the estimated 18.4 g for boys and 15.1 g for girls in this study. By 12 months of age, when mixed feeding has become well established, these differences were much less. A similar trend has been found recently in the United States (39). Sodium intakes were also down in the PGS, because of the lower sodium content of breastmilk and humanized formulas, compared to cow's milk, and greater use of home-cooked foods (often without added salt) rather than canned baby foods (28).

Sodium intakes in this study were lower than those reported from the United States as recently as 1972 (40). This difference is attributable to the lower sodium content of breast milk and humanized formulas compared to cow's milk and the greater use of home-cooked foods rather than canned baby foods. An increasing public awareness of the possible long-term consequences of excessive salt intake for the development of degenerative cardiovascular disease may also have contrib-uted to these lower salt intakes. Yeung et al. (41) studied sodium intakes in their prospective study of Canadian children and related the high intakes they found after 6 months of age to the salt content of home-made foods. They recommended that salt should not be added to home-made foods, or that infants should be given canned preparations that do not contain added salt.

Growth in the First 12 Months

There are three comparable Australian studies (11,15,42) in which weight of infants was recorded longitudinally. These provide interesting comparisons with the results of the present study, which are shown in Table 5.

Mean birthweights in PGS subjects were similar to those found by Bell and Lay (15) in the mid-1960s, by Boulton (43) in the late 1970s, and slightly less than by Clements (11) in 1933. Median weights at 3, 6, 9, and 12 months were much greater in the 1964 sample than in the other studies; this is shown clearly in Fig. 2. Similar patterns of growth were found in more than 1,000 breastfed Australian babies surveyed by questionnaire by the Nursing Mothers Association of Australia (42). It is tempting to suggest that the increased rates of growth in the 1960s were due to the early introduction of solids and the use of cow's milk formulas with added sugar, sometimes made excessively concentrated. This occurred soon before the resurgence of breastfeeding, which is now well established in Australia.

The recent longitudinal growth study of Canadian infants done by Yeung and his colleagues (44) has many similarities, and some important differences, when compared to our study, which was done independently in Perth at about the same time. The Canadian study was undertaken in Toronto and Montreal between 1977 and 1979, initially with 403 infants, in an attempt to provide data to develop Canadian

TABLE 5. *Mean body weights of Australian infants from studies published over the past 50 years[a]*

Age	Mean body weight (kg)				
	1933	1964	PGS	NMAA	Adelaide
Boys					
Birth	3.74	3.51	3.56	—	3.39
6 weeks	4.67	5.18	4.81	—	—
3 months	5.91	6.73	5.92	6.31	6.07
6 months	7.63	8.84	7.85	7.96	7.89
9 months	8.97	10.71	9.11	9.25	—
12 months	10.02	11.20	10.01	10.29	10.15
Girls					
Birth	3.62	3.45	3.47	—	3.25
6 weeks	4.52	4.95	4.60	—	—
3 months	5.73	6.22	5.61	5.71	5.62
6 months	7.49	8.18	7.44	7.26	7.31
9 months	8.71	9.40	8.56	8.45	—
12 months	9.73	10.48	9.50	9.49	9.56

[a]1933: A retrospective study by F. W. Clements of records from more than 1,000 infants attending Child Health Centres in Sydney (11). 1964: A comparative study from Sydney Child Health Centres, reported by Bell and Lay (15). PGS: This study; The Perth Growth Study. NMAA: A report from the Nursing Mothers' Association of Australia; information obtained by questionnaire (42). Adelaide: A prospective study of growth of infants in South Australia; reported by Boulton (43).

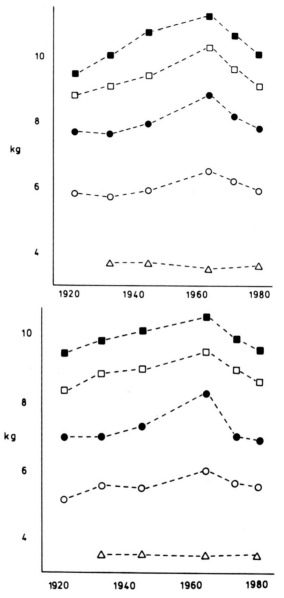

FIG. 2. Comparison of median weights of infants in Australia in the past 60 years. **Top**, boys; **bottom**, girls. (From Hitchcock et al., 31.)

"growth standards for infants" (44). The investigators found the most rapid period of growth to be in the first 3 months and that the percentile values for weight, length, and head circumference at birth and 1, 3, 6, 12, and 18 months (the upper limit) were similar to the National Center for Health Statistics (NCHS) values.

Median body weights for boys and girls from birth to 18 months of age were not significantly different from the NCHS values (Fig. 3).

Toronto and Montreal were chosen for this study because of their size (convenient for the study). Sampling was representative of Canadian French- and English-speaking societies; as in our own study, new immigrants were excluded. The survey method was pretested and validated, and a 4-day dietary record method chosen which recorded food consumption in household measures. Commercial brand names and home recipes were recorded. Nutrient intake calculations were done essentially as with the PGS project (45).

Some important points about infant feeding practices emerged from this detailed study of Canadian infants (46). For example, although their daily energy intakes were less than the Canadian recommended daily intakes (RDI) (47), their growth rates were considered normal, suggesting that the RDI was set too high. The authors found low iron intakes from 12 months onward, which they considered to be caused by "low intake of iron-fortified cereals." Their findings suggested that the widespread practice of vitamin supplementation was unnecessary, since the food intakes alone provided sufficient vitamins, e.g., vitamins A and C. Their findings stressed the importance of milk as a major source of energy, protein, fat, and most other nutrients. Milk consumption patterns are clearly different in North America and Australia, as the American practice of feeding skim milk and "2% milk" to infants from 6 months onward (41) is not (yet) prevalent here. Milk was the main source of dietary sodium for the Canadian infants, but by 7 months, table foods became a significant part of the diet. From then on, home-made foods became increasingly important sources of sodium, especially from salt added to

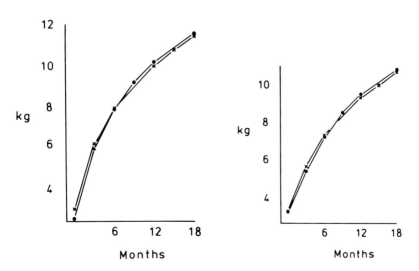

FIG. 3. Median body weights of boys **(left)** and girls **(right)** birth to 18 months, from NCHS charts *(circles)* and the Canadian study by Yeung et al. (44) *(crosses)*.

foods in their preparation or at the table, contributing to their high salt intakes (41).

We have commented previously on how the growth patterns found in our PGS subjects differed from British figures used in comparisons with studies of growth of infants from other countries (48). From 3 to 6 months of age, weight increments were significantly greater in Britain than in Perth. We suggested that this may be due to changes in feeding patterns between the 1950s, when the British figures were derived, and 1980, when the PGS data were obtained. This suggestion would fit with our experience in Australia relating artificial infant feeding and overfeeding in infancy in the 1950s and early 1960s to the perhaps aberrant growth rates observed then, when infantile obesity was increasing (49). This is in comparison with what we are seeing now that breastfeeding is again fashionable, or in the 1930s (11) when breastfeeding was the accepted norm in Australia. As seen below, patterns of growth in the PGS subjects are similar to the NCHS growth curves (50).

Nutrient Intakes After the First Year

Important changes were observed in PGS subjects in dietary patterns after 12 months of age. Daily consumption of cow's milk decreased from a mean of 490 ml at 12 months to 350 ml at 2 years and 300 ml at 3 years. Cheese consumption increased from 7 g/day at 1 year to 12 g/day at 2 to 3 years, but calcium intake was down in comparison to earlier studies. Milk consumption was approximately half that reported in the last comprehensive study of growth of Australian children (51); dietary calcium intake was down by one-third. Fruit juices, fruit juice drinks, cordials, and carbonated drinks seem to have helped displace milk consumption.

At 12 months of age, 15.7% of dietary energy came from protein and 45% from carbohydrate. By 2 years of age, the protein proportion had fallen to 13.8% and carbohydrate rose to 48.1%; this was virtually unchanged at 3 years. These patterns of contribution of dietary energy are similar to those found in older children and family groups in Western Australia (52–54), suggesting that dietary patterns are established as early as 2 or 3 years of age in our community (29).

Dietary intakes of major nutrients in these children are similar at the ages of 1 and 3 years to those of North American children studied in the 1950s (55) and to 3-year-old children studied in Britain from 1967 to 1971 (56,57). They also resemble the findings of Yeung and his colleagues (46) in their longitudinal study of more than 300 normal children from birth to 18 months in Canada.

Growth in the Second and Third Years of Life

The growth patterns found in our healthy children in the PGS have been compared with the official Australian growth charts (17) and with the international figures from the NCHS (50). Backward stepwise regression with a second degree polynomial model, including a dummy variable for each set of data, was used to compare percentile values for weight and length against other sets of reference values. F-tests were used to determine the significance of deleting variables from the regression equation. Variables were included in the equation if the F-value exceeded the 95% level (57).

There was no significant difference between the PGS and NCHS data for boys and girls, but the Australian NHMRC median weights are significantly heavier ($p<0.05$) from 6 months of age onward. Figure 4 shows the 50th percentile curves for weights of boys and girls from the PGS, NCHS (50), and NHMRC (17) data. As mentioned earlier, the recent prospective study of Canadian children from 0 to 18 months also fits with the NCHS and PGS patterns of growth (44) (Table 6). These mean body weights are similar to those found in the first year of life in a large, longitudinal growth study of Scandinavian children born between 1955 and 1958, except that both boys and girls tended to be heavier at 12 months of age and beyond (58).

It is not immediately clear why the Australian national reference values (17) are significantly higher from 6 months onward than these other three sets of data from well-documented, recent samples of healthy infants and children in well-nourished populations in industrialized countries. The sample on which the Australian reference values are based was obtained in Sydney in 1970–1972, and the ethnic distribution of the children measured is poorly documented. One reason we took extra care to define the ethnic origins of children in the PGS was the multinational pattern of our present population. Our study showed a strong trend back to breast-feeding; this has also occurred in other states of Australia (34,59–61). The NCHS figures were obtained from infants who were fed breast milk or a low-solute formula designed to simulate breast milk. We have suggested (31) that the return to more natural infant feeding and the decline of bottle feeding based on cow's milk may have a causal role in the return to patterns of growth in infancy and early childhood that were found in Australia in the 1930s, when breastfeeding prevailed (11). This is supported by the fact that the PGS, NCHS, and NHMRC figures show no differences in length-for-age in the first 3 years, although the NHMRC figures are heavier for age after 6 months. This suggests that the NHMRC sample was relatively overweight from 6 months onward, perhaps because of sampling procedures or infant feeding practices in Sydney at that time, or both.

These results have important implications, at least for Australia, with respect to the use of international sets of reference values for normal growth. One recent local example illustrates this point. We undertook an anthropometric survey of more than 600 Australian aboriginal children up to 30 months of age in an attempt to ascertain their current state of nutrition (62). There was a widespread fall-off in growth commencing in the second half of infancy. As can be seen in Fig. 5, however, the numbers (or proportions) of these subjects that could be considered underweight depend greatly on which set of reference values are used for comparison. For example, many more could be claimed to be "undernourished" using $<80\%$ standard-weight-for-age if the Australian growth charts (17) are used rather than the internationally used NCHS reference values. It may not be valid to compare aboriginal Australians to nonaboriginal Australians for other reasons, e.g., the relatively lighter aboriginal skeleton size compared to a European of comparable

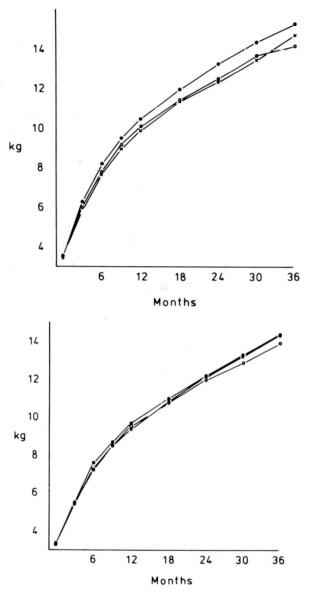

FIG. 4. The 50th percentile curves for boys **(top)** and girls **(bottom)** from the PGS *(crosses)*, NCHS *(open circles)*, and NHMRC *(solid circles)* growth charts.

stature (64). Thus it is probably best to use an independent, internationally accepted reference range of values, such as the NCHS figures.

    We should not think of international reference values for growth as "standards" like the gold standard. They should be used, as Waterlow (65) suggests, "like grids

TABLE 6. *Median body weights in the NCHS tables, the Perth study, and the Canadian study*[a]

Age	NCHS	PGS	Canada	Age	NCHS	PGS	Canada
Boys				Girls			
Birth	3.27	3.56	3.52	Birth	3.23	3.37	3.35
3 months	5.98	5.8	6.2	3 months	5.4	5.55	5.71
6 months	7.85	7.77	7.88	6 months	7.21	7.36	7.39
12 months	10.15	9.9	9.95	12 months	9.53	9.38	9.35
18 months	11.47	11.47	11.4	18 months	10.82	10.8	10.7

[a]NCHS, National Center for Health Statistics; PGS, Perth Growth Study; Canada, ref. 44.

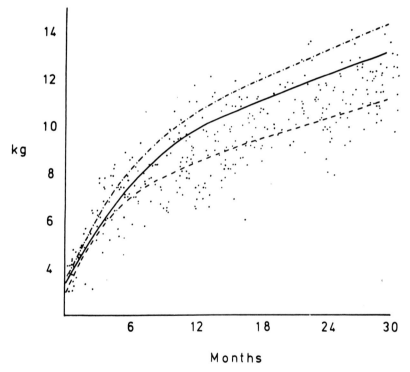

FIG. 5. Weight-for-age distribution of aboriginal children up to 30 months of age compared with NHMRC *(dotted, dashed line)*, NCHS *(solid line)*, and Kettle's *(dashed line)* median values (63). (From Gracey et al., ref. 62.)

on a map" as a guide to allow independent comparisons of sets of data from different communities in different parts of the world. They are acceptable in clinical pediatrics because they must be used to show changes in an individual's pattern of somatic growth; minor changes in median values and percentile distributions are unimportant. We should also recognize that adoption of international reference values does not imply that these are "goals" or "ideals"; they are simply independent reference points which allow objective comparisons of different groups of children, wherever they are. This is not widely appreciated, and poorly documented local standards are being established; in some places, double standards are being used. In places where undernutrition is prevalent, it could be argued that using a large cross-sectional sample of local children does that country or community a disservice by bringing down the 50th percentile value and, therefore, the expectations for growth potential in the minds of local health workers. There are few populations whose growth potential is restricted by their genes; African pygmies are one example. Growth potential for other populations responds to environmental circumstances; in most communities where undernutrition is prevalent, undernutrition and infections are the major factors that limit normal growth.

We have publicly cautioned against the development of a new, national growth standard for infants and children in Australia (66). The same arguments apply to similar countries who should adopt the international reference values (67).

ACKNOWLEDGMENTS

The PGS was made possible through the generous financial support of the TVW Telethon Foundation (Perth). The (Australian) NHMRC, Kellogg (Australia) Pty. Ltd., and Nestlé Nutrition S.A. have also given grants for the project. We thank our hospital's Dietetics Department for allowing us to use their facilities, and the mothers and children for their cheerful cooperation.

REFERENCES

1. Brailsford Robertson T. Studies on the growth of man. III. The growth of British infants during the first year succeeding birth. Am J Physiol 1916;41:535–46.
2. National Health and Medical Research Council. Dietary allowances for use in Australia–1971 revision. Canberra, Australia: Australian Government Publishing Service, 1971.
3. Hitchcock NE, Gracey M. Dietary patterns in a rural aboriginal community in South-West Australia. Med J Aust 1975;2(spec suppl):12–6.
4. Owles EN. A comparative study of nutrient intakes of migrant and Australian children in Western Australia. Med J Aust 1975;2:130–3.
5. FAO/WHO Expert Group. Requirements of vitamin A, thiamine, riboflavine and niacin. Rome: FAO food nutrition series, no 41, 1967.
6. Roche AF, Cahn A. Subcutaneous fat thickness and caloric intake in Melbourne. Med J Aust 1962;1:595–7.
7. Clements FW. Infant nutrition: its physiological basis. Bristol: John Wright, 1949.
8. Brailsford Robertson T. Studies on the growth of man. I. The pre and post-natal growth of infants. Am J Physiol 1915;37:1–42.
9. Southby R. A standard of weight for Australian infants. Med J Aust 1926;2:483–5.
10. Scantlebury V. Some aspects of infant welfare work in Victoria. In: Report of Australasian Association for the Advancement of Science, vol XIX, 1928.
11. Clements FW. The growth curve of Australian infants during the first year of age. Med J Aust 1933;1:543–9.
12. Dale J. The establishment of norms for heights and weights of infants and pre-school children in the city of Melbourne. In: National Health and Medical Research Council. Standard height–weight tables for Australians. Canberra, Australia: Commonwealth Department of Health, 1957.
13. Roche AF, Sunderland S. Melbourne University child growth study. Med J Aust 1959;1:559–62.

14. Bowden BD, Johnson J, Ray LJ, Towns J. Height and weight changes in Melbourne children compared with other population groups. Aust Paediatr J 1976;12:281–95.
15. Bell JW, Lay PM. The growth of Australian infants during the first year of life: a comparison, 1933 and 1964. Med J Aust 1968;1:541–4.
16. Jones DL, Hemphill W. Height, weight and other physical characteristics of New South Wales children. Part II. Children under 5 years of age. Health Commission of New South Wales, 1974;G79394-IG 5705.
17. National Health and Medical Research Council. Charts and tables of heights, masses and head circumferences of infants and children. Canberra, Australia: Australian Government Publishing Service, 1975.
18. Coy JF, Lewis IC, Mair CH, Longmore EA, Ratkowsky DA. The growth of Tasmanian infants from birth to three years of age. Med J Aust 1973;2:12–8.
19. Shukla A, Forsyth HA, Anderson CM, Marwah SM. Infantile overnutrition in the first year of life: a field study in Dudley, Worcestershire. Br Med J 1972;4:507–15.
20. Court JM, Hill GJ, Dunlop M, Boulton TJC. Hypertension in childhood obesity. Aust Paediatr J 1974;10:296–300.
21. Godfrey RC, Stenhouse NS, Cullen KJ, Blackman V. Studies of the cholesterol levels of Busselton school children and their parents. Aust Paediatr J 1972;8:72–8.
22. Lewis IC, Coy JF. Nutrition: a problem for paediatricians. Aust Paediatr J 1976;12:176–9.
23. Hitchcock NE, Owles EN. Australian growth studies: the Perth study. Proc Nutr Soc Aust 1980;5:71–78.
24. Congalton AA. Status and prestige in Australia. Melbourne: Cheshire, 1969.
25. Owles EN, Hitchcock NE, Gracey M. Feeding patterns of Australian infants: birth to one year. Hum Nutr Appl Nutr 1982;36A:202–7.
26. Thomas S, Corden M. Tables of composition of Australian foods. Canberra, Australia: Australian Government Publishing Service, 1970.
27. Waterlow JC, Thomson AM. Observations on the adequacy of breastfeeding. Lancet 1979;ii:238–42.
28. Hitchcock NE, Owles EN, Gracey M. Dietary energy and nutrient intakes and growth of healthy Australian infants in the first year of life. Nutr Res 1982;2:13–9.
29. Hitchcock NE, Owles EN, Gracey M, Gilmour A. Nutrition of healthy children in the second and third years of life. J Food Nutr 1984;41:13–16.
30. Hitchcock NE, McGuiness D, Gracey M. Growth and feeding practices of Western Australian infants. Med J Aust 1982;1:372–6.
31. Hitchcock NE, Owles EN, Gracey M. Breast feeding and growth of healthy infants. Med J Aust 1981;2:536–7.
32. Biering-Sørensen F, Jorgen H, Biering-Sørensen K. Breast feeding on the increase [Editorial]. J Trop Pediatr 1980;26:ii–iii.
33. Coles EC, Cotter S, Valman HB. Increasing prevalence of breast feeding. Br Med J 1978;2:1122.
34. Lawson JS, Mays CA, Oliver TI. The return to breast feeding. Med J Aust 1978;2:229–30.
35. Martinez GA, Nalezienski JP. The recent trend in breast feeding. Pediatrics 1979;64:686–92.
36. Fomon SJ. What are infants fed in the United States? Pediatrics 1975;56:350–4.
37. Myeres AW. A retrospective look at infant feeding practices in Canada: 1965–78. J Can Diet Assoc 1979;40:200–11.
38. Hankin ME. Infant feeding. Food Nutr Notes Rev 1965;22:47–55.
39. U.S. Department of Agriculture. Nationwide food consumption survey, 1977–78 [Abstract]. Food Nutr Notes Rev 1980;37:34–5.
40. American Academy of Pediatrics. Salt intake and eating patterns of infants and children in relation to blood pressure. Pediatrics 1974;53:115–21.
41. Yeung DL, Hall J, Leung M, Pennell MD. Sodium intakes of infants from 1 to 18 months of age J Am Diet Assoc 1982;80:242–4.
42. Shade E. Weight gains in breast fed infants. Nursing Mothers' Association of Australia Newsletter, April 3-9, 1980.
43. Boulton J. Nutrition in childhood and its relationships to early somatic growth, body fat, blood pressure, and physical fitness. Acta Paediat Scand 1981;Suppl. 284.
44. Yeung DL, Pennell MD, Hall J, Leung M. Growth and development of infants in Toronto and Montreal. Can J Public Health 1982;73:278–82.

45. Yeung DL, Leung M, Hall J, Medina D. Longitudinal survey of infant nutrition. J Can Diet Assoc 1979;40:288–95.
46. Yeung DL, Pennell MD, Hall J, Leung M. Food and nutrient intakes of infants during the first 18 months of life. Nutr Res. 1982;2:3–12.
47. Committee of Revision of the Canadian Dietary Standard. Dietary standard for Canada. Ottawa, Canada: Bureau of Nutritional Sciences, Food Directorate, Health Protection Branch, DNHW, 1975.
48. Hitchcock NE, Gracey M, Owles EN. Growth of healthy breast-fed infants in the first 6 months. Lancet 1981;ii:64–5.
49. Taitz LS. Infantile overnutrition among artificially fed infants in the Sheffield region. Br Med J 1971;1:315–6.
50. National Center for Health Statistics. NCHS growth charts monthly vital statistics report, serial no. HRA 76-1120. 1976;(suppl 25):1–22.
51. Cahn A, Neal K. Nutritional and dietary aspects of the Melbourne child growth study. Med J Aust 1959;2:549–54.
52. Hitchcock NE, Gracey M. Diet and serum cholesterol: an Australian family study. Arch Dis Child 1977;52:790–3.
53. Hitchcock NE, Gracey M. Nutrient consumption patterns of families in Busselton, Western Australia. Med J Aust 1978;1:359–62.
54. Hitchcock NE, Gracey M. Diet and nutrient intakes related to socio-economic status: a study of two groups of Western Australian school children. Food Nutr Notes Rev 1980;37:115–21.
55. Beal VA. Nutritional intake of children. I. Calories, carbohydrate, fat and protein. J Nutr. 1953;50:223.
56. Black AE, Billewicz WZ, Thomson AM. The diets of preschool children in Newcastle upon Tyne. Br J Nutr 1976;35:105–13.
57. Department of Health and Social Security. A nutritional survey of pre-school children, 1967–1968. London: HM Stationery Office, Report on health and social subjects no. 10, 1975.
58. Karlberg P, Taranger J. The somatic development of children in a Swedish urban community. A prospective longitudinal study. Acta Paediatr Scand 1976;(suppl):258.
59. Child Health Service, Tasmania. Tasmanian infant feeding survey, 1979–80, Hobart. Annual report, 1980.
60. Department of Health, Victoria. Director maternal, infant and pre-school welfare, Melbourne. Annual report, 1979.
61. Mothers and Babies Health Association, South Australia, Adelaide. Annual report, 1980.
62. Gracey M, Murray H, Hitchcock NE, Owles EN, Murphy BP. The nutrition of Australian aboriginal infants and young children. Nutr. Res. 1983;3:133–37.
63. Kettle ES. Weight and height curves for Australian aboriginal infants and children. Med J Aust 1966;1:972–7.
64. Abbie AA. Physical standards of nomadic aboriginal children. Med J Aust 1974;1:470–1.
65. Waterlow JC. Child growth standards. Lancet 1980;i:717.
66. Gracey M, Hitchcock N, Owles E. Normal growth in early childhood: comparison of international and Australian reference values. Proc Nutr Soc Aust 1982;7:154–7.
67. World Health Organization. A growth chart for international use in maternal and child health care. Geneva, 1978.

DISCUSSION

Dr. Whitehead: Figure 2 is a truly remarkable graph. It illustrates well the value of carrying out anthropometric surveys on a regular basis so that one can determine accurately trends of change. Your data, Dr. Gracey, indicate that there has been a peak in the size of children achieved at different ages. Skinfold thickness measurements carried out in the United Kingdom also indicate that we have gone through a peak. Do you know of any similar data from other countries?

Dr. Gracey: The studies by Taitz in the United Kingdom relate the recent trend to lower weight velocities to the phasing out of unmodified milks and the discouragement of overconcentrated feeding. Workers in the United States in the 1970s also found differences in weight gains between breastfed and artificially fed babies. I cannot say whether there is now a general reversal of these patterns in the Western world in the 1980s.

Dr. Anderson: The peak in England probably was related to the decline in breastfeeding and the change to early feeding of solids during the postwar years. A study in Dudley, Worcestershire (19), in 1972 of a large group of infants in their first year illustrated this growth increase. In the United States, dietary solids were introduced in very early infancy long before, and perhaps they had the growth peak earlier.

Dr. Barness: That is correct. The early introduction of solids in the United States began about 1935. This persisted until about 1978 when the Committee on Nutrition of the American Academy of Pediatrics recommended against these practices. The recommendation is that no supplemental foods be introduced before 4 to 6 months.

Dr. Guesry: When you take only breastfed babies in group D, do they behave like the babies in group A?

Dr. Gracey: Bell and Lay's sample, in 1964 (15), was selected to be representative of the Australian population at that time. From our own study, numbers are too small to assess, statistically, whether breastfed babies in group D behave like group A infants. We now know, from a prospective study of several hundred infants in Western Australia, that breastfeeding has a significant effect on weight gain in the first 12 months. From 0 to 3 months, there was no significant difference in breastfed or bottle-fed infants. After that, however, weight gains were greater in those artificially fed from birth or breastfed for only a short time when compared to those exclusively breastfed for 6 months or partially breastfed for 6 months or longer. [Hitchcock NE, Gracey M, Gilmour AI. The growth of breast fed and artificially fed infants from birth to 12 months. Acta P Scand 1985:74 (in press).]

Dr. Abdul Kader: With respect to Fig. 2, for the modality of weight, do you have a similar chart for the head circumference during these years? If so, what does it look like?

Dr. Gracey: Head circumferences in our study were not significantly different from our national growth charts. My interpretation of the data is that the children studied in the mid-1960s were relatively overweight, and that the cross-sectional sample taken in 1970–1972 to devise our national growth curves also included a considerable proportion of overweight children.

Dr. Mata: I am interested in Fig. 4, which shows the scattering of weight-for-height values of Australian aboriginal children today in comparison with the data of 1966, actually showing that your weight-for-height is improving; in other words, the children have become heavier. I would have expected malnutrition in your children. My impression is that your children are very slender, particularly in the legs, which is thought to be an adaptation to walking in deserts over the last 70,000 years. My question is: do you have in the original paper the same scattered diagrams for height and for weights separately? What do they look like?

Dr. Gracey: Yes; they look almost the same, which is the explanation for why you would have thought there was little malnutrition in these children because they are proportionately (i.e., weight-for-length) almost normal.

Dr. Mata: What impressed me more about Western Australia was that most women were tall, about 170 cm, and young girls were also very tall and very slender. That may represent a derivation of their good nutritional status, or it may be due to other factors. In Guatemala and Honduras, many people are stunted as adults, but among the aborigines, this is not so; it would be interesting to see if there is an inverse trend among adults. Do adults tend to be shorter today?

Dr. Gracey: You raised several important points. In the Kimberley region, in the tropical northwest of Australia, aboriginal children seem to be mostly short and light up to about 10 to 12 years of age; thereafter, there appears to be a period of catch-up growth. Why is this situation so different from what you see in Latin America? There is, generally, adequate food and money (from social welfare) in aboriginal communities, yet undernutrition is widespread in aboriginal children. On the other hand, there is a recently emerging problem of adult obesity in aborigines, particularly in women. I suspect the high level of environmental contamination in aboriginal communities and the heavy exposure of their children to repeated infectious diseases are important causes of growth retardation.

Dr. Nordio: With respect to the speculations concerning changes of infant growth during time, I do not think that changes within 10 to 20 percentiles are significant in terms of health. Growth and development should always be considered in the ecosystem context to avoid dangerous tunnel vision. In relation to population nutrition and health, the problem is to define valid and simple indicators to establish a risk-threshold for malnutrition, for hyponutrition in the developing countries, and for hyperunbalanced nutrition in the developed ones.

Dr. Gracey: It seems that the cutoff points that we normally use to assess risk are fairly crude.

Dr. Waterlow: Regarding the question of risk, the only studies of which I am aware are those from India (Kielmann AA, McCord C. Lancet, 1978;1:1247–50) and Bangladesh (Chen LC, Chowdury AKM, Huffman SL. Am J Clin Nutr 1980;33:531–5), in which cutoff points were established where the risk steeply rises. Personally, although I agree with the concept, I do not think that these data are particularly useful because the risk attached to a given height or weight deficit will vary according to the circumstances. It will be one thing in a country like Bangladesh where there is an enormous infectious load, and it will be different in a different country. Death is not the outcome in which we are normally most interested; one would like to have risks of morbidity and of some developmental failure, but these are difficult to establish.

Whether stunting is due to malnutrition or to infection is in a sense irrelevant; in the end, it is either a metabolic or a nutritional process that has gone wrong. There is evidence that the children are much less stunted in communities where they have a high protein diet, such as some of the tribes in Kenya and Northern Nigeria, people living on fish on certain islands, and so on. I do not know whether it is protein, minerals, or calcium but my hypothesis is that there is a nutritional cause for stunting. I cite a study by Fomon et al. (Fomon SJ, Filer LJ, Ziegler EE, Bergmann KE, Bergmann RL. Acta Paediatr Scand 1977;66:17–30), in which the authors fed a group of children dried skimmed milk. The children had a good protein intake and a poor energy intake, but there was absolutely no difference in height growth between those children and another group whose intake was adequate for both protein and energy; they were thin but tall. Your aboriginals, presumably, were living in past times on hunting and mainly on meat, rather than on starchy roots and such staples.

Dr. Gracey: Your comment about being unconcerned whether the cause is nutritional or infectious relates to the mechanisms involved in the eventual outcome. From a public health viewpoint, it is important to determine which mechanism is most important to help establish proper priorities in preventive programs.

Dr. Mata: I am puzzled with Fig. 4 because there must be about 20 to 30 datum points falling below the third to fifth percentile of the NCHS. A graph like that in Central or South America is associated with an infant mortality of about 60 per 1,000 and with 1 to 3% of chronic or severe malnutrition. In your aboriginal communities, however, the infant mortality is about 24 to 26 per 1,000. The birth rate has dropped tremendously, and primary health care has virtually eradicated polio and measles. My impression is that infection is not as common among Western Australian aborigines. Your communities consist of very small tribes, separated from one another by hundreds of kilometers, with limited possibilities for spread of infection.

Dr. Gracey: In the late 1960s and early 1970s, the incidence of infectious diseases in aboriginal children was very high, similar to the situation in developing countries such as India, Indonesia, and Bangladesh. This situation has changed in a dramatic way in the past 10 years. For example, the hospital admission rate for aboriginal infants for gastroenteritis in the Kimberley region in 1971 was 393%; by 1980, this rate had fallen to 24%. On a statewide basis, the annual rate, in Western Australia, declined from 171% per annum in 1971 to 36% in 1980. This is important in our consideration of risk factors. The improvements achieved in Western Australia are attributable to several interrelated factors, such as general standards of living, housing, hygiene, and the provision of comprehensive, community-based, preventive health programs.

Dr. Whitehead: We must consider the functional interpretation of growth achievements. If it is true that height and weight attainments of babies in the future are going to be less than they were during the bottle-feeding peak of the 1960s, people are bound to ask whether or not this matters in a functional sense. This has long been a problem for the developing world, where there have been a number of attempts to equate weight-for-age with, for example, immunological status. As far as the Western world is concerned, neurological and neuromotor development might be more important. Would the pediatricians here like to tell us of the functional parameters they would like to see measured along with the anthropometric ones?

Dr. Falkner: You have, as usual, picked out an important area where there are few hard data. The multidisciplinary teams engaged in longitudinal studies rarely relate their data from one discipline to another, for example, mental-behavioral development patterns related to neuromuscular development.

Dr. Waterlow: Cravioto et al. (Cravioto J, DeLicardie ER, Birch HG. Nutrition, growth and neurointegrative development: an experimental and ecologic study. Paediatrics 1966;38:319–72) have performed a variety of tests of neurosensory and neuromotor development and related them to deficits in height. The results show clearly that the stunted child is disadvantaged developmentally. The causal nexus, of course, is by no means clear.

Dr. Falkner: I was actually referring to the "normal child." There are few hard data on the mental development of normal children, in longitudinal studies, related to their somatic development. Such data are needed as a starting point.

Dr. Butte: We seem to have missed one important observation made by Dr. Whitehead: the exclusively breastfed infants tended to stay around the 25th percentile throughout the first year of life, even after complementary foods were introduced. Before we come to the conclusion that this represents normal growth, we must determine whether these mothers were imposing food restriction on their infants and whether the development of these infants was compromised in any way. These are the type of growth curves we associate with infants reared under less favorable conditions.

Dr. Whitehead: That is correct. Also, Dr. Waterlow was concerned that we should not automatically assume that trends within the professional classes in countries such as the United Kingdom inevitably set the ideal for everyone else.

It is going to be difficult indeed to produce any convincing relationship between different types of anthropometric growth and the functional capacities with which they may be associated. There may be a range of weights and heights for each individual which would be compatible with his health and well-being in the broadest sense.

Dr. Barness: We may be overemploying nutrition in child development.

Dr. Anderson: Dr. Whitehead and others have been discussing small variations in growth in the first 2 years of life and a recent slight falling off in rate; are they making too much of this? Is it not just a reversion to a growth pattern of several decades ago because of a change back to earlier feeding patterns? Is it also just a short-term variation? The Dudley study I mentioned previously showed that those overweight at 1 year were normal at 5 years. The comprehensive Child Development Study over 21 years in England should contain material of interest to nutritionists in this regard.

Nutritional Needs and Assessment of Normal Growth, edited by M. Gracey and F. Falkner. Nestlé Nutrition, Vevey/Raven Press, New York © 1985.

Environmental Factors Affecting Nutrition and Growth

Leonardo Mata

Instituto de Investigaciones en Salud (INISA), Universidad de Costa Rica, Ciudad Universitaria Rodrigo Facio, San Pedro, Costa Rica

Epidemiologic studies in tropical and subtropical regions highlighted the interaction between malnutrition and infectious disease and its contribution to determining morbidity and mortality in developing countries. There is no doubt that infectious diseases cause physiologic and biochemical alterations leading to malnutrition; on the other hand, a deficient nutritional status worsens the outcome of infection (1). However, the argument persists as to whether concurrent infections or deficient diets are the main contributors to the malnutrition, growth retardation, and premature death so commonly observed among children in impoverished societies (2).

Observations in Africa (3) and Costa Rica (4) indicated that poor child rearing practices, familial stress, and child abuse and neglect are important components in the multifactorial etiology of protein-energy malnutrition (PEM). A better understanding of the etiology of malnutrition and growth retardation of children in the tropics is fundamental for establishing priorities and policies aimed at prevention and control of infection and malnutrition.

Prospective observations in different parts of the world revealed that growth faltering invariably begins at about 3 to 6 months among breastfed infants in traditional societies, or even earlier when infants are prematurely weaned, as is the case of populations in transition adopting bottle-feeding (5). It is also known that as breast milk becomes insufficient, child rearing—a time-consuming occupation—deteriorates and children may not receive the nourishment and care required, particularly in deprived homes where mothers have other duties or engage in heavy work. It is not yet clear if onset of stunting is primarily related to (a) supplementation with inadequate foods when mothers' milk becomes insufficient, (b) infectious disease, (c) psychological stress, or (d) an interaction of several of these. Inadequate milk consumption without proper supplementation appears to be the rule in developing societies, but the striking event is the occurrence of infectious diseases (6) and of social stress during weaning.

In Latin America, among the communicable diseases of childhood, infectious diarrhea ranks first with respect to incidence and effects on nutrition and health, followed by acute respiratory disease, an important cause of morbidity and death in infancy. In third place rank measles, whooping cough, chickenpox, and tuberculosis. Malaria, kala-azar, viral fevers, and other illnesses strike children in particular ecosystems. The psychosocial factors are less known at present, and much research is needed.

FIELD STUDIES ON NUTRITION AND INFECTION

Long-term prospective studies concerning two indigenous populations in Central American highlands are described. The populations were devoid of malaria, trypanosomiasis, jungle fevers, and other tropical diseases. In Santa María Cauqué, Guatemala, infectious diseases are overwhelming; crowding, poverty, and underdevelopment favor their perpetuation (6). There is no awareness of child abuse and neglect, but child rearing practices are generally deficient. In Puriscal, Costa Rica, improved home environment, maternal technology, and health services and scattering of the population result in a low incidence of infectious diseases (7,8).

At the time of the study, most homes in Cauqué had only one room. Families slept in one or two beds or on mats on the floor. Preparation and cooking of food was done on a hearth on the dirt floor. Water had to be carried from public faucets and reservoirs. Few families had intradomiciliary water, and only one-third used latrines. Poverty, illiteracy, cohabitation with domestic animals, and crowding of families within the limited space of dwellings and of homes within the compact village structure favored transmission of infectious agents, especially enteric and respiratory (6,9) (see Table 1).

TABLE 1. *Differences in host and environment between Cauqué and Puriscal*

Variable	Cauqué, 1967	Puriscal, 1981
No. of people	1,000	24,000
Type of population	Rural, crowded	Rural, sparse
Percent literate	56	85
Percent using latrine or toilet	32	95
Percent having private piped water	7.4	84
Human milk intake (ml/day, 1–3 mo)[a]	674 ± 162	670 ± 152
Energy intake (kcal/day, 6 mo)	400	457 ± 142
Protein intake (g/day, 6 mo)	7	6.5 ± 2.5
Energy intake (kcal/day, 3 mo lactation)	2,078 ± 627	2,071 ± 666
Protein intake of the mother (g/day, 3 mo lactation)	59 ± 17	63.8 ± 25.5
Weight (kg 6 mo)	6.3 ± 6.7	7.8 ± 0.8
Length (cm 6 mo)	61.7 ± 0.3	66.0 ± 0.4
Weight of the mother (kg, 3rd trimester pregnancy)	52.8 ± 5.7	61.9 ± 5.7
Height of the mother (cm)	144.3 ± 4.9	153 ± 6
Percent low birth weight infants	42	8
Percent immunized against measles and DPT	0	95
Infant mortality per 1,000 live births	93	10

[a]Exclusively breastfed.

In rural Puriscal, living conditions are better. Homes are larger, and there is greater availability of intradomiciliary water, latrines, flushing toilets, and electricity. These, coupled with a high literacy rate, greater income, availability of health services, improved maternal technology, and ruralism (marked separation between homes) result in a low incidence of infectious disease (8,9) (Table 1).

In both places, the ecosystem and characteristics of the population remained relatively undisturbed by the studies. In Puriscal, however, hospital interventions were carried out to improve incidence and duration of breastfeeding, making it similar to Cauqué, at least during the first 6 months of life (7). Food consumption by pregnant and lactating women and by children during healthy periods in Puriscal was about the same as in Cauqué. However, marked differences were noted between the two populations regarding incidence of infectious diseases, occurrence of malnutrition, growth retardation, and mortality of children, all of which were markedly greater in Cauqué.

Infection and Infectious Disease

Cauqué mothers are common carriers of enteric organisms and are a source of infection for their infants from birth onward. This is favored by traditional delivery at home in the squatting or kneeling position and by exposure of neonates to maternal feces (6,10). Infections occur as early as the first few days or weeks after birth and usually are asymptomatic, probably as a result of protection afforded by human colostrum and breast milk; nonbreastfed infants in similar environments frequently suffer serious infectious morbidity. By contrast, intestinal infection in Puriscal neonates is virtually absent, since mothers are relatively free of enteric infection and almost all deliveries are in clinics or hospitals, thereby reducing opportunities for fecal contamination at delivery (7).

Customarily, Cauqué infants are exclusively breastfed until 4 to 9 months. The burden of infection is so large, however, that diarrheal disease begins in the early months, increasing with age as breast milk and transplacental immunities fade away and infants start consuming contaminated foods (11). Infants are infected with enteric viruses and pathogenic bacteria and parasites. By 1 year of age, most are carriers of a wide variety of pathogenic agents, as revealed by weekly examination of feces during the first 3 years of life (10). At 3 years of age, more than 50% carry enteroviruses, and more than 25% excrete *Shigella* and *Giardia* (Fig. 1). Undernourished children also show abnormalities of the intestinal flora and colonization of the upper intestine (12). Puriscal infants also are exclusively breastfed, although for a shorter time than Cauqué infants; the rate of infection is markedly lower (8).

Diarrhea among Cauqué children averages 7 episodes per child per year in the first 3 years of life, contrasting with the low number (2–3) of episodes in Puriscal children (Table 2). The maximum incidence and severity of diarrhea and other infectious diseases in Cauqué are observed during weaning (9).

The enormous infection burden observed in Cauqué can be accounted for by deficient sanitary conditions and traditional practices which potentiate communic-

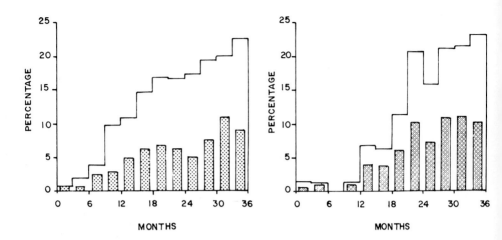

FIG. 1. Infection with *Giardia* **(left)** and *Shigella* **(right)** in a cohort of 45 Cauqué children from birth to 3 years of age. Rates were derived from weekly fecal examination or from cultures of feces; (□) prevalence, (▥) incidence.

TABLE 2. *Incidence of infectious diseases in Cauqué and Puriscal infants[a]*

Age (months)	No. of infants	Person-months	Enteric[b]	Respiratory[c]
Cauqué, 1964–1969				
0–5	45	270	33.3	15.9
6–11	45	270	63.0	23.0
Puriscal, 1979–1981				
0–5	115	690	4.2	5.5
6–11	114	684	7.5	7.7

[a]Values per 100 person-months.
[b]Diarrhea and dysentery.
[c]Laryngotracheobronchitis, bronchitis, and bronchopneumonia.

ability of enteric and respiratory agents. Since children excrete as many as 10^6 to 10^9 Shigellae per gram of wet feces during bouts of diarrhea and shedding may extend over several months (6), poor village children living in crowded conditions are at a disadvantage when compared to village children in sparse rural situations or to urban children in good environments because they are exposed to large doses of virulent organisms. This might account for the greater severity of the disease in tropical areas, regardless of nutritional state.

Few comprehensive studies on the epidemiology of respiratory disease in poor traditional societies have been conducted (13). Mortality due to respiratory disease is high among infants, especially if they are weak or undernourished. Measles, whooping cough, chickenpox, rubella, and mumps are generally severe in indige-

nous populations; they have great public health significance due to their malnourishing effect, disability, and mortality (8,10,12,14).

Nutritional Implications

The negative effects of infectious disease on the nutritional state consist of
reduced food consumption, nutrient losses, metabolic alterations, hormonal imbalances, and alterations in immune function. They are manifested as wasting, stunting, reduced activity, acute malnutrition, and death.

Reduced food consumption is best illustrated by enteric disease resulting from
attachment, colonization, or invasion of mucosal cells, initiating pathophysiologic
processes in susceptible individuals. Anorexia, fever, diarrhea, and vomiting result
in reduced food consumption in Cauqué children, which is complicated by food
withdrawal and inappropriate treatment and feeding during convalescence. Marked
reduction in energy intake coincides with infectious diseases (15,16) among fully
weaned 2-year-old children (Fig. 2). Energy and protein consumption are reduced
by 21 and 24%, respectively, during bouts of diarrhea (Table 3). It is estimated
that as much as 16% of dietary calories and 18% of protein are not consumed by
Cauqué children as a result of infections, since children are ill during one-fourth
to one-third of their entire first 3 years of life (6). The impact is considerable for
children at risk of becoming malnourished, or who are already malnourished, as
food consumption often is below recommended levels (6,15,16). Similar results

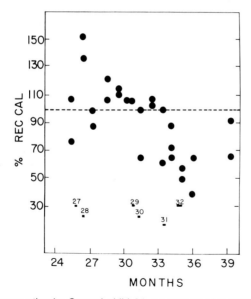

FIG. 2. Energy consumption by Cauqué child 24, as percent of recommendation by weight
(%REC CAL). *Dots*, means of daily diet values; *numbers*, illnesses; *bars*, duration of illness.
Episodes 27 and 29 (diarrheas), 30 (rubella), 31 (fever, respiratory disease), and 32 (cellulitis,
bronchitis) were associated with reduced consumption.

TABLE 3. *Mean daily food consumption with respect to diarrhea by Guatemalan and Ugandan preschool children*

| Health condition | Guatemala[a] | | Uganda[b] |
	Energy (MJ)	Protein (g)	(Energy, MJ)
Well	3.82	25	3.52
Diarrhea	3.02	19	1.89
Percent difference, well–diarrhea	21	24	46

[a]From Mata et al. (9).
[b]From Whitehead (17).

were obtained in other societies of different ethnic backgrounds (18,19). Anorexia also occurs with acute respiratory disease, dysentery, whooping cough, and measles, but reduced food consumption is observed even with mild infections (10,15,19).

Altered digestive-absorptive processes are observed in diarrhea due to the rapid transit through the gut. The surface epithelium can be coated by *Giardia* or bacteria or damaged by invading viruses, bacteria, or parasites, with a resultant alteration in function. Mucosal lesions concurrent with bacterial colonization are observed in persons living in the tropics (12,20,21); jejunitis and the accompanying malabsorption of sugars, fats, and vitamins disappear spontaneously after settlement in an environment with better sanitation (22). Enterotoxins stimulate formation of cyclic AMP or cyclic GMP, impairing absorption of sodium and water. Certain bacteria split bile salts, reducing micelle formation and fat absorption and increasing the bile acids pool, which irritates the mucosa. Bacteria and parasites are capable of sequestering nutrients needed by the host. The intestine can be regarded as a secreting organ; diarrhea then is an abnormal hypersecretory state with losses of fluid, electrolytes, and protein. Hypersecretion is caused by (a) imbalances in digestive-absorptive processes, (b) changes in hydrostatic pressure, (c) synthesis or increase in enterotoxins, bile, fatty acids, hormones, and neurotransmitters, and (d) greater calcium permeability (23).

Practically all metabolic pathways become altered during the course of infection (24), even mild or asymptomatic. The most important alterations are negative nitrogen balance, protein-losing enteropathy, and abnormal nutrient metabolism. The stress of fever, dehydration, cramps, tenesmus, and anxiety and the need to satisfy gluconeogenesis result in release of corticosteroids and mobilization of amino acids from muscle. Protein losses probably relate to thinning and alterations of the intestinal wall (20) and occur in various specific diarrheas, as with *Shigella*, enterotoxigenic *Escherichia coli*, and rotaviruses (25). There are important losses of sodium, potassium, bicarbonate, chloride, and phosphate during enteric and systemic infections. There is an increased synthesis of (a) liver enzymes, (b) foreign protein, lipid, and carbohydrate (in viral replication), and (c) acute phase reactant proteins *(nutrient diversion)*. Also, there is a depression of levels of circulating trace elements (zinc, iron, and copper) and concentration in hepatic cells *(nutrient sequestration)*. Furthermore, there is an increased expenditure of energy sources and vitamins *(nutrient overutilization)* (24,26).

A wasting and stunting effect results from repetitive infections and infectious processes, particularly in children who normally do not consume an optimal amount of food. Progressive deterioration of the nutritional status manifests as weight stagnation, weight loss, and impaired linear growth. These effects are evident in individual growth curves of Cauqué and Puriscal children observed from birth to preschool age. In Cauqué, about 40% of infants were of low birthweight, breast-feeding was universal, and the association of diarrhea with weight faltering and stunting was clear. There was no adequate knowledge of oral rehydration, and other forms of handling severe dehydration were not accepted by the community during the study period, contributing to the severity of the disease (6).

In general, growth during exclusive breastfeeding exhibited a velocity comparable to that of the National Center for Health Statistics-Centers for Disease Control (NCHS-CDC) reference curves. At about 3 to 6 months, with onset of supplementary feeding, there was a tendency to falter. Often, foods were poorly prepared, bulky, and contaminated. Inadequate supplementation after mother's milk became insufficient (4–6 months) resulted in subtle starvation of infants remaining at the breast. However, marked inflections in growth curves during weaning often corresponded to concurrent infectious diseases, particularly diarrhea.

Figure 3 (left) shows the body length curve and diarrheal episodes of a Cauqué child who had adequate intrauterine growth. Episodes of diarrhea were associated with weight loss or weight stagnation, regardless of their etiology. Obviously, losses of water, electrolytes, plasma, and cells during diarrhea had a negative effect on nutrition. Acute weight loss of the order of 5 to 10% or more was common (6). Furthermore, wasting (deficit of weight for height) persisted for weeks or months, contributing to the genesis of marasmus. This often was complicated by inadequate feeding during convalescence, although it is known that in some cases, even with good child care attitudes, the anorexia is so marked as to neutralize maternal efforts to restitute proper nourishment. Wasting and stunting also occurred with other diseases, notoriously with measles and whooping cough. The malnourishing capacity of illnesses that attack once in a lifetime (e.g., measles) can be more pronounced than that of diarrhea.

In general, impaired growth was more evident if infants had fetal growth retardation or were prematurely weaned, as Fig. 3 (right) shows for another Cauqué child. Several episodes of diarrhea associated with a variety of agents occurred in this child, together with periods of arrest in linear growth. One double infection with *Shigella* and *Salmonella* occurred without diarrhea and yet coincided with marked growth retardation lasting for more than 2 months. At the age of 2 years, the child was, as the previous case, considerably stunted.

The situation of Puriscal children studied more recently (1979–1981) was markedly different in that only 6% had low birthweight. Sanitary conditions, education, and hygiene were significantly better than those in Cauqué. There had been a deterioration of breastfeeding in Puriscal and in Costa Rica in general, evident at

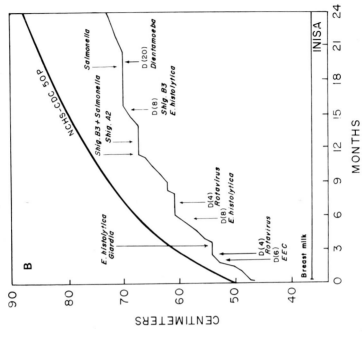

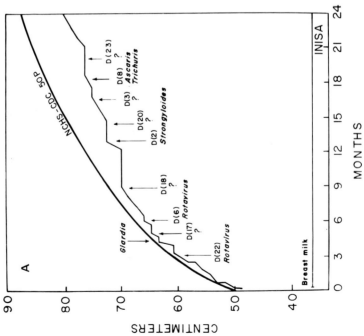

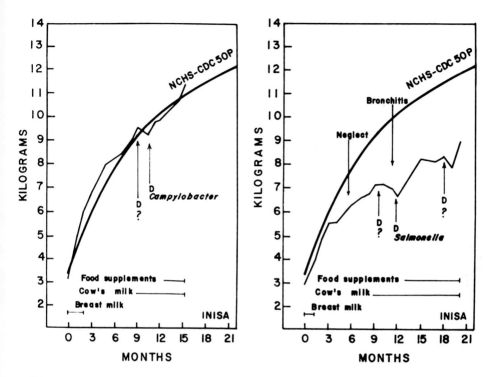

FIG. 4. Growth of Puriscal weaned children. **Left:** Child born with adequate weight (boy 060; birthweight, 3180 g). One bout of diarrhea caused weight loss. **Right:** Child with low birthweight who became undernourished due to neglect, and became very ill after episodes of diarrhea, eventually requiring hospitalization (boy 106; birthweight, 2905 g).

the beginning of the study; hospital and field interventions initiated in 1977 resulted in the fact that more than 90% of infants were breastfed for 1 to 2 months (7). Puriscal infants usually had fewer infections, and these were milder than in Cauqué, probably because of smaller inocula and fewer sources of infection resulting from improved hygiene and scattering of dwellings (ruralism).

Most Puriscal children are immunized against polio, measles, pertussis, diphtheria, and tuberculosis (9), and a low rate of diarrhea was observed in breastfed infants (see Table 2). Furthermore, diarrhea generally did not show a marked negative impact in breastfed children. However, weaned Puriscal children experienced weight loss and growth retardation as a result of infectious diseases, particularly diarrhea. Figure 4 (left) depicts a prematurely weaned Puriscal child with adequate fetal growth who developed diarrhea associated with weight loss. Another child prematurely weaned and suffering from an episode of neglect and several bouts of diarrhea exhibited marked weight loss and required hospitalization (Fig.

FIG. 3. Growth of Cauqué breastfed children. **Left:** Child born with adequate weight (boy 040; birthweight , 2711 g; length, 47.7 cm). Periods of growth arrest were associated with diarrhea of various etiologies. **Right:** Child who had fetal growth retardation (boy 002; birthweight, 2369 g; length, 45.1 cm). Marked stunting was evident at 1 year of age.

4, right). No marked inflections in the growth curve of Puriscal breastfed infants could be attributed to infections (9).

Thus the main environmental difference between the two settings appears to be the higher frequency of prematurity and fetal growth retardation and the considerably greater risk of infection and infectious morbidity in Cauqué than in Puriscal. There were no marked differences in the food consumption of mothers and children in the two populations. In fact, breast milk intake by Cauqué infants was slightly greater than in Puriscal. Cauqué women consume about 0.5 kg corn per day, and their calorie and protein consumption is similar to that of Puriscal women (see Table 1).

If infection is such an important determinant of malnutrition, marked differences in growth are to be expected among the two cohorts. Mean weight curves computed for 133 cohort Cauqué infants born in the period from 1964 to 1967 (6,9) were compared with mean weight curves for 277 cohort Puriscal infants born during the period from 1979 to 1981. Children in both cohorts were consecutively born during the stated periods and were classified according to fetal maturity. Term-adequate-for-gestational age Cauqué infants were notoriously smaller at 4 months of age than their Puriscal counterparts, who matched the 50th percentile of the NCHS reference curve throughout infancy (Fig. 5). Furthermore, term-small-for-gestational age Cauqué infants exhibited an even greater growth retardation as compared with Puriscal infants, who followed the corresponding track of the NCHS curve. It should be noted that large-for-gestational age infants were not observed in Cauqué, a reflection of the marked fetal growth retardation in this village (6). It is evident that in Cauqué, postnatal infection in addition to fetal growth retardation causes much of the postnatal growth failure of both body weight and length.

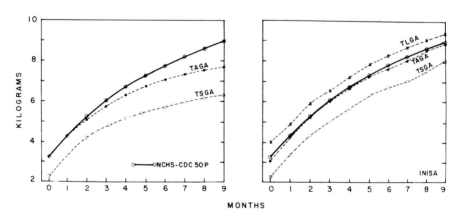

FIG. 5. Mean weight curves of Cauqué **(left)** and Puriscal **(right)** cohort infants observed prospectively from birth to 9 months of age. TLGA, term-large; TAGA, term-adequate; and TSGA, term-small-for-gestational age. Comparison is with the 50th percentile of the NCHS curve. Note that TLGA infants were not observed in Cauqué. Most children in Cauqué had shifted to lower percentiles of the NCHS curves. Growth velocity in Puriscal followed the recommended curves.

Severe malnutrition and death related to repetitive infectious diseases and chronic malnutrition were clearly evident in village children observed longitudinally. The marasmic state, which persists for months, is similar to that resulting from food shortage or child abuse. Marasmic children become critically ill under the stress of acute watery diarrhea, dysentery, measles, and other infectious diseases, as they do after episodes of social and psychologic perturbation in the home.

Decreases in serum albumin concurrent with infections (measles, hookworm, diarrhea) may precipitate kwashiorkor. It has long been known that outbreaks of severe PEM appear in the community a few weeks after epidemics of diarrhea, measles, and malaria (19,27), sometimes independent of food availability (6,28,29).

Children in poor villages may suffer from infectious diseases for one-fourth to one-third of their entire infancy and preschool age. These diseases represent the main determinant of acute malnutrition and are responsible for the death of children who are weak or premature, with fetal growth retardation, or with immunologic, biochemical, or organic deficiencies.

Regarding nutrition and resistance to infection, the most important host factor curtailing infection in the first months of life is breastfeeding (5). Other antiinfectious host defense mechanisms are gastric acidity, intestinal motility, intestinal microflora, and specific immune responses. Adequately nourished individuals can cope better with dehydration, nutrient losses, and other consequences of infection; they also exhibit a competent cell-mediated immunity, a good amplification of the immune response, and an integrity of natural barriers (1).

Impaired immunocompetence is observed in intrauterine growth retardation. Small-for-gestational age infants exhibit a higher incidence of infection and mortality in the first years of life (6,30). Postnatal undernutrition, whether of a nutritional origin (as in famine) or due to nutrition-infection interactions (common in the tropics), is accompanied by alterations in resistance (dryness of skin and mucosa, hypochlorhydria, and intestinal dysbacteriosis). Severely undernourished children may show a decreased lymphoid cell mass, an impaired T- and B-immunocyte function, and diminished synthesis of complement and secretory immunoglobulin A (31,32).

Undernourished Cauqué children experienced a higher attack rate of diarrhea, a greater severity and mortality due to infections, and greater difficulty in controlling and recovering from infection than did Puriscal children (6,33). Infectious disease and the carrier state (in shigellosis and measles) were generally longer in undernourished than in well-nourished individuals (6). Severely malnourished children show an absent or diminished T-cell response, and children may die of measles without evidence of delayed hypersensitivity (34).

Severe undernutrition under conditions of extreme food deprivation may result in depletion of the immune system; starved individuals may develop fulminant infectious disease upon nutritional recuperation (35,36). On the other hand, infection may alter immune function in a variety of ways, including exacerbation of immune function, secondary immunodeficiency, and immunological paralysis (37).

CHILD ABUSE AND MALNUTRITION

Studies in traditional human societies and in wild animals show that severe aggression and killing within the species is a rare phenomenon. Furthermore, malnutrition and other deficiencies are not observed or occur only rarely both in humans living under selvatic conditions or in sylvan animals (38). When natural disaster, man-made alterations of the ecosystem, and abrupt changes in lifestyles occur, however, social distress, such as child abuse, appears, often related to family disruption, alcoholism, poverty, and other forms of deprivation (39). The phenomenon, claimed to be typical of industrial nations, was not observed in traditional Santa María Cauqué (6) but is known to occur in traditional societies profoundly disturbed when placed at a disadvantage. In Costa Rica and other Latin American nations in transition, child abuse appears to be increasing, particularly during the present economic and social crisis (40).

An analysis of the 33 cases admitted to the National Children's Hospital during 1977 revealed that young age of the mother, unwanted pregnancy, low birthweight, mother-infant separation, and familiar poverty and deprivation were background features of the syndrome, often interlaced. These factors generally occurred in abused children in excess of expectation. On the other hand, malnutrition was three to four times more frequent in abused than in nonabused children of the same age (6) (Table 4). Since malnutrition develops after several weeks or months of deprivation, whereas physical abuse is an acute phenomenon, the occurrence of chronic malnutrition in abused children must be interpreted as the result of prolonged deprivation in the home environment. Thus child neglect and abuse induce malnutrition more often than suspected. In fact, in rural, peri-urban, and slum communities, malnutrition relates to low education, poor family planning, unwanted pregnancy, high-risk pregnancy, premature delivery, failure to breastfeed, deficient maternal technology, and child neglect and abuse. For instance, a recent study in Costa Rica, where most of the malnutrition associated with infectious diseases has been drastically reduced, showed that child abuse was a factor present in about one-half of all the severe cases of PEM admitted to the National Children's Hospital (40) (Table 5). Pediatricians in other Latin American countries are reporting a similar situation, and child neglect and maternal incompetence have been described in Colombia as a cause of premature death (41,42).

TABLE 4. *Nutritional status of battered children[a]*

Status	Battered (prevalence, %)	Nonbattered[b]
<80 Weight/height (wasted)	17	5
<90% Height/age (stunted)	36	8

[a]National Children's Hospital, Costa Rica, 1977.
[b]Children of same age group, National Nutrition Survey, 1978.

TABLE 5. *Determinants of PEM in 112 children[a]*

Determinant[b]	Number	Percent frequency
Infectious diseases		
Diarrhea[c]	81	72
Lower respiratory illness	39	35
Intestinal parasitosis	24	21
Otitis media	21	19
Alterations in central nervous system	57	51
Child abuse	43	38
Congenital defects	30	27
Metabolic diseases	3	2.6

[a]National Children's Hospital, 1981. From P. Jiménez, E. Mohs and L. Mata *(unpublished)*.
[b]More than one factor could be present in any single case.
[c]More than one-half the cases lasted for more than 6 weeks.

CONTROL OF INFECTIOUS DISEASES AND MALNUTRITION

If infectious diseases are major determinants of chronic and acute malnutrition, one would expect that, provided there is no shortage of food, a significant reduction in the former would lead to a significant decrease in the rate of malnutrition in any given country. Indeed, a remarkable decline in mortality due to infectious disease and eventually to malnutrition has been recorded in several less developed countries in the Americas and in Asia, apparently independent of significant changes in food consumption. Costa Rica is a good example, particularly because the decrease in morbidity and mortality from leading infectious diseases—especially diarrhea—occurred within a span of 15 years (43,44) and was not accompanied by a demonstrable improvement in energy intake. Table 6 indicates the changes in food consumption, infection, mortality, and nutrition in Costa Rica that took place over 11 years. While the quality and quantity of food consumed per caput did not change significantly (45), the rate of infection of intestinal parasites was sharply reduced (44). Mortality due to diarrhea (44), and less markedly pneumonia and influenza, also decreased sharply. As a consequence, childhood mortality decreased in parallel to the reduction of diarrheal diseases and other infectious and parasitic diseases (43,44). Also, the prevalence of severe weight deficit (less than 75% weight for age, or second and third degree malnutrition, Gomez classification) declined significantly, and the reduction in severe PEM was so marked that the malnutrition ward of the National Children's Hospital could be closed. What is striking about these changes is the apparent lack of correlation between food consumption and the changes in the prevalence of malnutrition.

It can be concluded that the control of infection will eventually lead to the control of malnutrition. The decline in infection in Costa Rica has been the result of significant investments in education, environmental sanitation, and primary health care (Table 7). Income, electricity, roads, and other parameters of socioeconomic development have improved (43,44,46).

TABLE 6. *Changes in food consumption, infection, mortality, and nutritional status in Costa Rica, 1966–1978*

Parameter	1966	1978	Percent change
Per capita food consumption			
Energy (kcal)	1,894	2,020	+6.6
Protein (g)	53.6	54.0	+0.7
Iron (mg)	15.4	14.4	−6.5
Intestinal parasites[a]			
Ascaris (%)	21.7	3.5	−83.9
Trichuris (%)	56.7	4.6	−91.9
Hookworm (%)	10.2	2.9	−71.6
Mortality[b]			
Diarrhea (per 100,000)	104.4	11.8	−88.7
Pneumonia, influenza (per 100,000)	144.7	76.1	−47.4
Infant (per 1,000)	69.8	17.7	−74.6
1–4 yr (per 1,000)	5.5	0.7	−87.3
Nutritional status			
<75% Weight for age	13.5	4.1	−69.6

[a]For 1966, children 2–4 years old; for 1982, all ages.
[b]For diarrhea, all ages; for pneumonia and influenza, children <2 years.

TABLE 7. *Changes in host and environment in Costa Rica, 1960–1980*

Parameter	1960	1980	Percent change
Percent literate	84.4	90.1	+7
Percent in school, 18–23 year olds	4.0	21.0	+425
Birth rate per 1,000	48.3	31.2	−35
Global fecundity, children	7.3	3.7	−49
Percent with low birth weight	12.5	7.0	−44
Percent deliveries in hospitals	50.0	90.7	+81
Maternal mortality per 1,000	1.4	0.3	−79
Percent with water connection			
Rural	34.0[a]	62.0	+82
Urban	90.0[a]	98.0	+9
Percent with primary health care, rural	10	50.0	+400

[a]Data for 1966.

COMMENTS

It may be equivocal to assume that malnutrition predisposes to infection, as infection depends on exposure of the host to the agent and follows the laws of probability. This is substantiated by the high attack rate of enteric infection, diarrhea, and weight loss among well-nourished travelers to tropical regions (47), which incriminates the environment and its high contamination potential—much more than the nutritional status—as the crucial element in the multifactorial cause of malnutrition.

In traditional societies, breastfeeding is part of the culture and generally leads to adequate nutrition and growth during the first 3 to 6 months of life, even among low birthweight infants (6). During this period, the child is sufficiently protected from infection and from its negative nutritional impact by inherent nutritional and immune properties, by correction or amelioration of dehydration by the continuous supply of breast milk, and by imposing a mechanical barrier to environmental contamination. As weaning begins, exposure to infection increases and results in concurrent diseases and a deterioration of the nutritional state. In transitional societies, many infants are not breastfed or are weaned early in life, and the deleterious effect of infection may become quite obvious shortly after birth, particularly in deprived environments. Under such conditions, recurrent diseases induce weight loss and growth retardation, leading to chronic or acute malnutrition very early in life. It is worth noting that early diarrhea becomes an important determinant in the multifactorial cause of mental retardation in such circumstances.

The nutritional damage induced by diarrhea is pronounced if oral rehydration or other treatments are not available, as is the case in many villages throughout the world. Recurrent diarrhea, anorexia, and fever, coupled with diets of low biological value and unhygienically prepared (48), induce marasmus or precipitate kwashiorkor. Death also occurs among well-nourished children, however, if they become dehydrated and do not receive prompt fluid therapy. The risk of death is greater for pre-term and small-for-gestational age infants or for those with chronic or severe malnutrition (6,49). Well-nourished children may also die from diarrhea, bronchopneumonia, and other infectious diseases.

Prospective community studies emphasize the importance of environmental sanitation and home technologies for promotion of child nutrition and health (6,9), as opposed to food distribution programs and isolated nutritional interventions (44,50). Supplementation of the village diet in Santa María Cauqué with one of the best existing supplements (soya flour, lysine, vitamins, iron) on a daily basis over 4 years did not result in any change in the nutrition of children and women in the reproductive years (51). In contrast, societies with good education, personal hygiene, primary health care, and sanitation showed remarkable improvements in child nutrition and survival (Costa Rica, Cuba, Kerala in India, Sri Lanka, and Western Australia aborigines). It should be stressed, however, that populations suffering from acute food shortages are to be excluded from such generalizations, and that food distribution should receive immediate consideration in the case of demonstrated acute food shortage (e.g., during and after natural and man-made disasters).

A practical way to know whether infection or diet should be the target for intervention is to examine both the community prevalence of undernutrition across all age groups and behavior of mortality. When food supply is limited as a result of natural disaster or war, undernutrition and mortality increase in all ages and sometimes in all social classes. The usual situation in the developing world, however, is different; there is no limitation in diet as, in fact, most children in Asia and

Latin America consume around 80% of the calories and protein recommended by WHO/FAO, a level compatible with normal growth of children in industrial and transitional societies (52). On the other hand, undernutrition in most developing countries is virtually confined to infants and very young children and more rarely to the very old who live in isolation (6). A logical explanation for the malnutrition observed in children in developing countries is the continuous stress resulting from infection and social pathology, more than a limitation in food intake. In this regard, observations in Uganda and Costa Rica revealed that psychosocial factors leading to voluntary and involuntary child abuse and neglect induce chronic malnutrition and precipitate its severe forms (3,40). Deficient maternal technology (15), or maternal incompetence (42), favor infection, poor feeding, poor care, and premature death.

Epidemiologic evidence indicates that prevention and control of infection, particularly enteric disease, correlate with improved nutrition. For instance, a decrease in diarrheal disease deaths in Costa Rica was highly correlated with a decline in infant mortality and a secular positive trend in height of children (48). During the observation period, no drastic changes in individual food consumption were recorded that could account for the significant gains in nutrition and infant mortality. Nevertheless, there was a dramatic reduction in deaths due to diarrheal and respiratory diseases, measles, whooping cough, and other communicable diseases. These changes were concurrent with a marked increase in per capita income, education, sanitation, and primary health care.

It is expected, then, that improvement in water supplies and sanitation, in primary health services (including promotion of breastfeeding, oral rehydration, immunizations, treatment, family planning), and education (especially of women) will result in a betterment of the world nutrition situation without necessarily demanding an increase in food consumption. This comment, as said before, does not apply to areas where there is a proven acute shortage of foodstuffs.

ACKNOWLEDGMENTS

Recognition is given to the staffs of INCAP (Guatemala) and INISA and the National Children's Hospital (Costa Rica), particularly to Drs. Juan J. Urrutia, Edgar Mohs, and Patricia Jiménez. Support was received from the University of Costa Rica, the Costa Rican Ministry of Health and National Council for Research and Technology, the USAID, the British ODA, and the Rockefeller Foundation.

REFERENCES

1. Scrimshaw NS, Taylor CE, Gordon JE. Interaction of nutrition and infection. Monograph 57. Geneva: World Health Organization, 1968.
2. Waterlow JC. Observations on the suckling's dilemma—a personal view. J Hum Nutr 1981;35:85–98.
3. Goodall J. Malnutrition and the family: deprivation in kwashiorkor. Proc Nutr Soc 1979;17:22.
4. Mata L. Child malnutrition and deprivation: observations in Guatemala and Costa Rica. Food nutri 1980;6:7–14.

5. Jelliffe DB, Jelliffe EFP. Human milk in the modern world. Psychological, nutritional and economic significance. New York: Oxford University Press, 1978.

6. Mata LJ. The children of Santa María Cauqué. A prospective field study of health and growth. Cambridge, Massachusetts: The MIT Press, 1978.

7. Mata L, Allen MA, Jiménez P, et al. Promotion of breast-feeding, health, and growth among hospital-born neonates, and among infants of a rural area of Costa Rica. In: Chen LC, Scrimshaw NS, eds. Diarrhea and malnutrition. Interactions, mechanisms and interventions. New York: Plenum, 1983:177–202.

8. Mata L, Jiménz P, Allen MA, et al. Diarrhea and malnutrition: breast-feeding intervention in a transitional population. In: Holme T, Holmgren J, Merson MH, eds. Acute enteric infections in children. New prospects for treatment and prevention. Amsterdam: Elsevier/North Holland, 1982:233–51.

9. Mata L. Malnutrition and concurrent infections. Comparison of two populations with different infection rates. In: Mackenzie JS, ed. Viral diseases in South-East Asia and the Western Pacific. Sydney: Academic Press, 1982:56–76.

10. Mata LJ, Urrutia JJ, Cáceres A, Guzmán MA. The biologic environment in a Guatemalan rural community. In: Proceedings of the western hemisphere nutrition congress III. New York: Futura, 1972:257–64.

11. Capparelli E, Mata L. Microflora of maize prepared as tortillas. Appl Microbiol 1975;29:802–6.

12. Mata LJ, Jiménez F, Cordón M, et al. Gastrointestinal flora of children with protein-calorie malnutrition. Am J Clin Nutr 1972;25:1118–26.

13. Kloene W, Bang FB, Chakroborty SM, et al. A two years respiratory virus survey in farm villages in West Bengal, India. Am J Epidemiol 1970;92:307–20.

14. Mata LJ, Urrutia JJ, Albertazzi C, Pellecer O, Arellano E. Influence of recurrent infections on nutrition and growth of children in Guatemala. Am J Clin Nutr 1972;25:1267–75.

15. Mata L. The malnutrition-infection complex and its environment factors. Proc Nutr Soc 1979;38:29–40.

16. Mata LJ, Kronmal RA, Urrutia JJ, García B. Effect of infection on food and the nutritional state: perspectives as viewed from the village. Am J Clin Nutr 1977;30:1215–27.

17. Whitehead RG. Malnutrition and infection. In: Isliker H, Schurch B, eds. The impact of malnutrition on immune defense in parasitic infestation. Bern: Hans Huber, 1981:15–25.

18. Cole TJ, Parkin JM. Infection and its effect on the growth of young children: a comparison of the Gambia and Uganda. Trans R Soc Trop Med Hyg 1977;71:196–8.

19. Martorell R, Yarbrough C, Yarbrough S, Klein RE. The importance of ordinary illnesses on the dietary intakes of malnourished children. Am J Clin Nutr 1980;33:345–50.

20. Molla A, Molla AM, Sarker SA, Khatoon M, Rahaman MM. Absorption of nutrients during diarrhoea due to *V. cholerae*, *E. coli*, rotavirus and *Shigella*. Working paper 19. Dacca: ICDDR,B, 1981.

21. Gracey M. The contaminated small bowel syndrome. Am J Clin Nutr 1979;32:234–43.

22. Lindebaum J, Gerson CD, Kent TH. Recovery of small-intestinal structure and function after residence in the tropics. I. Studies in Peace Corps volunteers. Ann Int Med 1971;74:218–22.

23. Field M. Water electrolyte and carbohydrate transport. In: Proceedings of the 74th Ross conference of pediatric research. Columbus: Ross Lab, 1977:114–25.

24. Beisel WR. Magnitude of the host nutritional response to infection. Am J Clin Nutr 1977;30:1236–47.

25. Wahed MA, Rahaman MM, Gilman RH, Greenough WB, Sarker SA. Protein-losing enteropathy in diarrhoea: application of α_1-antitrypsin assay. Working paper 22. Dacca: ICDDR,B, 1981.

26. Beisel WR. Trace elements in infectious processes. Med Clin N Am 1976;60:831–49.

27. Gordon JE, Wyon JB, Ascoli W. The second year death rate in less developed countries. Am J Med Sci 1967;254:357–80.

28. McGregor IA, Rahman AK, Thompson B, Billewicz WZ, Thomson AM. The growth of young children in a Gambian village. Trans R Soc Trop Med Hyg 1968;62:341–52.

29. Chambers R, Longhurst R, Bradley D, Feachem R. Seasonal dimensions to rural poverty: analysis and practical implications. Inst Dev Stud, England: University of Sussex, 28 p, 1979.

30. Chandra RK. Fetal malnutrition and postnatal immunocompetence. Am J Dis Child 1975;129:450–5.

31. Neumann CG. Maternal nutrition and neonatal immunocompetence. In: Jelliffe DB, Jelliffe EFP,

eds. Advances in international maternal and child health. Oxford: Oxford University Press, 1982;2:16–27.

32. Faulk WP, Mata LJ, Edsall G. Effects of malnutrition on the immune response in humans: a review. Trop Dis Bull 1975;72:89–103.

33. Chen LC, Alaudin-Chowdhury AKM, Huffman SL. Anthropometric assessment of energy-protein malnutrition and subsequent risk of mortality among preschool age children. Am J Clin Nutr, 1980;33:1836–45.

34. Morley D. Severe measles: some unanswered questions. Rev Infect Dis 1983;5:460–2.

35. Murray MJ, Murray AB. Starvation supression and refeeding activation of infection. Lancet, 1977;1:123–5.

36. Murray MJ, Murray AB. Cachexia: a "last ditch" mechanism of host defence? J Coll Phys Lond 1980;14:197–9.

37. Targett GAT. Malnutrition and immunity to protozoan parasites. In: Isliker H, Schurch B, eds. The Impact of malnutrition on immune defense in parasitic infestation. Bern: Hans Huber, 1981:158–79.

38. Mata LJ, Mohs E. As seen from national levels: developing world. Chapter 23. In: Margen S, Ogar RA, eds. Progress in human nutrition, vol II. Westport: Ari, 1978:25–64.

39. Turnbull CM. The mountain people. New York: Touchstone, 1972.

40. Mata L, Quesada AV, Saborío F, Mohs E. El niño agredido y la desnutrición: observaciones epidemiológicas en Costa Rica. Rev Med Hosp Nal Costa Rica, 1980;15:137–48.

41. Scrimshaw SCM. Infant mortality and behavior in the regulation of family size. Popul Dev Rev 1978;4:383–92.

42. Wray JD, Aguirre A. Protein-calorie malnutrition in Candelaria, Colombia. I. Prevalence, social and demographic causal factors. J Trop Pediatr 1969;15:76–98.

43. Mohs E. Infectious diseases and health in Costa Rica: the development of a new paradigm. Pediatr Infect Dis 1982;1:212–6.

44. Mata L. The evolution of diarrhoeal diseases and malnutrition in Costa Rica. The role of interventions. Assignment children. 1983;61/62:195–224.

45. Ministry of Health: Encuesta Nacional de Nutrición. Costa Rica: Department of Nutrition, Ministry of Health, 1983.

46. Rosero-Bixby L. Social and economic policies and their effects on mortality: the Costa Rican case. Paris: International union for the scientific study of population, 1983.

47. Lee JA, Kean BH. International conference on the diarrhea of travelers—new directions in research: a summary. J Infect Dis 1978;137:355–69.

48. Mata L, Kronmal RA, Villegas H. Diarrheal diseases: a leading world health problem. In: Ouchterlony O, Holmgren J, eds. Cholera and related diarrheas. Basel: Karger, 1980:1–14.

49. Chandra RK, Newberne PM. Nutrition, immunity and infection. New York: Plenum, 1977.

50. Mata L. The nature of the nutrition problem. In: Joy L, ed. Nutrition planning, the state of the art. New York: Science and Technology Press, 1978:91–9.

51. Urrutia JJ, García B, Bressani R, Mata L. Report of the maize fortification project in Guatemala. Guatemala: INCAP, PAHO/WHO, 1978:28–68.

52. Waterlow JC, Thompson AM. Observations on the adequacy of breast-feeding. Lancet, 1979;2:238–42.

DISCUSSION

Dr. Zoppi: Dr. Mata, in 1972, you published a paper on intestinal colonization in infants living in a rural area. After the changes you report in your chapter, how did the intestinal ecosystem of today's infants in Costa Rica compare with those reported 10 years ago?

Dr. Mata: We measured the microflora in Guatemalan children because we were trying to find an explanation for diarrhea. We have not done similar studies of the microbiota in Costa Rica, but we have found differences in the pathogens. For instance, in Guatemala, 20% of children shed *Giardia*, while in Costa Rica, less than 5% do so. The incidence of diarrhea is less in Costa Rica than in Guatemala. We find areas in Costa Rica that are poor, but there are no marked differences in nutrient intake within Costa Rica, while there are differences in delivery of primary health care, infection, housing, and living conditions.

Dr. Lechtig: This chapter makes a persuasive case for infection as an important determinant of nutritional and health status. I doubt any of us would disagree with this conclusion. We should not assume that food supplementation programs will always produce a nutritional improvement. There are food supplementation programs that produce such a high proportion of replacement in dietary intake—sometimes as much as 75% of the supplement is replacing the home diet—that no improvement in nutrition is detected. If these programs are abruptly withdrawn, the condition of the participating populations could easily deteriorate because of the high degree of replacement and corresponding dependence on the supplements. It is also evident that many of these programs are used for political, economic, or other reasons not directly related to the nutritional condition of the participants. This is a good argument to improve design, implementation and continuing evaluation but not to conclude that food supplementation programs are not useful at all.

In the data you present, it appears that the dietary intake of pregnant women and infants at 6 months of age was notably higher in Puriscal than in Santa María Cauqué. Would this difference explain part of the differences in physical growth in these two populations? In addition to infection rates, there are many other important differences between these two populations, i.e., maternal height and weight, parents' education, family income, home dietary intake, and use of available health services.

Dr. Waterlow: You have convinced me that in those two populations, malnutrition no longer exists in children, although perhaps it does in mothers. It would be useful to know the proportion of intakes that are below a certain level, because it is difficult to judge from these averages whether or not there has been a shift in distribution which, after all, is what matters. The limitation of food supply could play a more important role in such countries as India, Bangladesh, and Nepal.

Dr. Mata: The striking fact is to find that Puriscal women are about 5 kg heavier and about 10 cm taller, although they are eating the same diet as Cauqué women, with no correlation between maternal weight, maternal consumption, and birthweight. This made us skeptical about the relationship between pregnancy diet and birthweight; thus we sought other variables.

The most dramatic evidence of the lack of correlation is in Kerala, where intakes are about 1,600 to 1,700 calories; birthweights are relatively good, and the infant mortality is lower than in most less-developed countries, except Cuba. In Kerala, people have democracy; they have raised the level of education of women. Regarding infection, for many years, I also supported the view that malnutrition would diminish resistance, but this is challenged by immunologists today. In our symposium in Lutry, it was virtually concluded that what infection does is not only to cause wasting and stunting in children, but also to alter the immune apparatus, in some cases producing immunological paralysis. Chandra's and our own data show that small-for-date children show a decreased survival and a tendency to develop prolonged infectious disease in postnatal life. The decreased survival extends beyond infancy into the second and third years of life.

Dr. Butte: If we look at the intakes reported for mothers in Santa María Cauqué and Puriscal, the mothers in Cauqué were consuming more energy on a body weight basis; however, there are very different distributions of birthweights in the two villages. Would you attribute the lower birthweights in Cauqué to intrauterine infection?

Dr. Mata: Intrauterine infection has been postulated by Lechtig and myself after showing that 20% of all consecutive neonates in Guatemala have exceedingly high levels of immunoglobulin M (IgM). We used the levels of IgM as an indicator of intrauterine infection, but our observations were not confirmed by others. Eventually, McGregor in the Gambia and investigators in Colombia found exactly the same thing. Lechtig, Delgado, and I did another study in which we drew blood from the femoral vein and showed that in four villages in Guatemala, 20% of consecutive newborns also had elevated IgM. The only way to explain this is by fetal antigenic stimulation, whether by intrauterine infection or by toxin or antigens.

Dr. Whitehead: Your values for energy intake during pregnancy in Guatemala (2,100 kcal/kg/day) and Costa Rica (2,200 kcal/kg/day) are high for the developing world. Have you an explanation for how things apparently are so good?

Dr. Lechtig: Work from our group in the four rural villages in Eastern Guatemala clearly indicated that supplement intake was causally related to better physical growth at birth and during the first 5 years of life. Supplement intake could explain from 30 to 50% of the gap in growth. In the same populations, it was evident that the number of days with diarrhea was inversely related to birthweight and postnatal growth in weight and height. Actually, diarrhea could explain up to 30% of the growth gap. Data in Fig. 4 of my chapter indicate that both the food supplementation to the lactating mother and the use of primary health care services (mainly for diarrhea, respiratory diseases, and immunizations) were directly related to the proportion of infant deaths. It is clear, therefore, that in this population, a primary health care approach that includes simple measures to improve dietary intake and to control diarrhea and respiratory and preventable diseases may be effective in decreasing early mortality and improving physical growth.

The issue is not whether infection or nutrition is important; in poor populations, both factors are important, and the characteristics of their interaction vary across populations and within the same population in different time periods. Thus food supplementation alone may not be the most effective program to deal with these complex interactions. I would expect notably greater impact from integrated nutritional programs that include simple measures, such as control of infectious diseases, promotion of breastfeeding and appropriate weaning, growth monitoring, improved schooling programs, and long-term self-sufficiency in food availability at the family level.

Dr. Mata: Comments by Dr. Butte and remarks by Dr. Whitehead on the quality of the mothers and how they protect their babies from the environment, with respect to feeding, care, and so forth, seem to represent the most important determinant, perhaps even more so than infection and nutrition. We have labeled this component "maternal technologies"; others have called it "maternal competence." One British professor called it "the art and craft of being a good mother."

Nutritional Needs and Assessment of Normal Growth, edited by M. Gracey and F. Falkner. Nestlé Nutrition, Vevey/Raven Press, New York © 1985.

Early Malnutrition, Growth, and Development

Aaron Lechtig

Edificio Seguradoras, Brazilia 70-072, Brazil

A large segment of the world population lives on deficient protein-energy intakes and suffers from physical growth retardation, low psychological test performance, and a high prevalence of infant and preschool age mortality. To ascertain the extent to which these events are causally related, the available data on the relationship between early malnutrition and physical growth should be explored, and the implications of early malnutrition and growth retardation for mortality and mental development of the offspring should be analyzed.

In the following discussion, early malnutrition includes protein-energy malnutrition (PEM) during intrauterine life, breastfeeding, weaning, and postweaning periods up to the first 5 years of age. Thus it includes children of mothers malnourished during pregnancy and lactation as well as those malnourished during the weaning period and preschool years. The discussion focuses mostly on data from major intervention studies: Bogota (1), Guatemala (2), India (3), Mexico (4), Montreal (5), New York (6), Taiwan (7,8), and the Dutch famine study (9). Although emphasis is put on the integration of existent knowledge, the implications for current action programs are also reviewed.

EARLY MALNUTRITION AND PHYSICAL GROWTH

To explore the effects of early malnutrition on growth requires a better understanding of the nature of the variables used to measure prevalence and incidence of malnutrition. Data in Table 1 indicate that the risk of delivering a low birthweight (LBW) baby (below 2.5 kg) is three times higher in developing than in developed countries. Data in Table 2 clearly show that the risk of physical growth retardation as measured in terms of weight for age (categories II and III of the Gomez classification) during preschool age is 40 times higher in developing countries than in developed nations. Because of this increased risk, developing countries contribute 95 and 99% of all the growth retardation observed at birth and at 5 years of age, respectively, in the world. Further analysis suggests an association between per caput gross national product and energy available per caput per day with physical growth retardation at birth and at 5 years of age (12).

There seems to be a general pattern of physical growth retardation in poor populations, which usually begins during fetal life. In low income rural populations, where duration of breastfeeding averages more than 12 months, the prevalence of

TABLE 1. *Estimated number of LBW babies born during 1980[a]*

Degree of development	Population[b] (millions)	No. of births[c] (millions)	LBW babies[c]	
			%	No. (millions)
Developing countries	3,314 (75.6%)	109.0 (86.6%)	19.0	20.71 (95%)
Developed countries	1,068 (24.4%)	16.8 (13.4%)	6.8	1.14 (5%)
Total:	4,382 (100.0%)	125.8 (100.0%)	17.4	21.85 (100.0%)

[a]LBW, ≤2.5 kg.
[b]World Development Report (10).
[c]Lechtig and Klein (11).

TABLE 2. *Estimated number of children less than 5 years of age with moderate or severe deficit in weight for age during 1980[a]*

Degree of development	No. of children less than 5 years of age (millions)[b]	Percentage with moderate or severe deficit in weight for age	No. of children malnourished (millions)[c]	Deaths under 5 years of age[c,d]	
				%	No. (millions)
Developing countries	499 (86.2%)	28.0	139.7 (99.6%)	3.5	17.2 (98.3%)
Developed countries	85 (13.8%)	0.7	0.6 (0.4%)	0.3	0.3 (1.7%)
Total:	584 (100.0%)	24.0	140.3 (100.0%)		17.5 (100.0%)

[a]Defined by a deficit greater than 25% in weight for age (Gomez II and III).
[b]World Development Report (10).
[c]Lechtig and Klein (11).
[d]Calculated from unpublished United Nations document ESA P WP 55, and from Population Reference Bureau Inc.

growth retardation increases between the third and seventh month of age and continues to increase up to the third or fourth year. In poor urban populations, where the prevalence of early weaning has been steadily increasing during the last two decades, the situation is worse: prevalence of growth retardation increases from the first month of age. Later, in those children surviving after 4 years of age, it is common to find proportionally stunted individuals, in other words, children with normal weight for height but low height for age and, therefore, low weight for age.

Effect of Early Malnutrition on Prenatal Growth

Results of recent intervention studies suggest an effect of maternal nutrition during pregnancy on fetal growth as measured by birthweight (2,13). In Bogota, the increment was 77 g for those mothers supplemented during more than one trimester. In Guatemala, the average increment was 111 g in the well-supplemented groups. In India and Mexico, the mean increments were 298 and 180 g, respectively, while in Montreal, it was 41 g. In New York, an increment of 41 g was observed only in the group receiving the low-protein beverage (complement), while a decrement of 32 g was found in the group receiving the high-protein beverage (supplement). In the same study (New York), the expected decrease in birthweight due to heavy smoking was not observed, probably because the food supplementation overcame the decrease in birthweight produced by smoking. In Taiwan, the increment in birthweight was 100 g when newborns of women consuming more than 50% of the supplement were compared with the control group. Finally, in the Dutch famine study, the mean birthweight decreased 298 g from the prefamine levels before increasing 271 g when diet improved. All these studies reported changes in birthweight in the expected direction after the dietary modification, an impressive result given the variety of ethnic, cultural, and sociogeographic situations represented.

At least in five studies (Bogota, Guatemala, Montreal, New York, and the Dutch famine), the observed improvement in birthweight was greater in those women with poorer nutrition, as measured by lower weight for height (Bogota), lower prenatal weight (Montreal and New York), and rations below 1,500 kcal/day (Dutch famine). Data in Fig. 1 from the Guatemalan study indicate that the impact of food supplementation during pregnancy on birthweight was greater in mothers from the lower socioeconomic strata within the village and with lower height, results that add support for the nature of the relationship between the dietary changes and birthweight (14).

There remained the possibility in the Guatemalan study that mothers delivering heavier babies were those who also tended to collaborate more with the program. The sibling analysis presented in Fig. 2 explores the possibility that a constant maternal factor might be responsible for both the high consumption of food supplement during pregnancy and heavier newborns. The figure shows that when caloric supplementation during the later pregnancy was lower than during the preceding pregnancy, the birthweight of the later babies was lower than that of the preceding ones. On the other hand, when caloric supplementation during the later pregnancy was more than 20,000 calories higher than during the preceding pregnancy, the later newborns were heavier than the preceding ones. Consequently, this analysis indicates a positive association between changes in caloric supplementation and changes in birthweight in consecutive pregnancies of the same mother ($r = 0.298$, $N = 94$, $p < 0.01$, $b = 22$ g birthweight per 10,000 supplemented calories). Data in Table 3 from sibling analyses performed with the extended sample followed up to 1977 indicate a similar result ($r = 0.111$, $N = 469$ pairs, $p < 0.01$, $b = 22$ g birthweight per 10,000 supplemented calories).

As expected, in Bogota, New York, and Taiwan, the changes in birthweight were not statistically significant ($p > 0.05$); these studies were not designed to detect changes of this magnitude and, therefore, sample sizes were inadequate. In all

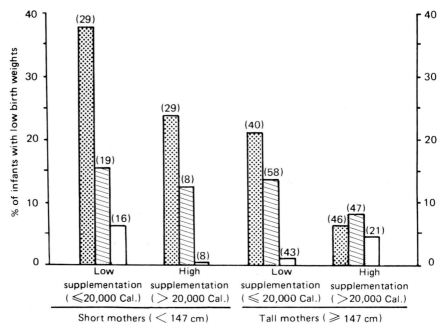

FIG. 1. Influence of maternal height and caloric supplementation during pregnancy on the relationship between socioeconomic score and proportion of infants with LBW (▒) low, (◨) intermediate, (□) high; number of cases in parentheses.

cases, failure to reject the null hypothesis was attributed to small numbers and not to unexpected direction of the results.

Estimates of the dose-response relationships expressed in grams of birthweight per 10,000 net supplemented calories during pregnancy (equivalent to 112 additional calories during the third trimester of pregnancy) are +41 g in Bogota, +41 g in Guatemala, +71 g in India, +36 g in Mexico, +28 g in New York (complement), +35 g in Taiwan, and +29 g in cohorts conceived and born after the famine in the Dutch study. In the latter study, the estimated dose-response relationship was +47 g per net increase of 10,000 calories during pregnancy. The dose-response values computed for Bogota, Guatemala, Mexico, and Taiwan (41,41,36, and 35 g, respectively), are consistent with the relatively similar nutritional conditions of these populations, as estimated by weight and height. The higher estimate for India (71 g) may be explained by the higher prevalence and severity of malnutrition in this sample and by decreased physical activity due to hospitalization of the supplemented group in order to perform the dietary intervention. The low value observed in New York (28 g) is not unexpected given the nutritional condition of this sample, the best among these studies.

Finally, the smaller range observed in the dose-response relationships as compared with the range of mean increments in birthweight (28–71 compared with

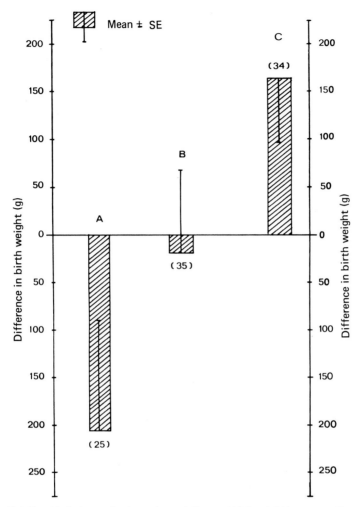

FIG. 2. Relationship between food supplementation and birthweight in consecutive pregnancies. A, 40,000–0 kcal; B, 100–20,000 kcal; C, 20,000–120,000 kcal. Number of pairs of pregnancies in parentheses. Difference between groups A and C, $p<0.01$. (From Lechtig et al., ref. 20.)

40–298 g, respectively) is also suggestive of the nutritional nature of the observed relationship between dietary modification and birthweight. The dose-response values observed in these studies (from 28 to 71 g of birthweight per 10,000 net supplemented calories during pregnancy) are similar to the dose-responses expected from: (a) the relationship between maternal weight gain during pregnancy and birthweight (28–80 g of birthweight per 10,000 kcal); (b) the relationship between differences in prepregnant weight and differences in birthweight between two consecutive pregnancies (25–40 g of birthweight per 10,000 kcal); (c) the relationship between food intake, body composition, and physical activity (36–84 g of birthweight per 10,000 kcal); (d) the available data from the Leningrad famine

TABLE 3. *Correlation between supplemented calories during pregnancy and birthweight*

Sample	n	r	b (g birthweight/ 10,000 supplemented calories)
All populations (Jan. 1969–Sept. 1977)	905	0.092[b]	18.6
Jan. 1969–Feb. 1973	387	0.132[b]	26.6
Feb. 1973–Sept. 1977	548	0.053	11.1
Within siblings[a]	469 pairs	0.111[b]	22.2

[a]Correlation value between differences in caloric supplementation between both pregnancies and differences in birthweight between both babies: the latter minus the preceding sibling.
[b]$p < 0.05$; [‡]$p < 0.01$.

(− 33 g of birthweight per net decrease of 10,000 kcal during pregnancy); and (e) the relationship between home diet and birthweight in white, middle class populations in the United States (33 g of birthweight per 10,000 additional kcal during pregnancy) (16).

Furthermore, if in the sample from the Indian study, home diet had increased to the recommended standards for pregnant women during the last two trimesters of pregnancy (from 1,800 to 2,200 kcal/day) at the dose-response computed for that population (71 g/10,000 net supplemented kcal during pregnancy), the average birthweight would have increased from 2.5 to 3.1 kg. In Guatemala, an increment of home diet up to the recommended standards during the last two trimesters of pregnancy (from 1,400 to 2,200) with the same dose-response relationship (41 g/ 10,000 net supplemented calories) would increase birthweight from 2.9 to 3.5 kg. Thus the effects of food supplementation on birthweight appear to be consistent with usual expectations. An unanswered issue is why these populations did not increase their intake up to the recommended levels of energy intake.

In Guatemala, mothers with high supplementary intakes had a net increment of about 140 kcal/day over the low supplement group (1,400 kcal/day). This represents only 20% of the gap in energy intake [expected requirement: 2,200 kcal/day (17)], and about 10% only of the home dietary intake. Obviously, this was not a typically hungry population. Indeed, low energy density was not the main factor of the unexpected low amount of supplement ingested during pregnancy. Two supplements (high protein-high energy in two villages, and no protein-low energy in the other two) were freely available and accessible at central places of distribution. Although large differences in energy intakes were observed in children between the two supplements, this was not the case in pregnant women in whom no significant differences in either net or total supplement intake were observed.

It was clear in the Dutch study that mothers with intakes below 1,500 kcal could easily increase their intake of energy up to the recommended level, which in this case was similar to levels observed before the famine. Under conditions of chronic malnutrition, however, this increment is narrow and does not reach recommended levels of intake. Therefore, the gap (recommended minus observed) is reduced in only 20 to 50% of individuals. It appears that the same adaptive mechanisms that allowed the mother-fetus diad to survive and develop new equilibrium points at lower levels of energy intake: in other words, lower energy requirements.

Evidence in this direction has been recently presented by Sukhatme and Margen (18). The same mechanisms, perpetuated through generations would limit the ability of chronically malnourished women to rapidly increase their usual intake up to current recommended levels. The practical implication of this hypothesis is not that current recommendations are too high but that it may take several decades or a generation to increase the dietary intake of chronically malnourished pregnant women up to the recommended levels currently ingested by middle class women in developed countries. In other words, it may become unrealistic in terms of consumption to set intake objectives for chronically malnourished populations based on current dietary energy recommendations. Similarly, it may take several decades of nutritional improvement to reach fetal growth standards similar to those accepted in developed countries.

When computed in the same way, the expected dose-response relationships in infants are 134, 55, and 34 g per 1,000 net supplemented calories during the first, second, and third year of age, respectively. Thus the magnitude of the effect of food supplementation during pregnancy on birthweight (28–71 g) is not small when compared to the expected effect of diet on infant weight during the years of most rapid physical growth. Weight gain in the mother during pregnancy is notably smaller in chronically malnourished populations than in well-nourished ones. It is not infrequent to find an average weight gain of 6 to 7 kg in the former compared with 10 to 12 kg in the latter populations (10).

When estimates of dose-response relationships are made in terms of total maternal weight gain, the resultant figures indicate high efficiency rates. Except for Taiwan, all reviewed longitudinal studies (Bogota, Guatemala, India, Mexico, Montreal, New York, and Dutch famine) showed an increment in weight gain during pregnancy associated with nutritional supplementation. In Guatemala, for 10,000 net supplemented calories during pregnancy, 1.008 kg of maternal weight gain was deposited. Of this increased maternal weight gain, 41 g corresponded to increased birthweight (19). Thus the estimated efficiency of supplemented calories was about 60%, of which 3% was increase in birthweight and 97% was maternal and related fetal tissue (16). The relationship between maternal weight gain and birthweight (41 g of birthweight per kilogram of maternal weight gain) was close to the maximum values expected for the mean prepregnant weight of the study population, which was 46.7 kg (expected range: 36–42 g of birthweight per kilogram of weight gain during pregnancy for prepregnant weight of 45.8–49.8 kg) (20).

The same dose-response relationship may have different public health implications, depending on the birthweight distribution and the net amount of supplemented calories during pregnancy (16). In Guatemala, for example, the proportion of LBW babies decreased from 33% in a small sample at the beginning of the study to 13% at the end of the intervention. This reduction in LBW babies may be larger in populations in which the proportion of LBW babies is 40%, as in Mayan Indian populations, and very low if the proportion of LBW babies is around 7%, as in white, middle class populations of the United States.

Influence of Sex on Response of Birthweight to Dietary Change

In three studies (India, Mexico, and Montreal), there were no published data on the influence of sex of the newborn on the response of birthweight to dietary change. The New York study reported no clear sex differences, while the Bogota, Guatemala, and Taiwan studies presented data suggesting that the effect of dietary improvement is greater in males than in females. In the Bogota study, supplemented mothers who delivered male newborns gained more weight during pregnancy and had a greater dietary intake than those who delivered female newborns. In the same study, however, the influence of sex was not observed in the unsupplemented group. Finally, in the Dutch famine study, it was observed that birthweight was greater in males than in females during the famine period. In conclusion, there is some evidence that males may benefit more from prenatal supplementation. The best explanation is that the male fetus grows more rapidly in late pregnancy and therefore is more likely to be vulnerable to shortages of food supply and to benefit from extra food.

Timing of Food Supplementation During Pregnancy

In all these studies, nutritional intervention during the last trimester was sufficient to produce the observed effect in birthweight. In the Dutch study, the effects of famine on fetal growth occurred only in those women exposed in late pregnancy and not in those exposed during the first two trimesters, a finding consistent with the rapid increase in fetal weight during the last trimester. This is also in agreement with the observation that large variations in fetal weight between developed and developing countries do not exist before 36 weeks of gestational age (see Falkner, *this volume*). Therefore, additional food provided at least during the third trimester of pregnancy can improve birthweight.

Data from Guatemala suggest that the total amount of food supplement consumed during pregnancy is a more important factor than the gestational age at which supplementation is begun. In this context, the information available indicates that mothers with high subcutaneous fat, as measured by tricipital skinfold, had heavier and fatter newborns than mothers with low subcutaneous fat (3,667 versus 3,420 g in males and 3,491 versus 3,338 g in females, respectively), other conditions being equal. At the same time, mothers with high muscle area, as measured by arm circumference corrected by tricipital skinfold, had heavier, leaner, and longer newborns than mothers with low muscle area (3,667 versus 3,322 g in males and 3,492 versus 3,211 g in females, respectively) (21). Thus the observation that indicators of maternal energy and protein mass are positively related to birthweight provides additional support to the hypothesis that maternal "reserves" may be used to some extent for fetal growth.

Maternal Nutrition Threshold

A clear association has been observed between energy intake and birthweight below 1,800 kcal/day. As a consequence, the probability of detecting an effect on birthweight in populations with chronic malnutrition will increase, the lower the home diet intake is below 1,800 kcal/day and the higher the net increase in nutrient intake achieved by the program. When famine occurs in a previously well-nourished population, maternal stores will help to adapt to the shortage in energy intake; therefore, the threshold would be lower, around 1,500 kcal/day, as suggested by the Dutch study.

A related question refers to the ability of these populations to survive under chronically energy-restricted diets. In developing countries, it is usual to find women populations with average energy intakes during pregnancy within the range of 1,400 to 1,800 kcal. Despite this intake being at least 700 kcal below the commonly accepted energy requirements (17), it is usually able to protect the prepregnancy weight against a steady decrease. Thus in Guatemala, pregnant women with an average daily intake of 1,500 kcal had a mean prepregnant weight of 47 kg and mean weight gain of 6 kg during pregnancy. They delivered babies with a mean birthweight of 2.9 kg, with a rate of LBW babies around 20% (16). The usual values for well-nourished populations are 64, 12, and 3.3 kg, and 7%, respectively (10).

Increased efficiency of utilization of dietary energy from an average of 37% to upper levels of 55% could also play a key role in this adaptive process (18). Thus if other conditions are equal, two populations may have similar pregnancy outcomes with grossly different mean dietary intakes (i.e., 2,500 and 2,000 kcal) if they develop proportionally improved efficiency rates to use dietary energy. Therefore, it appears that in these chronically malnourished populations, survival is achieved at the price of low prepregnancy weight. However, this ability of the reproductive process to adapt to chronic energy restriction, remarkable as it is, should not serve as an excuse for public health inaction. When the limits of this capacity for homeostasis are exceeded, because of either lower intake or greater expenditure (increased physical activity or infectious disease during pregnancy), the adaptive balance achieved may disappear and acute malnutrition may occur. The implication is that thresholds, as requirements, are probably of a dynamic nature and not fixed conditions, since equilibrium may be achieved at different levels of intake (18).

Effects on Other Parameters of Prenatal Growth

The Dutch famine study reported an effect of prenatal famine exposure during the third trimester of pregnancy on infant length and head circumference at birth. Except for this study, no information is available on the effect of maternal food supplementation on other anthropometric parameters besides birthweight. Birthweight was the main outcome investigated because of its known relationship with infant mortality and because measurement error was lower than for circumference, skin-fold, length, and length/weight ratio. Information on the effect of maternal mal-nutrition on other anthropometric measurements may shed light on the nature of fetal growth affected by maternal nutrition and on the predictivity of parameters of fetal growth on later outcomes in childhood. For example, data in Table 4 from a recent study in Guatemala clearly indicate that a low arm circumference at birth (less than 9.0 cm) has equal or better value than low birthweight (<2.5 kg) to predict mortality during the first 15 days of life (22).

Stability of the Long-Term Impact of Improved Maternal Nutrition on Birthweight

Little is known of the long-term stability of the food supplementation effects. Data in Table 4 from the Guatemalan study suggest that the impact of supplementation per additional calorie decreased as the intervention continued over a period of 9 years. Although no clear explanation is available, the observation does not appear to be produced by a systematic decrease in measurement reliability; indeed, it may be related to the inhibition of adaptive mechanisms.

The study population had chronic moderate malnutrition, which gradually developed adaptative mechanisms resulting in survival at lower levels of energy intake. In other words, this population increased its efficiency to use energy, the main limiting nutrient in dietary intake. The nutritional intervention increased energy intake, which was reflected in improved growth and other functions with a relatively high level of efficiency due to the adaptive mechanisms mentioned before. Over several years, however, nutritional improvement gradually became a routine component of dietary intake. In some way, this routine provision of supplementary food inhibited some of the mechanisms that had protected essential living functions over

TABLE 4. *Comparison of predictivity of early death between low arm perimeter at birth and LBW*

Arm perimeter	Early death (0–15 days)	Alive at 15 days	Total
Low birthweight (<2.5 kg)			
Low (<9.0 cm)	25	238	263
High (≥9.0 cm)	0	5	5
Total	25	243	268
High birthweight (≥2.5 kg)			
Low (<9.0 cm)	2	90	92
High (≥9.0 cm)	0	370	370
Total	2	460	462
Total	**27**	**703**	**730**

decades of chronic nutritional deprivation. The final result was a decline in the efficiency of using the additional energy for growth, as measured by dose-response estimates. Independent of the mechanisms responsible for the apparent diminished impact, these data provide additional support to the recommendation that food supplementation programs be implemented as short-term interventions dealing with acute, emergency situations. As soon as possible, they should gradually be replaced by long-lasting interventions aimed at increasing food purchasing power, food availability, nutrition education, and self-sufficiency at the family level.

Implications of LBW for Postnatal Growth

Studies on long-term effects of intrauterine growth retardation (IUGR) indicate different degrees of recovery when the environment is favorable in terms of food and sanitation, a finding explained by the existence of different types of IUGR infants. These infants with adequate weight for their shorter height or stunted babies show a trend to remain shorter and lighter during the first years after birth (23–25), suggesting that height has a lower probability for recovery than does weight. In contrast, "wasted" IUGR infants (with low weight for their height) may be able to recover by gaining weight during the first months after birth. Thus under appropriate nutritional conditions, postnatal growth tends to stabilize the relationship between weight and height. Similar to postnatal growth retardation, IUGR represents a mixture of different conditions depending on the onset, duration, and severity of the nutritional deprivation during pregnancy (25). These factors are important to determine the prognosis in terms of physical growth and functional outcomes and the most appropriate type of nutritional and health interventions.

In populations with chronic moderate malnutrition, about two-thirds of the LBW babies are babies with low weight for gestational age. Of these babies, two-thirds show proportionate body size. In other words, about one-half of the LBW babies are stunted infants, with high probability of long-term growth retardation. Despite compensatory mechanisms resulting in higher growth rates than normals, most tend to remain below the 10th percentile of the international standards for weight and height up to 3 years of age (26–28). In contrast, in populations suffering in famine, where most LBW babies are wasted, there is a greater probability of compensation if appropriate nutritional programs are implemented after birth.

Early Malnutrition and Postnatal Growth

A positive impact of food supplementation on physical growth of the offspring has been observed in studies in Bogota, Guatemala, and Mexico. However, differentiation between the relative importance of prenatal versus postnatal maternal supplementation has proved difficult. No effect of supplementation during pregnancy on postnatal physical growth was detected in the New York study, where data suggest that there was no severe PEM. No data on this question are available from the studies from India, Montreal, and Taiwan. Finally, in the Dutch study, a small excess in frequency of obesity was reported in males born to women exposed to famine early in pregnancy. On the contrary, severe nutritional deprivation in the latter part of pregnancy and the first few months of life led to a lower rate of obesity. In Colombia, the investigators reported an effect of supplementation on weight and height, beginning at between 3 and 6 months and continuing up to 36 months of age. The prevalence of severe physical growth retardation at 36 months of age, as measured by adequacy of weight for age (Gomez II and III), was reduced from 20.6 to 8.8%, with a corresponding increment in category I and normals. Similar changes were observed in terms of height for age: the proportion of children with adequacy of less than 90% decreased from 54.0 to 39.7%.

Data from the Guatemalan study indicate that the proportion of children with physical growth retardation in weight, height, and head circumference at 1 year of age was lower at the end (1976) than at the beginning (1969) of the program.

A supplementary intake was clearly associated with better growth in height and weight up to the first 5 years of life (29). No clear trends were detected in arm and calf circumferences. All skinfold measures (triceps, subscapular, and medium calf) decreased with increased supplementation, mainly due to the increment in height and length of the extremities. These data also suggest that height and weight may be useful indicators of the effect of nutritional intervention in children up to 5 years of age. Head circumference may be a useful indicator of nutritional impact, particularly during the first year of life, even better than weight or height.

It is clear from the above longitudinal studies that food supplementation of malnourished and lactating mothers and their offspring resulted in significant increases in rate of growth in terms of weight, height, and head circumference during fetal and postnatal life up to the first 3 to 5 years of age. This effect was also reflected in important reductions in the prevalence of children with severe malnutrition (II and III as measured by Gomez) (weight for age), as well as in the prevalence of less than 90% of adequacy in height for age. Notwithstanding the validity of these effects, the increments observed represent only one-third to one-half of the difference between the control groups and samples from high socioeconomic strata in the same countries or according to international growth standards. This modest impact of well-conducted nutritional programs could be explained by the high rate of substitution of home dietary intake (probably including breast milk) by the food supplements. In many food supplementation programs carried out in chronically malnourished populations, this replacement is about one-half or more of the supplemented energy intake. Estimations made during pregnancy suggest that if all the differential in energy intake could be fulfilled, most of the gap in birthweight could be covered. The inference with respect to postnatal growth, however, is different. In Bogota and Guatemala, where total nutrient intake was estimated, the supplements fulfilled two-thirds of the differential in energy intake and all the differential in protein intake, but only one-third of the gap in postnatal growth was filled.

The best explanation for this observation is the high incidence of common infectious diseases of mild to moderate severity, particularly diarrhea. In Guatemala, it was found that 10% of the retardation in growth was associated with diarrheal disease (30). Further analysis of these data suggest that this figure was conservative, the real effect of diarrhea being about 30% or more of the gap in physical growth. Much of the nutritional impact of diarrhea is mediated through decreased dietary intake in mothers and children (31,32). In children, the presence of these infectious episodes is associated with a decrement of 19% of the dietary intake, or about 175 kcal and 4.8 g of protein per day. When the prevalence of these clinical infections is taken into account, this figure represents at least one-fifth of the mean energy deficit for the same population (33). In pregnant mothers, infectious diseases account for a decrease of about 400 kcal/day, or 25% of usual dietary intake (31). Other mechanisms of the impact of infections on growth are related to food utilization and include vomiting, malabsorption, and unfavorable metabolic effects (34,35). These common infections are important causes of the growth deficit observed in low income populations. Their prevention and treatment should be considered in all programs aimed at improving nutrition.

The IUGR and ethnic differences among groups could also contribute to the modest impact of nutritional programs. As mentioned before, stunted IUGR babies show a trend toward long-term growth retardation, despite appropriate postnatal nutrition and health care. On the other hand, ethnic differences in the growth of preschool children have been reported. In a recent study, children of African and European descent were heavier and taller than Chinese and Indian children. African children were also of greater weight for height than Indian children (36). The conclusion is that although most of the differences in size at preschool age is attributable to malnutrition and infection, the contribution of ethnic differences may become increasingly important as nutrition and general health conditions improve.

The practical implication of the above findings is that food supplementation programs may have a greater impact on physical growth when they are integrated with the following:

1. Primary health care programs aimed at preventing and treating common infections, including immunizations, environmental sanitation, and oral rehydration treatment for diarrhea;
2. Effective promotion of breastfeeding, protection against early weaning, and appropriate weaning practices;
3. Nutrition and health promotion programs, including monitoring of physical growth to decrease home diet substitution and improved food utilization and distribution within the family;
4. Increased self-sufficiency in food availability at the family level.

Early Malnutrition and Permanent Stunting

There are indications that suboptimal nutrition during early life can lead to permanent stunting. Adult populations who suffer from early PEM are consistently shorter and lighter, suggesting long-term stunting as a consequence of early malnutrition (14). The difference of 12 cm at 7 years of age between Guatemalan girls from poor rural villages and middle class girls from the United States is similar to that observed between adult women from both population groups (14). Data from Indian populations indicate that girls who were severely malnourished at preschool age grew faster in height than the standards after 5 years of age (37). However, the difference in weight did not disappear; it went from 20.1 cm at 5 years to 15.3 cm at 18 years of age.

The most important compensatory mechanism reported in populations with chronic malnutrition is the delay of 1 to 2 years in the onset of menarche in girls and about 3 years in the onset of sexual maturation in boys (38–40). As a consequence, the delayed pubertal growth spurt and epiphyseal fusion allow for a longer period of higher rate of growth in the malnourished girls and boys. Nevertheless, most of the growth retardation observed at 7 years of age in chronically malnourished children seems to persist up to adult age, making stunting the most commonly detectable effect of early malnutrition. When stunting is not accompanied by wasting, there may not be current malnutrition but only a long-term effect or a sequela of early malnutrition.

There are indications that permanent stunting could occur across generations. In Guatemala, parent-child correlations in attained height were similar to those reported for well-nourished populations, a finding explained through similarities in environmental conditions. Thus parents who suffered early malnutrition and infection are likely to have offspring with similar problems (41). In girls, permanent stunting is reflected in shorter mothers with higher risk of delivering IUGR babies, thus perpetuating stunting through generations (42). As a consequence, generational stunting may be the result not only of parent-child similarities in environmental conditions but also of biological mechanisms operating at least during pregnancy.

It should be noted that adult stunting may increase the probability of surviving and carrying out physical work with lower dietary intake because of smaller body size. The available data also indicate smaller differences in life expectancy after 7 years of age between developing and developed countries and between high and low socioeconomic strata within the same country, despite large differences in availability of health services among the compared groups. Consequently, the main goal from a public health point of view must be to eradicate physical growth retardation not for the sake of bettering growth in itself but because growth retardation is associated with morbidity, mortality, and suboptimal mental development in present and future generations. It should be remembered when combating early malnutrition that disease and suboptimal development are associated also with overnutrition. There may exist an optimal zone between these two extremes, and there may be variations across populations in the location of this optimal zone.

Energy or Protein

Another important question is whether the addition of energy or protein is associated with the increase in growth rate. In India, there was no additional effect on birthweight when the protein content of the diet increased from 60 g (protein-calorie ratio: 9.6%) to 90 g (protein-calorie ratio: 14.3%). Similar results have been observed in India for postnatal growth in weight and height (43). In Guatemala, the effect of the high-protein-energy supplement was similar to the energy supplement in terms of birthweight, placenta weight, and postnatal growth in weight and height (16,20,29,44,45). In New York, the high-protein supplement did not produce an effect on birthweight.

In Bogota, Guatemala, India, Mexico, Taiwan, and the Netherlands during the famine, the average home energy intake during pregnancy (1,400–2,000 kcal/day) was below requirements (about 2,200 kcal/day) and provided a small margin for physical activity. In contrast, with the exception of Bogota, mean protein intake (43–80 g/day) was usually similar or higher than that required for maintenance and tissue synthesis (about 54 g/day). Thus analysis of the dietary data in these populations showed that energy rather than protein was the main limiting nutrient in mothers and children. Under conditions of energy limitation observed in Guatemala, a daily net supplementation of 200 kcal during the last trimester of pregnancy with no additional protein would increase the daily retention of nitrogen and produce a corresponding increment in birthweight (from 72 to 168 g) in addition to the associated increment in weight gain during pregnancy. Under these conditions, a very large increment of protein intake would be required to produce a similar increment in nitrogen retention and birthweight. Results from Guatemala on the relationship between food supplementation and urea/creatinine ratio in the urine in lactating mothers and their breastfed babies support this hypothesis (13).

This conclusion is also corroborated by analysis of postnatal growth suggesting adequacy of protein and deficiency of energy in preschool children (46). As net supplemented energy increases, protein intake may gradually become the main limiting nutrient, and further energy supplementation alone would not produce an effect on birthweight unless accompanied by protein supplementation.

The relative importance of protein and energy for physical growth depends on which is the main limiting nutrient in the home diet. Other factors, such as placental and mammary gland transport, body composition, physical activity, prevalence of common infections, and nutrient availability from maternal stores during pregnancy and lactation, may also be important in determining the relative contribution of deficiencies in energy and protein to physical growth. Thus it is inappropriate to infer from the Guatemalan and Indian studies that protein-rich supplements will not be needed or that the dietary energy gap should be filled exclusively with energy-rich supplements. The protein/calories ratio usually reached by populations with unlimited access to a wide choice of foods is 11%, a ratio that probably represents the physiological equilibrium of the diet. There are no reasons to lower the protein content of the supplements beyond this level. Protein-rich supplements may be desirable in populations where the protein/calorie ratio is notably below 11%, such as in the New Guinean population, where the main staple is sweet potato. The implication is that the nutrient content of each supplement must be defined in terms of the characteristics of the diet of that population. Where this information is missing, calories from protein should account for 11% of total calories. When designing interventions to meet the nutritional needs of the population at risk, care should also be taken to meet the self-perceived needs of the target group by involving participants and program workers in program planning, implementation, and evaluation.

PHYSICAL GROWTH RETARDATION

Growth Retardation and Mortality

Since the first report (47), a constant association between growth retardation in weight for age and infant (0–11 months) and childhood (1–4 years) mortality has been reported. In poor populations, moderate to severe malnutrition usually is associated with death at preschool age in about one-half the cases (48). In Brazil, for example, it is common to find that one-third to one-half of the children born in malnourished populations do not reach the age of 5 years. Data in Table 2 indicate that in 1980, developing countries contributed 99% of all children with moderate to severe deficit in weight for age and 93% of all deaths below 5 years of age. Being born in a developing country increases 40 times the risk of growth retardation and 12 times the risk of death during the first 5 years of age when compared with developed countries. Mechanisms of association between early malnutrition and mortality are depression of cell-mediated immunity as well as high duration and intensity of exposure to infection. Higher infant mortality is also mediated through increased incidence of LBW babies and, in poor populations with early weaning, the marasmic type of malnutrition.

Unexpectedly, no consistent association has been found between the provision of supplements and duration of diarrhea in Bogota and Guatemala. Given the high validity and reliability of the measures used to estimate supplemental intake and the duration of diarrhea, it was concluded that diarrhea was not affected by the improvement in nutritional status produced by the food supplement.

The association between growth retardation and risk of death is influenced by age (49), degree of wasting measured by the adequacy of weight for height (50), and availability of health care services and nutritional programs (45). As expected, the younger, more wasted, and neglected the malnourished child, the higher the risk of dying (51).

Data on the potential impact of nutritional programs on mortality come from studies in Bogota and Guatemala. In Bogota, the food supplementation program was associated with a 50% decrease in perinatal mortality. In Guatemala, food supplementation during pregnancy and lactation and simplified health care at the primary level were associated with a marked reduction in infant and child mortality. Similar effects on infant and preschool child mortality have been reported in other studies, and the rate of decrease in mortality was notably more rapid than in similar areas where there was no intervention (52). Although in these studies there was no clear indication about the most effective component of each intervention, the following features were particularly effective: an integrated approach that included elements of nutrition and health care, maternal nutrition, maternal immunization against tetanus, monitoring of growth, nutrition, and health, immunization of children against common contagious diseases, early treatment and referral of acute respiratory infections and diarrhea, widespread coverage, greater use of paramedical personnel, and effective training programs.

In Guatemala, infant mortality was negatively associated with length of lactation independent of age of death. Furthermore, weight at birth, actual weight, height, and head and arm circumference at 15 days and 3 months of age were also negatively related to risk of death during the first year of life. Later, these anthropometric variables proved to be useful risk indicators for primary health care programs (53). Because of the consistency of the association between growth and mortality, anthropometric measurements have become simple and useful tools, not only for somatic classification but also for gross prognosis of the child's capacity to survive during infancy and preschool age. This selection allows concentration on public health programs for those children who are in greatest need.

Early Malnutrition, Growth Retardation, and Suboptimal Mental Development

Effects During Infancy

In developed countries, an association between birthweight, head circumference at birth, and subsequent cognitive function has been reported (54). Some studies also have reported effects of the nutritional intervention on behavioral and cognitive variables independent of birthweight (6,55). In Bogota, visual habituation at 15 days of age was faster in the group receiving prenatal supplementation than in the control infants. High-protein supplementation during pregnancy was similarly associated with better scores in habituation, dishabituation, and length of play episodes measured at 1 year of age in New York. Thus the two studies exploring habituation (New York and Bogota) reported faster habituation processes in the infants of the supplemented groups.

The Mexican study revealed significantly improved psychomotor development throughout the first years of life in the group supplemented during pregnancy. Results of the Taiwan study indicated no effect of the supplement on the Bayley mental scale scores at 8 months of age; however, there was an impact on the motor scores.

Data in Table 5 from the Guatemalan study indicate that food supplementation during pregnancy and mother's third trimester weight, head circumference, and birth interval were positively associated with psychomotor development of the baby at 6 months of age. Other important maternal variables were negatively associated with psychomotor development: duration of breastfeeding, parity, morbidity, and immunoglobulin levels in cord blood. These associations were not due to colinearity with birthweight. Furthermore, in these populations, retardation in psychomotor

TABLE 5. *Variables significantly related to sixth-month composite infant score performance*[a]

Variables	Subscales (correlation coefficient)	
	Mental	Motor
Caloric supplementation during pregnancy ($N = 351$)	0.11[b]	0.12[b]
Mother's third trimester weight ($N = 205$)	0.16[b]	0.06
Mother's head circumference ($N = 351$)	0.13[b]	0.13[b]
Parity ($N = 351$)	0.05	0.13[b]
Birth interval (9–37 mo) ($N = 256$)	0.18[b]	0.19[b]
Months lactating during pregnancy ($N = 141$)	0.22[b]	0.02
IgM level ($N = 155$)	0.15	0.17[b]
Morbidity of mother during pregnancy ($N = 214$)	0.12	0.14[b]

[a]Adapted from Lasky et al. (56).
[b]$p < 0.05$.

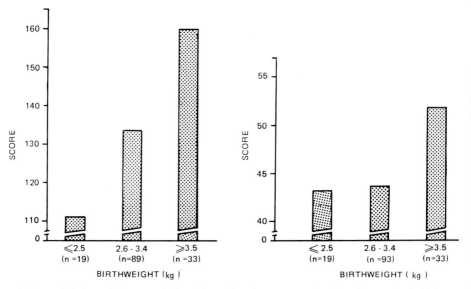

FIG. 3. Relationship between birthweight and performance on the Brazelton scale: (**left**) habituation, $r = 0.273$, $p < 0.01$, $n = 141$; (**right**) alertness, $r = 0.116$, N.S., $n = 145$.

development seemed to be indicative of extremely impaired functioning: infants who died in the first 3 years of life had significantly lower scores in the mental and motor subscales at 6 months of age than did infants who survived (56).

Data in Figs. 3 and 4 indicate an association between birthweight and three of the four Brazelton psychomotor variables (habituation, motor fitness, tremors, and startles). Data in Fig. 5 show a similar association between birthweight and mental and motor variables at 6 months of age. Although the LBW category was consistently related to lower psychomotor test performance, this association seemed to

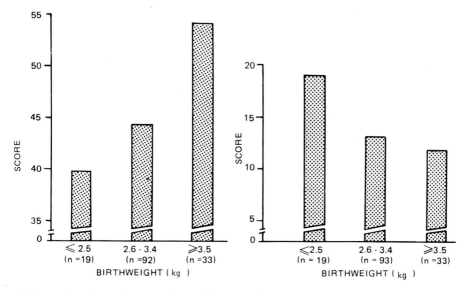

FIG. 4. Relationship between birthweight and performance on the Brazelton scale (B): **(left)** motor fitness, $r = 0.281$, $p<0.01$, $n = 144$; **(right)** tremors and startles, $r = 0.174$, $p<0.05$, $n = 145$. (*Note:* the lower the score, the more advanced the behavior.)

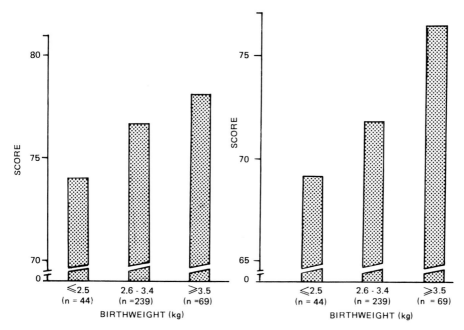

FIG. 5. Relationship between birthweight and performance in the composite infant score at 6 months of age: **(left)** mental, $r = 0.103$, N.S., $n = 352$; **(right)** motor, $r = 0.163$, $p<0.01$, $n = 352$.

persist among newborns weighing more than 2.5 kg. These associations between birthweight and psychomotor development held after controlling for measured potential confounding factors and were also observed within siblings of the same mother ($r = 0.266$, $n = 65$ pairs, $p < 0.5$) (55). Thus the findings in Mexico, Taiwan, Bogota, and Guatemala are consistent in that nutritional effects during infancy were most evident on motor performance. In Guatemala, intermediate variables of fertility and indicators of maternal morbidity were also associated with psychomotor performance of the infant.

There was an association between early malnutrition, LBW, and low psychomotor test performance up to 1 year of age in the study populations. Overall, a miscellaneous set of positive effects on psychomotor development were associated with food supplementation during pregnancy and lactation, and the information available suggests that these effects are attributable to the nutrition intervention. The finding of effects primarily on the motor subscales should not be surprising; improvement in neuromotor and sensorimotor functions characterizes development at this age and therefore would be most affected by malnutrition.

There is a lack of information on the effects of maternal malnutrition on maternal function during the first year of life. Early bodily contacts, the quality of holding, and eye-to-eye communication are important components of the quality of early physical care, and most of these components may be affected by chronic maternal malnutrition, particularly energy deprivation. Some related data suggest lower levels of exploratory activity and attachment behavior, especially distance interaction and a heightened need for physical closeness to the mother. Lower psychomotor activity, a decrement of the overall time spent in play, and an increase in the time spent sucking at the breast have also been reported. These characteristics could interfere with other motivational determinants that lead to increased exploration and social contacts (57).

In Bogota, lower levels of irritability and higher levels of visual attention at 15 days of age were reported in infants from supplemented mothers. Lower levels of apathetic behavior were also reported at 4 and 8 months of age among infants from women supplemented during pregnancy. In the Bogota and Mexican studies, increased levels of activity and demand for attention on the part of the infants from supplemented mothers were also reported. Reports from these two studies also indicated higher levels of caretaker-infant interaction in the infants from mothers supplemented during pregnancy. Increased environmental stimulation and exploratory behavior may be mechanisms by which improved nutrition could affect intellectual and behavioral development. Functional isolation may be one of the most important steps mediating the causal relationship between early malnutrition and mental development.

Effects on Cognitive Development During Preschool Age

Most of the early studies on the effects on cognitive development during the preschool years indicated a clear effect of severe malnutrition. However, they usually involved severely malnourished children recovering in the hospital and did not take into account the effects of hospitalization (58–61). Recent studies have reported similar improvements in psychological test performance in well-nourished children recovering in the hospital from other illnesses. This would suggest that at least part of the rise in developmental quotients observed in malnourished children during recovery may not be due to improved nutrition. Results of studies exploring this possibility indicate positive effects in malnourished children who underwent programs of structured psychosocial stimulation during hospitalization for recovery and later at home for at least 6 months. In Jamaica, severely malnourished children benefiting from similar programs made significant improvements in their developmental quotients in the hospital and at home and continued to do so after discharge. Six months after the intervention, they were significantly ahead of the malnourished group, who received standard hospital care only, and were no longer behind hospitalized, well-nourished children (62).

Impact of Nutritional Supplementation During the Perinatal Period on Cognitive Function 5 to 7 Years Later

A recent study (55) indicated that children supplemented during the perinatal period showed significant enhancement of most cognitive variables examined when compared with their siblings, who were supplemented after 1 year of age. The perinatal supplemented children showed better scores in IQ, attention span, visuomotor synthesis, and school grade-point average at the first year of school in reading, writing, and arithmetic. They also were significantly taller for their age than their siblings, although no significant differences were observed in birthweight. The major problem in interpreting these data is the possibility that the above-mentioned differences could result from differences in variables correlated with the study design, namely, age at testing, parity, family size, and maternal age. Other factors, such as emotional stress, social deprivation, total amount of supplementation, health care, and nutritional counseling, could have operated systematically; thus results might not be due to the timing of nutritional supplementation.

In the Bogota study, results indicated that children who were supplemented since the third trimester of pregnancy performed better than those who did not in the Griffith test of infant development and in the Cannon-Escalona scale up to 36 months of age. This association was particularly clear in motor skills in girls. It is important to note, however, that the effect on behavior seemed to be contemporaneous. The authors noted that although the intervention reduced the gap in cognitive performance between lower and upper socioeconomic classes, a disparity still remained by the end of the study at 3 years of age (63).

In the Guatemalan study, children in the high-protein-energy supplement group scored better than those in the energy supplement group in cognitive tests measuring vocabulary, motor control, memory, and visual ability at 3, 4, and 5 years of age. Results of multivariate analysis suggested that pregnancy and the first 2 years of age were critical periods for later mental development.

Data in Table 6 from the Guatemalan study indicate that the three supplement variables (supplement intake during pregnancy and lactation and supplementation of the child) were associated with cognitive performance. This association was independent and in addition to that observed for indicators of social environment. Mother's supplementation during pregnancy and lactation was significantly associated with cognitive test performance in males and females up to 5 and 4 years of age, respectively. Child's supplementation was associated with cognitive scores in males and females up to 6 and 7 years of age, respectively. Additional analysis indicated that supplement intake plus head circumference and height of the child statistically explained about 10% of the variance in cognitive composite scores at all study ages. These data, albeit limited, provide support for the causal nature of the association between early nutrition and cognition at preschool age. The data also indicate that both factors (maternal and early child nutrition) were important in contributing to the child's cognitive competence (64).

Long-Term Effects on Mental Development

Does early malnutrition cause low cognitive test performance at school age? Different sets of data collected during the 1970s have helped to better understand this complex question. Birthweight has been found to correlate with subsequent cognitive function, particularly when large samples are studied. This relationship may not be linear, however, the impact of birthweight on IQ being clearer in infants with very LBW (below 1,500 g) (54,65).

Studies that have attempted to isolate early malnutrition from social environmental factors include prospective studies of middle class children who suffered early postnatal malnutrition because of specific medical conditions (66–68), retrospective studies of poor children with severe early malnutrition raised later in favorable social environments (59,69–71), and retrospective studies of army recruits

TABLE 6. *Correlations between supplementary intake and cognitive composite score[a]*

Supplementary intake	Cognitive composite score									
	Age (years)									
	Males					Females				
	3	4	5	6	7	3	4	5	6	7
During pregnancy	0.14[c]	0.14[c]	0.11[b]	0.04	0.04	0.12[b]	0.09	0.02	0.01	0.05
During lactation	0.09	0.12[c]	0.03	0.01	0.01	0.12[b]	0.12[b]	0.08	0.02	0.09
Of the child	0.11[b]	0.19[c]	0.13[c]	0.15[c]	0.08	0.10[b]	0.10[b]	0.07	0.03	0.11[b]

[a]Adapted from Freeman et al. (64).
[b]$p < 0.05$.
[c]$p < 0.01$.

who experienced war-related famine as infants and were subsequently reared in middle class homes (72). All suggest that access to various social support systems could play an important role in compensating for low psychological test performance in children with early severe malnutrition.

Several reports indicate that children who suffered malnutrition during the first 6 months of age could gain considerable compensation in personal strength from their social surroundings. Most of the deficit in psychological test performance observed in children with early malnutrition during the first 5 years of life was no longer detectable in children from 6 to 12 years of age (66–68,73). Functioning in school and at home did not reveal higher difficulties in previously malnourished children when compared to controls, despite the fact that malnourished subjects showed early developmental retardation. Furthermore, no association has been reported between supplementation of school children and school achievement in developed countries (74).

In the Dutch study (9), psychological test performance was not associated with exposure to famine during pregnancy. There was a small excess of central nervous system defects in 19-year-old males born to mothers exposed to famine early in pregnancy but not in those born to mothers exposed to famine during the latter part of pregnancy. Although there the possibility exists that unmeasured mental functions were affected by exposure to famine, a more likely explanation is that the effect of prenatal nutritional deprivation was compensated by the favorable social stimulation conditions of postnatal life.

Few data are available concerning the implications for future competence in psychological test performance during the first 5 to 7 years of life in chronic malnourished populations. Data from the Guatemalan study reveal that performance in preschool tests is associated with how intelligent the children seemed to be to village adults and how they will eventually perform in primary school (75).

Data in Table 7 from the Guatemalan study present the results of multiple regression analysis computed for each of the 11 psychological tests composing the 7-year test battery. The independent variables in the regression model were sex, head circumference, and height at 7 years of age as indicators of nutritional status, as well as the quality of the house and maternal characteristics as indicators of family socioeconomic status. The maternal characteristics included indicators of vocabulary, modernity and school experience. In 7 of the 11 regressions, psychological test performance was predicted by the model at a statistically significant level ($p < 0.05$). In 5 of these 7 tests, the child's height and/or head circumference were related to psychological test performance at 7 years of age, after controlling for the family socioeconomic indicators. These results were observed in the fully longitudinal sample, followed from conception to 7 years of age. The amount of variance statistically explained by nutritional and socioeconomic indicators ranged between 3 and 11%, and their effect was about one-third to one-half of a standard deviation. The tests significantly associated to these factors are extremely varied and include measurements of verbal ability, memory, perceptual analytic capacity, and motor control.

TABLE 7. *Relationship between 7-year psychological test performance and preschool nutritional and family socioeconomic status*

Dependent variable[a]	Independent variables		p	r^2
	Nutritional status[b]	Family socioeconomic status[d]		
Vocabulary naming	× [c]	×	0.0001	0.11
Verbal influences	×	×	0.0001	0.08
Digit memory	—	×	0.0562	0.03
Embedded figures	×	×	0.0069	0.05
Incomplete figures	—	×	0.0034	0.08
Block designs	×	—	0.0001	0.11
Draw-a-line slowly	×	—	0.0005	0.07

[a]Predicted variable. Tests with no significant association: discrimination learning, conservation of matter, conservation of area, and conservation of quantity.
[b]As measured by head circumference and height at 7 years of age.
[c]×, $p < 0.05$ for the partial F of corresponding independent variable.
[d]As measured by quality of the house and maternal characteristics.

Data in Table 8 from the same study present the results of multiple regression analysis predicting intellectual ability at school age. The independent variables were child's age at the time of testing and sex, as well as preschool age nutritional status, socioeconomic status, and intellectual ability. These variables were entered in the order described, followed by the score measuring school performance. Nutritional indicators at 7 years of age were not associated with psychological test performance, and socioeconomic indicators at 7 years of age were consistently associated with school age cognitive test performance. In other words, in these rural villages, children with better cognitive test performance at school age were those who attended school for longer periods of time, performed better in school, came from higher socioeconomic strata, had higher psychological test performance at 7 years of age, but did not have better nutritional status at age 7. This was surprising given the general poverty and the high prevalence of chronic malnutrition and poor health conditions in these villages. In addition, no relationship was found between preschool nutritional status and school performance. The conclusion from this carefully controlled study was that if nutrition and growth play a role, it is through their relationship with the intellectual ability up to 7 years of age. Another important finding was the strong association between school performance and psychological test performance throughout a variety of psychological tests.

In summary, from this array of different study designs and populations, the available evidence suggests that children stunted because of early PEM show various indications of suboptimal mental development up to 7 years of age produced by the interaction between malnutrition and inadequate social environment, an interaction that entails deep implications for public health interventions. Psychological

TABLE 8. *Relationship between school age cognitive test performance, preschool intellectual ability, nutritional and family socioeconomic status, and school experience*

Dependent variables	Independent variables					
School age cognitive test[a]	Preschool intellectual ability[b]	Preschool nutritional status[d]	Preschool family socioeconomic status[e]	School performance[f]	p	r^2
Syllogism						
Verbal rationale	$\times$ [c]		$\times$	$\times$	0.0001	0.28
Correct responses	$\times$		$\times$	$\times$	0.0001	0.33
Verbal Inferences	$\times$	$\times$	$\times$	$\times$	0.0001	0.44
Vocabulary naming	$\times$		$\times$	$\times$	0.0001	0.50
Digit memory	$\times$		$\times$	$\times$	0.0001	0.48
Block design	$\times$		$\times$		0.0001	0.24
Matrix test	$\times$				0.0001	0.29
Embedded figures	$\times$		$\times$	$\times$	0.0001	0.17

[a]Predicted variable measured at ages 9–15. Tests with no significant association: conservation of volume, conservation of weight, and discrimination learning.
[b]As measured by composite score of psychological test performance at 7 years of age.
[c]$\times$, $p < 0.05$ for the partial F of corresponding independent variable.
[d]As measured by head circumference and height at 7 years of age.
[e]As measured by quality of the house and maternal characteristics when the child was 7 years of age.
[f]As measured by composite score based on school performance at ages 9–15.

test performance at 7 years of age in turn is associated with intellectual performance and school performance up to 15 years of age. Thus the improved scores in psychological tests observed in preschool children with better nutrition up to 7 years of age may be associated with improved competence for the tasks of adult life. In contrast, a history of early malnutrition usually associated with unfavorable social environment and poor schooling will probably result in poor competence for adult tasks.

SUMMARY AND CONCLUSIONS

This chapter discusses the relationship between early malnutrition and survival, physical growth, and mental development, as well as the implications for action programs. Early malnutrition refers to PEM during intrauterine, breastfeeding, weaning, and postweaning periods up to 5 years of age. The main conclusions are as follows.

Children with early malnutrition have a higher probability of long-term physical growth retardation, suboptimal mental development, and early mortality than well-nourished children. Malnutrition results in physical growth retardation, which in turn is associated with a higher risk of mortality and low psychological test performance. To a large extent, the associations with growth retardation and mortality are due to complex interactions between early malnutrition and infection, while those involving mental development result from the interaction between malnutrition and inadequate social environment. These effects are greater when malnutrition began earlier, lasted longer, and was more severe, and when social neglect and environmental deprivation continued to prevail. They appear to be of a long-term nature and are indicative of a continuing deleterious process that may be modified by improving nutrition, environmental sanitation, health care, and social environment.

In populations with PEM, either acute or chronic, appropriate food supplementation of pregnant and lactating mothers and of their weaning children decreased the incidence of intrauterine and postnatal growth retardation in weight, height, and head circumference. The effect on growth was greater in populations with severe malnutrition and in those where the intervention was applied earlier, during pregnancy and lactation, and continued in the weaned children. However, improvements in postnatal growth rates were not proportional to the increments in total nutrient intake produced by food supplementation, probably because of the high prevalence of diarrhea.

Food supplementation programs, integrated with primary health care services, improved indicators of mental development and the probability of survival of the offspring. Primary health care programs carried out by auxiliary personnel contributed to reduce infant and child mortality and to decrease the duration of common child diseases, including severe malnutrition. Cost-effectiveness estimations for these integrated interventions are lower the earlier in life the intervention is implemented. Furthermore, access to appropriate school and social support systems in part compensates for long-term deficits in intellectual development of children with early malnutrition.

In summary, the distribution of physical growth retardation and mortality in children under 5 years of age is associated with food availability at country and social stratum level. Planned changes in dietary intake of pregnant and lactating women and their children, integrated with primary health care services, were followed by improvement in growth rates, mortality, and psychological test performance up to school age. There was a clear time sequence between the dietary modification and the observed improvement in growth rate and functional outcomes. These associations were consistent across different populations and study designs. There was a defined dose-response relationship between additional intake and pre- and postnatal growth. Causal mechanisms for these associations between malnutrition and growth retardation and low psychological test performance have been identified. They include not only metabolic processes related to nutrition and growth but also complex interactions of nutrition with infection and inadequate social environment. Finally, there is no evidence for noncausal explanations of these associations. Thus stunting and suboptimal mental development may represent part of the price to be paid for adaptation and survival when dietary intake is chronically restricted through generations. This adaptative capacity of the reproductive process should not serve as an excuse for inaction.

Food supplementation alone may not be the most effective way to deal with these complex interactions between malnutrition, infection, and inadequate social environment. Improvements in nutrition usually follow positive changes in education, purchasing power, health care services, food availability at the family level, and environmental sanitation. Isolated vertical programs exclusively aimed at distributing food may have little impact on growth and functional outcomes. A greater impact is expected from integrated nutritional programs, including: (a) immunizations, environmental sanitation, and oral rehydration for diarrhea; (b) effective promotion of breastfeeding and appropriate weaning practices; (c) nutrition and health promotion, including monitoring of physical growth to decrease home diet replacement and improve food utilization and intrafamily food distribution; (d) development of adequate social environment and improved schooling programs; and (e) improvement of self-sufficiency in food availability at the family level.

Investments in these integrated nutritional programs would alleviate the heavy burden on development programs incurred by malnutrition and would produce economic returns important enough to stimulate social and economic development.

In these integrated nutritional programs, the nutrient content of the food supplements should be tailored to provide the most limiting nutrients in the home diet. When information on the main limiting nutrients is missing, the mean protein/energy ratio of the supplements should be close to 11%. Food supplementation programs should also be designed to meet the desired and self-perceived needs of the target group by involving participants and program workers in program planning, implementation, and evaluation.

No evidence has been detected of harmful effects of protein-energy supplementation provided through regular foods within the recommended dietary allowances. However, economic and social dependency on the program, inhibition of breastfeeding, stimulation of early and inappropriate weaning, inhibition of self-sufficiency on the part of the population being served, adverse changes in eating habits, and inhibition of the local food industry may counteract program impacts, particularly in long-term operations. For these reasons, food supplementation programs should be implemented as short-term interventions to deal mostly with acute, urgent components of the nutritional problem. They should be gradually replaced by community development interventions aimed at increasing self-sufficiency in food availability at the family level.

REFERENCES

1. Mora JO, de Paredes B, Wagner M, et al. Nutritional supplementation and the outcome of pregnancy. I. Birthweight. Am J Clin Nutr 1979;32:459–62.
2. Lechtig A, Delgado H, Martorell R, Yarbrough C, Klein RE. Materno-fetal nutrition. In: Roslyn B, Alfin-Slater D, and Kritchervsky D, eds. Human nutrition. A comprehensive treatise. New York: Plenum, 1979:79–127. (Jelliffe DB and Jelliffe EFP, eds. Nutrition and growth; Vol. 2).
3. Iyengar L. Proceedings of the 9th international congress of nutrition, Mexico, 1972. Basel: Karger, 1975;2:53–58.
4. Chavez A, Martinez C. The effect of maternal supplementation on infant development. In: Lechtig A, ed. Effects of maternal nutrition on infant health: implications for action. Arch Latinoam Nutr 1979;29(4)(suppl 1):143–153.
5. Rush D. Nutritional services during pregnancy and birthweight: a retrospective matched pair analysis. J Can Med Assoc 1984 (in press).
6. Rush D, Stein Z, Susser MA. Controlled trial of prenatal nutrition. Supplementation defended. Pediatrics 1980;66:656–8.

7. Blackwell RQ, Chow BF, Chinn KS. Prospective maternal nutrition study in Taiwan: rationale, study design, feasibility and preliminary findings. Nutr Rep Int. 1973;7:517–32.

8. Herrat RM, Hsueh AM, Icheson RA. Influence of maternal diet on offspring: growth, behaviour, feed efficiency, and susceptibility (human). Final report on contract AID/CSD 2944, 1979. Washington DC: Agency of international development.

9. Stein Z, Susser M, Saenger G, Marolla F. Famine and human development: the Dutch hunger winter of 1944/45. New York: Oxford University Press, 1975.

10. World Development Report. Washington DC: The World Bank, 1982.

11. Lechtig A, Klein RE. Guia para interpretar la ganancia de peso durante el embarazo como indicador de riesgo de bajo peso al nacer. Bol San Pan 1980;89(6):489–95.

12. Lechtig A, Irwin M, Klein RE. Societal implications of early protein-energy malnutrition. Prevention in childhood of specific adult health problems. Section 2, chapter III. Undernutrition. Geneva, Switzerland: WHO, 1980:43–51.

13. Lechtig A, Klein RE. Pre-natal nutrition and birthweight: is there a causal association? In: Dobbing J, ed. Maternal nutrition in pregnancy: eating for two? London: Academic Press. 1981;131–156.

14. Lechtig A, Delgado H, Lasky RE, et al. Maternal nutrition and fetal growth in developing societies—socio-economic factors. Am J Dis Child 1975:129:434–7.

15. Lechtig A, Yarbrough C, Delgado H, Martorell R, Klein RE, Behar M. Effect of moderate maternal malnutrition on the placenta. Am J Obstet Gynecol 1975;123:191–201.

16. Lechtig A, Yarbrough C, Delgado H, Habicht J-P, Martorell R, Klein RE. Influence of maternal nutrition on birthweight. Am J Clin Nutr 1975;28:1223–33.

17. FAO/WHO. Energy and protein requirements. Report of a joint FAO/WHO Ad Hoc expert group. Geneva, Switzerland: WHO. WHO technical report series no. 522, 1973.

18. Sukhatme PV, Margen S. Autoregulatory homeostatic nature of energy balance. Am J Clin Nutr 1982;35:355–65.

19. Lechtig A, Martorell R, Delgado H, Yarbrough C, Klein RE. Food supplementation during pregnancy, maternal anthropometry and birthweight in a Guatemalan rural population. J Trop Pediatr Env Child Health 1978;24:217–22.

20. Lechtig A, Habicht J-P, Delgado H, Klein RE, Yarbrough C, Martorell R. Effect of food supplementation during pregnancy on birthweight. Pediatrics 1975;56:508–20.

21. Frisancho AR, Klayman JE, Matos J. Influence of maternal nutritional status on pre-natal growth in a Peruvian urban population. Am J Phys Anthrop 1977;46:265–74.

22. Vaquera M, Townsend J, Arroyo JJ, Lechtig A. The relationship between arm circumference at birth and early mortality. J Trop Pediatr 1983;29:167–174.

23. Cruise MO. A longitudinal study of the growth of low birthweight infants. Pediatrics 1973;51:620–8.

24. Holmes GE, Miller HC, Hassanein K, Lasky SB, Goggin JE. Post-natal somatic growth in infants with atypical fetal growth patterns. Am J Dis Child 1977;131:1078–83.

25. Davies DP, Platts P, Pritchard JM, Wilkinson PW. Nutritional status of light-for-date infants at birth and its influence on early post-natal growth. Arch Dis Child 1979;54:703–6.

26. Grantham-McGregor SM, Desai P, Buchanan E. The identification of infants at risk of malnutrition in Kingston, Jamaica Trop Geogr Med 1977;29:165–171.

27. Urrusti-Sanz J, Yoshida Ando P, Frenk S, et al. Crescimiento post-natal del nino con desnutricion intrauterina. Arch Invest Med (Mex) 1978;9(2):439–46.

28. Alvarez ML, Alvear J, Cousino L, Saitua MT. Influencia del medio en la desnutricion infantil. Arch Latinoam Nutr 1980;30:254–63.

29. Martorell R, Lechtig A, Yarbrough C, Delgado H, Klein RE. Energy intake and growth in an energy deficient population. Ecol Food Nutr 1978;7:147–154.

30. Martorell R, Yarbrough C, Lechtig A, Habicht J-P, Klein RE. Diarrhoeal diseases and growth retardation in preschool Guatemalan children. Am J Phys Anthrop 1975;43:341–6.

31. Lechtig A, Habicht J-P, Guzman G. Morbilidad materna y crecimiento fetal en poblaciones rurales de Guatemala. Arch Latinoam Nutr 1972;22:255.

32. Mata LJ, Kromal RA, Urrutia JJ, Garcia B. Effects of infection on food intake and the nutritional state: perspectives as viewed from the village. Am J Clin Nutr 1977;30:125.

33. Martorell R, Yarbrough C, Yarbrough S, Klein RE. The impact of ordinary illnesses on the dietary intakes of malnourished children. Am J Clin Nutr 1980;33:345–50.

34. Beisel WR, Sawyer WD, Ryll ED, Crozier D. Metabolic effects of intracellular infections in man. Ann Int Med 1967;67:744.

35. Briscoe J. The quantitative effect of infection on the use of food by young children in poor countries. Am J Clin Nutr 1979;32:648.
36. Ashcroft MT, Desai P. Ethnic differences in growth potential of children of African, Indian, Chinese and European origin. Trans R Soc Trop Med Hyg 1977;70:433–8.
37. Nadamuni NA, Swaminathan MC, Narasinga BS. Effect of nutritional deprivation in early childhood on later growth: a community study without intervention. Am J Clin Nutr 1981;34:1636–7.
38. Satyanarayana K, Nadamuni NA. Nutrition and menarche in rural Hyderabad. Ann Hum Biol 1979;6:163–5.
39. Satyanarayana K, Nadamuni NA, Narasinga Rao BS. Adolescent growth spurt among rural Indian boys in relation to their nutritional status in early childhood. Ann Hum Biol 1980;7:359–66.
40. Kulin EM, Bwibo N, Mutie D, Santner SJ. The effect of chronic childhood malnutrition on pubertal growth and development. Am J Clin Nutr 1982;36:527–36.
41. Martorell R, Yarbrough C, Lechtig A, Delgado H, Klein RE. Genetic-environmental interactions in physical growth. Acta Paediatr Scand 1977;66:579–84.
42. Lechtig A, Delgado H, Yarbrough C, Habicht J-P, Martorell R, Klein RE. Simple assessment of the risk of low birthweight to select women for nutritional intervention. Am J Obstet Gynecol 1976;125:25–34.
43. Gopalan C, Swaminathan MC, Kumari VKK, Rao DH, Vijayaraghavan K. Effect of calorie supplementation on growth of undernourished children. Am J Clin Nutr 1973;28:281–6.
44. Lechtig A, Rosso P, Delgado H, et al. Effects of moderate maternal nutrition on the levels of alkaline ribonuclease activity in the human placenta. Ecol Food Nutr 1977;6(2):83–90.
45. Lechtig A, Klein RE. Maternal food supplementation and infant health: Results of a study in rural areas of Guatemala. In: Aebi H and Whitehead R, eds. Maternal nutrition during pregnancy and lactation. Bern; Switzerland, Nestlé foundation publication series no. 1, 1980;285–313.
46. Martorell R, Yarbrough C, Lechtig A, Delgado H, Klein RE. Upper arm indicators of nutritional status. Am J Clin Nutr 1976;29:46–53.
47. Gomez F, Ramon-Galvan R, Cravioto J, Frank S. Malnutrition and kwashiorkor. J Paediatr 1954;43(suppl 100):336.
48. Puffer RR, Serrano CV. Characteristicas de la mortalidad en la ninez. Washington DC: PAHO scientific publications no. 262, 1973.
49. Kielman AA, Taylor CB, Parker AL. The Narangwal nutrition study. A summary review. Am J Clin Nutr 1978;31:2040–57.
50. Lechtig A, Ibarra A, Gupta M, Klein RE. Indicadores de riesgo de morir durante el primer ano de vida en areas rurales de Guatemala. Arch Latinoam Nutr 1980;30(4):677–81.
51. Waterlow JC. Childhood malnutrition, the global problem. Symposium on protein-energy malnutrition. Proc Nutr Soc 1979;38:1–9.
52. Gwatkin RD, Wilcos JR, Wray JD. Can health and nutrition interventions make a difference? Washington DC: Overseas Development Council, monograph no. 13, 1980.
53. Lechtig A, Townsend JW, Pineda F, Arroyo JJ, Klein RE, de Leon R. SINAPS: The Guatemalan program of primary health care. In: Jelliffe DB, ed. Advances in international maternal and child health. New York. Oxford University Press, 1983:146–73.
54. Drillien CM, Thomson AJM, Burgoyne K. Low birthweight children at early school age: A longitudinal study. Dev Med Child Neurol 1980;22:26–47.
55. Hicks LE, Langhan RA, Takenaka J. Cognitive and health measures following early nutritional supplementation: a sibling study. Am J Public Health 1982;72:1110–8.
56. Lasky RE, Lechtig A, Delgado H, et al. Birthweight and psychomotor performance in rural Guatemala. Am J Dis Child 1975;129:566–70.
57. Graves PL. Nutrition and infant behaviour. A replication study in the Katmandu valley, Nepal. Am J Clin Nutr 1978;31(3):542–51.
58. Cravioto J, DeLicardie ER, Birch HG. Nutrition, growth and neurointegrative development: an experimental and ecologic study. Pediatrics 1966;38:319–72.
59. Hertzig MF, Birch HG, Richardson SA, Tizard J. Intellectual levels of school children severely malnourished during the first two years of life. Pediatrics 1972;49:814–24.
60. Monckeberg F. Effects of early marasmic malnutrition on subsequent physical and psychological development. In: Scrimshaw NS, Gordon JE, eds. Malnutrition, learning and behaviour. Cambridge, Massachusetts: MIT Press, 1968;278–89.
61. Stoch MB, Smythe PM. Undernutrition during infancy and subsequent brain growth in intellectual

development. In: Scrimshaw NS, Gordon JE, eds. Malnutrition, learning and behaviour. Cambridge, Massachusetts: MIT Press, 1968:278–289.

62. Grantham-McGregor S, Steward NE, Scofield WN. Effect of long term psychological stimulation on mental development of severely malnourished children. Lancet 1980;2:785–9.

63. Water RP, Vuori-Christiansen L, Ortiz N, et al. Nutritional supplementation, maternal education and cognitive development of infants at risk of malnutrition. Am J Clin Nutr 1981;34:807–13.

64. Freeman HE, Klein RE, Townsend J, Lechtig A. Nutrition and cognitive development among rural Guatemalan children. Am J Public Health 1980;70:1277–85.

65. Lipper E, Leek, Caartber LM, et al. Determinants of neurobehavioural outcome in low birthweight infants. Pediatrics 1981;67:502–80.

66. Beardslee WR, Wolff PH, Hurwitz I, Parikh B, Shwachman H. The effects of infantile malnutrition on behavioural development: a follow-up study. Am J Clin Nutr 1982;35:1437–41.

67. Valman HB. Intelligence after malnutrition caused by neonatal resection of ileum. Lancet 1974;1:425–7.

68. Lloyd-Still JD, Hurwitz I, Wolff PH, Shwachman H. Intellectual development after severe malnutrition in infancy. Pediatrics 1974;54:306–11.

69. Richardson SA, Birch HG, Ragheer C. School performance of children who were severely malnourished in infancy. Am J Ment Defic 1973;77:623–32.

70. Richardson SA, Birch HG, Ragheer C. The behaviour of children at home who were severely malnourished in the first two years of life. J Biosoc Sci 1975;7:255–67.

71. Richardson SA. The reaction of severe malnutrition in infancy to the intelligence of school children with differing life stories. Pediatr Res 1976;10:57–61.

72. Stein Z, Susser M, Saenger G, Marolla F. Nutrition and mental performance. Science 1974;178:708–13.

73. Lloyd-Still JD. Clinical studies on the effects of malnutrition during infancy and subsequent physical and intellectual development. In: Lloyd-Still JD, ed. Malnutrition and intellectual development. Littleton, Massachusetts: Publishing Sciences Group, 1976.

74. Gietzen D, Veermeersch JA. Health status and school achievement of children from Head Start and Free School Lunch programs. Public health report, 1980;95:362–8.

75. Nerlove SB, Roberts JM, Klein RE, Yarbrough C, Habicht J-P. Natural indicators of cognitive development: an observational study of rural Guatemalan children. Ethos 1974;2:265–95.

DISCUSSION

Dr. Briend: It does not seem possible to derive from your data the conclusion that food supplementation during pregnancy results in a lower rate of LBW babies. One would have to know the birthweight rate before intervention, and this is not available. The correlation that was observed between maternal food supplementation during pregnancy and birthweight is fairly low and explains only 1% of the variance of birthweight. The fetus and the placenta themselves are oxygen consumers; they may consume as much as 8 or 10% of maternal oxygen. One may assume, therefore, that women who are giving birth to babies with a higher birthweight are bound to consume more food. Since the amount of food consumed by women is determined by self-selection, there could be a bias in this study. Women who took more food during pregnancy had babies with higher birthweights, but a causal relationship could not be derived from this observation. This kind of correlation between maternal food intake and birthweight was observed in many other circumstances, first by Thompson in 1959. He derived no cause-effect relationship from this observation. We should be as cautious as he was.

Dr. Lechtig: As mentioned before, the magnitude of this effect is low when expressed in terms of the proportion of the birthweight variance statistically explained by ingestion of food supplements: 1 to 2%, depending on the groups analyzed. On the other hand, when this effect is estimated in terms of proportion of LBW babies, the results are impressive. In the Guatemalan study, the proportion of LBW babies decreased from 33% in a small sample at the beginning of the study in 1969 to 13% at the end of the intervention in 1977. The proportion of LBW babies decreased from 19% in the low supplementation group to 10% in the group with high supplementation. Thompson's data were based on measurements of home diet, while the Guatemalan study was based on direct recording of daily supplement intake throughout pregnancy.

The problem with self-selection in the design of the Guatemalan study was pointed out more than a decade ago (Lechtig A, Arroyave G, Habicht JP, Béhar M. Nutricion materna y crecimiento fetal. Arch Latinoam Nutr 1971;21:505), but it was not possible to change the design. Because of this "inborn" design problem, the analytical approach indicated for longitudinal quasiexperimental cohort studies was carried out as follows: (a) reliability and validity of the two main variables (daily supplement intake during pregnancy and birthweight) proved to be very high: about 0.99; (b) extensive statistical analysis failed to identify maternal characteristics that could "confound" the relationship observed between food supplement ingestion and birthweight; (c) since the relationship was also observed within pairs of consecutive siblings of the same mother, we discounted the possibility that maternal factors constant to the mother (e.g., maternal height) could be responsible for the observed association; (d) obviously, there still remained the possibility of confounding factors not related to the mother but to each pregnancy within the same mother. Of those factors that could change from one pregnancy to the other, several were measured: parity; changes in home diet; diseases, including diarrhea; changes in socioeconomic status; and indicators of subclinical intrauterine infection. None of these variables was shown to be responsible for the observed association between food supplementation and birthweight. Moreover, anthropological and time-activity surveys showed no evidence of significant changes in patterns of physical activity of the study mothers. Thus we concluded that, because of the observed replication of similar findings across different types of analysis, the most suitable interpretation of this association was one of a cause-effect relationship between food supplementation and birthweight.

In well populations, where food availability is not a problem, regulators of fetal growth may influence maternal intake; therefore, the size of the baby may be the cause and not the effect. The reverse is expected to occur in poor populations where nutrient availability limits dietary intake and socioeconomic factors regulate nutrient availability. As observed in many poor populations, socioeconomic characteristics not directly caused by fetal growth are the main limiting factors of nutrient availability and, in turn, the main determinants of nutrient intake. The observation that in malnourished populations food supplementation during pregnancy is associated with higher birthweight contributes additional support to this cause-effect hypothesis. Thus dietary intake may operate as both cause and effect of fetal growth, depending on the nutritional characteristics of the population studied. In poor populations, such as those of Northeast Brazil, intense physical work increases energy expenditure but not dietary intake; therefore it will decrease fetal growth more than expected from the low dietary intake alone. A high incidence of diarrhea usually increases energy expenditure and decreases dietary intake. This double action decreases fetal growth further than expected from "usual" intake alone. Thus these two variables, intense physical work and high incidence of diarrhea, contribute to a greater magnitude of the apparent relationship between low dietary intake and high incidence of LBW babies. It is clear that in these two examples, neither physical work nor incidence of diarrhea are acting as effects but as important contributing causes of fetal growth retardation in addition to low dietary intake per se.

If we provide food supplements alone to such a population without decreasing physical activity and incidence of diarrhea, the effect on birthweight, important as it may be, would not fill the gap observed between poor and well-nourished populations. This does not mean that it is not important to improve dietary intake in malnourished populations, but that other factors limit fetal growth in these populations, in addition to dietary intake.

One must be careful in reviewing some data. Dr. Lechtig mentioned that the experiment in India had a high effectiveness, attributable to the low food intake of these women before supplementation. As far as I know, however, this effect was measured by comparing birthweights among mothers admitted to the hospital a few weeks before delivery to receive the food supplement and among outpatients. In one of the first studies carried out on birthweight and published in Paris in 1898, it was shown that admitting a woman to a hospital a few weeks before delivery, without any other intervention, was enough to observe a birthweight 200 g heavier than among outpatients. I am reluctant to ascribe the effects observed in the quoted study in India to the nutritional intervention by itself and suggest that maternal rest may have played a role.

The dose-response relationship in the Indian study was notably higher than that observed in Guatemala or Colombia (71 versus 41 g/10,000 kcal). This increased impact suggests an effect of resting on birthweight in addition to the effect of improved dietary energy intake. The effect of resting would be equivalent to saving about 125 kcal/day. In other words, in this specific case, the effect contributed by resting to birthweight (in addition to the effect of dietary improvement) could be explained by the amount of energy saved. Of course, this inference does not discount other mechanisms of action.

Dr. Mata: Birthweight as an indicator of fetal growth is a variable that exhibits secular changes. This has been obvious in the Japanese population, where there has been a tremendous increase in mean birthweight and a marked increase in the incidence of LBW over the last three decades. In Costa Rica, a country where we have been able to obtain reliable data over a long period of time, we also can compare changes. Considering the frequency of birthweight distribution, which is the most obvious way to measure changes over time, and the data of 1970 and 1975 for Costa Rica, we find a bell-shaped distribution. This is different from that of Guatemala, where the distribution is skewed to the left, denoting the common fetal growth retardation. The only way to deal with Dr. Lechtig's design would be to compare two villages that have supplements with two other villages that do not have supplements and present the results graphically. With a large number of babies, it is possible to see several LBWs at the beginning and at end of the period.

Dr. Lechtig: As we have mentioned repeatedly, the demonstration in the Guatemalan study of an effect of dietary intake on birthweight does not mean that other maternal and environmental factors are not important. In poor populations of developing countries, a high prevalence of LBW babies is the outcome of stunted and wasted mothers because of malnutrition through generations, current low dietary intake, short birth intervals, frequent episodes of diarrhea, bacteriuria, malaria, and hard physical work during pregnancy. Thus dietary improvement plus interventions focused on malaria in Africa, or plus oral rehydration, diarrhea prevention, and birth spacing in Bangladesh, or plus actions aimed at decreasing physical work in the hilly slums of Rio de Janeiro will have a stronger effect than food supplementation in the Harlem population in New York City, for example, where dietary intake and anthropometry do not suggest a high prevalence of malnutrition. A far more effective intervention in this population to decrease prevalence of LBW babies would be one focused on birth spacing, cigarette smoking, and drug control. Obviously, effectiveness of these interventions will vary across populations, depending on epidemiological and nutritional profiles as well as their economic and social feasibility.

Secular trends in fetal growth usually are associated with improved socioeconomic status, dietary intake, sanitation, hygiene, and maternal education, as well as with decreased incidence of diarrhea, short birth interval, and physical activity during pregnancy. However, developing countries require faster and less expensive ways to solve their problems. Today, there are many more babies with LBW than 20 years ago. Thus the issue, from a public health point of view, is not whether secular trends exist but what are their main causal mechanisms. Further knowledge of these mechanisms may help to improve new interventions aimed at avoiding fetal growth retardation in developing countries.

Dr. Barness: Please explain the adverse effects of supplementation.

Dr. Lechtig: The New York study reported an excess of premature babies and of neonatal deaths in the group with high-protein supplementation (estimated protein/energy ratio: 34%). This finding, observed particularly in the group of women with prior LBW infants, led the authors to conclude that high-protein supplements could be toxic for those women. I do not see any nutritional reason to provide protein in such high concentration to this population. I cannot see why protein could be toxic for adult women or for mothers with a prior LBW baby.

Before arriving at such a conclusion, one must discard other alternatives that require careful consideration: the presence of contaminants (toxic agents per se) in the canned beverages provided as food supplements, differential use of available health services by these mothers, and changes in home intake due to high-protein supplementation, among several other alternatives. As far as I know, the authors have not published any data on these possibilities.

Dr. Whitehead: I have commented on our experience with a maternal supplementation program in the Gambia and its effect on birthweight. It is relevant to make a more general comment about other changes that have occurred in the village of Keneba in the Gambia. Twenty years ago, Sir Ian McGregor showed that in that village, 50% of children died before the age of 5 years. Furthermore, by 2 years, two-thirds of surviving children would be judged undernourished by international standards. Initially, our program involved the introduction of medical service provided by a doctor and a nurse. This resulted in a profound improvement in mortality rates, but morbidity rates and growth patterns were virtually unaffected. We then introduced a baby supplementation program. Although this did result in a somewhat improved growth rate, the differences were only marginal when considered in relation to the magnitude of our input. We did not begin to see any dramatic improvement in the growth rates of babies during the first 12 months of life until we introduced the maternal supplementation program during pregnancy. Exactly why our children are on the average 750 g larger by 1 year is not clear. Perhaps the greater weight at birth creates a better start in life for the children. We are currently looking at morbidity patterns to see whether or not there is any evidence that the children are now less ill during infancy than they used to be. Nevertheless, it seems that increased maternal dietary intake during pregnancy is a cost-effective way of subsequently improving the health of babies.

Dr. Lechtig: I agree that the evidence of the effect of maternal dietary intake on fetal growth is clearer in famine situations, such as Leningrad or Holland, than in populations with chronic moderate malnutrition. At first glance, the distinction between acute and chronic malnutrition appears obvious. In the two extreme situations, there are clear differences in onset (abrupt versus gradual), duration (short versus long), and severity (severe versus moderate). The limit becomes less clear when they are analyzed closely. The current world economic recession is slowly producing decreased dietary intake in many poor areas of the world. In Brazil, for example, the rate of LBW babies has increased in São Paulo and the northeast during 1982–1983, compared with 1978–1979. Does the 5-year drought of northeast Brazil result in a long episode of acute malnutrition or the gradual deterioration of a previously chronically malnourished population? How could we classify the lactating mothers of Guatemala who lose an average of 369 g of weight per month compared to their prepregnancy weight? The results of our energy expenditure studies in this population indicate that they were "compensating" for the greater energy expenditure through weight loss more than through higher energy intake.

Is seasonal variation an acute episode of malnutrition or a chronic situation of intermittent cycles of food deprivation? Each episode of diarrhea during pregnancy could also be considered acute malnutrition. However, we describe the whole picture as endemic diarrhea associated with chronic moderate malnutrition.

The problem for most poor populations in developing countries may be related to thresholds. Whenever dietary intake during pregnancy is below the threshold required to support fetal growth, there will be an effect on birthweight. These thresholds probably vary across and within populations. They may represent points of "dynamic" equilibrium influenced by nutrient expenditure, maternal nutrient reserves, and time for adaptation, among other variables. In the famines of Holland and Leningrad, where most mothers were previously well nourished, this threshold could be located around 1,500 kcal/day. In many poor populations of developing countries, this threshold oscillates around higher levels: about 1,800 kcal/day. This difference could be explained by the smaller maternal nutrient reserves in these populations. Thus the conclusions from this hypothesis are as follows: (a) in malnourished populations, appropriate nutritional programs during pregnancy can decrease the incidence of LBW babies; (b) this effect will be greater the lower the level of nutrition in that population (acute, severe) and the higher the magnitude of the nutritional treatment; and (c) in poor populations, there are other important factors of fetal growth retardation (e.g., diarrhea, intense physical work, bacteriuria, smoking) which should be controlled through specific interventions.

Dr. Whitehead: It is unlikely that one could ever force, or indeed persuade, people to eat something they do not like or do not see the need for. Our understanding was based on a biscuit of high caloric and nutrient density produced for us by the village baker using local techniques. We claim that it is because we introduced such a biscuit as a snack food that the consumption of traditional foods was so little reduced despite the supplement. Interestingly, in parallel studies carried out in Cambridge, there too we found that women increased their food intake during pregnancy and lactation largely by consuming energy dense foods, such as cake and biscuits.

Dr. Lechtig: In the Guatemalan study, we provided two beverages of different caloric density: Atole (0.9 kcal/ml) and Fresco (0.3 kcal/ml). The two supplements were freely available for each village, and attendance and intake were voluntary. No significant differences were found between Atole and Fresco intake in terms of net energy supplementation (106 and 82; pooled SD; 87 kcal/day) or in total energy intake (1,588 and 1,526; pooled SD; 453 kcal/day). Mothers drank more than twice as much Fresco as Atole. As a result, supplement energy intakes overlapped considerably in the Atole and Fresco villages. The situation in children was very different, those in the Atole group ingesting more supplemental energy than those in the Fresco group.

Dr. Guesry: I draw your attention to the danger of concluding too rapidly on any medical or nutritional intervention done on pregnant women, especially at the end of pregnancy. Every additional week at the end of pregnancy increases the birthweight of the baby by about 150 g.

Dr. Lechtig: In the Guatemalan study, food supplement intake was associated with an average increment of 5 days in length of gestation. This effect amounted to 71% of the difference in length of gestation between poor rural populations from Guatemala and middle class groups from the United States. The proportion of preterm babies decreased from 16.8 to 6.6%. In the Dutch study, length of gestation decreased 2 days during famine and increased 4 days afterwards. These findings are consistent with prior reports of decreased duration of gestation in mothers from poor populations and in mothers with low prepregnancy weight.

In the Guatemalan and Dutch studies, the changes in length of gestation explained partially, but not totally, the effects of dietary intake on birthweight. Two conclusions arise: (a) there is an effect of maternal nutrition on duration of gestation; and (b) changes in birthweight associated with dietary intake are a consequence of both increased length of gestation and increased fetal growth rate per se.

Dr. Pierson: With respect to the role of the sex of the fetus in the effect of supplementation, males seem to be benefiting more than females from the prenatal supplementation. It may be an anabolic effect due to the male gonads which occurs in the last week of gestation and continues after birth.

Dr. Lechtig: As mentioned, the effect of dietary intake was greater in males than in females in Bogota, Taiwan, and Guatemala. During the last weeks of pregnancy, the male fetus has greater potential for growth and therefore is more likely to benefit from dietary improvements.

Dr. Waterlow: What happens to these calories? I assume that your 10,000 kcal was a net supplement after allowing for any displacement of food in the family. It is difficult to understand what is happening to these calories unless there is an increase in the mother's physical activity, or unless she is simply "burning them off." The effect cannot be accounted for by the gain in either mother's or fetus' weight.

Dr. Lechtig: In Guatemala, about 1 kg of maternal weight was gained per 10,000 net supplemented calories, or about 55 additional calories per day. Of that 1 kg of weight gain, 41 g corresponded to an increase in birthweight per se. Thus the efficiency of supplemented calories to build maternofetal tissues was high: about 60%. The other 40% (about 22 kcal/day) was spent in physical activity and increased resting metabolic rate. The computed relationship between maternal weight gain and birthweight was also close to the maximum expected values. A similar effect of food supplementation on maternal weight gain during pregnancy was also reported in Bogota, India, Mexico, Montreal, New York, and the Dutch famine study. Therefore, the dose-response relationships presented in my chapter are compatible with current nutritional theory. The main problem is that our expectations for a nutritional effect on birthweight were excessively high 15 years ago when most of these longitudinal studies were designed. At that time, it was assumed that food supplementation would solve all differences in physical growth related to poverty.

On one hand, we have learned that the picture is more complicated than simple, linear, aristotelic logic suggested. On the other hand, we also learned that nutritional supplementation may indeed be important when appropriately implemented in malnourished populations.

Subject Index

A

N-Acetylneuraminic acid, in human milk, 32
Adipose tissue, brown, in newborn infants, 73,102
Alcohol consumption, Australian growth studies, 145
Allometry coefficient, 4
American Academy of Pediatrics Committee on Nutrition
  growth of low birthweight infants, 45
  protein intake, maximal and minimal values, 30
  trace element requirements for healthy neonates, 35
  vitamin E requirements, 31
Amino acids
  metabolism in low birthweight infants, 47
  requirements of healthy neonates, 26–29
Anthropometry
  Australian growth studies, 145,155–157
  measures of growth monitoring, 128–131
Australian growth studies, 139–158
  anthropometry of aboriginal children, 155–157
  early child growth studies, 140–143
  local conditions, 144
  Melbourne University Child Growth Study Unit, 141
  Perth Growth Study
    anthropometric findings, 145
    body weights in first year, 151–154
    breastfeeding patterns, 146,150
    data collection, 145
    dietary energy and nutrient intakes, 47,150,154
    food consumption patterns, 147–148
    growth in second and third years, 154–158
    nonmilk food, 146
  Tasmanian child growth surveys, 142–143

B

Bicarbonate metabolism during infectious diseases, 170
Bifidus factor, 28
Bile salts, in low birthweight infants, 50
Biological value (BV), protein nutrition, 29,30
Biotin deficiency, propionic acid excretion test, 34

Birthweight
  and maternal food supplementation, 186–195
  optimal, ethnic factors, 2,3
  and psychomotor development, 201–204
Blood flow; *see* Placenta
Blood pressure elevation in obese children, Australian growth studies, 142
Body weight
  loss in healthy infants, 129
  water percentage, 23
Bone
  growth monitoring, 131
  lesions in preterm infants, 54,55
Breastfeeding
  Australian growth studies, 146,150
  changes in attitudes, 85
  during first four months of life, energy and protein intakes of infants, 63–79
  infection resistance, 175,179
  secular trends, 85–118
Brown fat; *see* Adipose tissue

C

Calcium, in low birthweight infants, 54–56
Canada
  infant feeding practices, 151–153,155
  malnutrition studies; *see* Malnutrition
Cannon–Escalona scale, school-age children, and nutritional supplementation during perinatal period, 205
Carbohydrate requirements
  healthy neonates, 32
  low birthweight infants, 48–50
Carnitine, in human milk, 32
Cheese consumption after first year, Australian growth studies, 154
Chickenpox, in malnourished children, 166,168
Child abuse, and malnutrition, 176
Children
  preschool, cognitive development, effects of early malnutrition, 204–205
  school age, cognitive function, effect of nutritional supplementation during perinatal periods, 205–206
Chloride, metabolism during infectious diseases, 170
Cholesterol
  in human milk, 32
  serum levels, Australian children, 142

Chromium, essential trace element, 35
Cognitive development
    in preschool age, effect of early
        malnutrition, 204–205
    in school age, effect of nutritional
        supplementation during perinatal
        period, 205–206
Colostrum
    protease inhibitors, 29
    protein content, 28
Copper
    deficiency, with zinc excess, 35
    in infectious diseases, 170
Cortisol, in human milk, 36
Costa Rica, malnutrition and growth
    retardation; *see* Environmental factors
Cow's milk
    amino acid content, 27
    fatty acids, 31
Crying, and energy utilization, 25
Cyclic nucleotides, in infectious diseases, 170

D

Developing countries, *see also* individual
    countries; Malnutrition
    breast and complementary feedings, 94–97
    energy requirements of pregnant women,
        12–15
    growth retardation and mortality, 200–201
    low birthweight deliveries, 185–186
    milk output, 92
Diabetes, maternal, and fetal size, 7
Diarrhea, infectious diseases of children; *see*
    Environmental factors
Dietary patterns, Australian growth studies,
    154
Digestibility of milk, and protein requirements,
    27,46
1,25-Dihydroxycholecalciferol, vitamin D
    deficiency, 34

E

Education, and environmental factors, 179–180
Energy intake
    Australian growth studies, 147
    in early preschool period, 107–109
    exclusively breastfed infants, 73–74, 86–90
    low birthweight infants, 52–53
    versus protein, and growth rate increase,
        198–200
    requirements
        for healthy neonates, 24–26
        of pregnant women, 12–15
Environmental factors, 165–180
    child abuse and malnutrition, 176
    infection control and malnutrition, 177–180
    nutrition and infection studies
        digestion–absorption changes, 170
        fecal contamination at delivery, 167

food consumption, 169–170
        growth curves, 171
        immune system deficits, 173–175
        infection and infectious disease, 167–169
        metabolic alterations, 170
        respiratory disease, 168
Enzymes
    in milk, 29
    synthesis, in infectious diseases, 170
Epidemiology
    environmental factors affecting nutrition and
        growth, 165–180
    perinatal mortality, 1–2
Epidermal growth factor, in human milk, 36
Ethnic factors
    early malnutrition and postnatal growth,
        195–197
    optimal birthweight, 2,3

F

Fat
    absorption
        in low birthweight infants, 50–52
        neonatal, and calcium, magnesium, and
            fat-soluble vitamin absorption, 35
    brown, in newborn infants, 73,102
    growth patterns, 131
    maternal, and fetal weight, 5,11
Fatty acids, plasma levels, during pregnancy,
    11
Feces, neonatal contamination at delivery, 167
Fels Research Institute, growth standards, 112
Fetus
    allometry coefficient, 4
    birthweight statistics, 2
    growth curves, 126–128
    growth-limiting factors, 3–6
    head growth curves, 1
    male, rapid growth in late pregnancy, 192
    and maternal weight, 4–6
    normal growth, 1–3
    nutritional victim, 9–11
    optimal birth weight, 1–3
    oxygenation, regulation of birthweight, 4–7
    perfect parasite, 11–12
    preterm growth faltering, 8–9
Folic acid deficiency, formiminoglutamic acid
    excretion test, 34
Food
    intakes, in late infancy, 99–104
    nonmilk, Australian growth studies, 146
    reduced consumption with infectious
        diseases, 169–175
    shortage, and fetal growth, 9–11
    supplementation
        breast-complementary, and energy intakes,
            94–97
        during pregnancy, and prenatal growth,
            186–195
        reduced iron absorption, 35

Formiminoglutamic acid excretion, test of folic acid deficiency, 34

G

Galactosemia, carbohydrate supplementation, 32
Gambia
  energy intake of breastfed infants, 86–87
  maternal energy intake, 14
Genetic influences
  growth patterns, 125,127
  parental size factor, 130
Glucose regulation of fetal metabolism, 7
Glutathione reductase in erythrocyte, riboflavin status, 35
Griffith test of infant development, and nutritional supplementation during perinatal period, 205
Growth; *see also* Australian growth studies; Environmental factors
  correlation with body weight and total energy intake, 109
  curves, and infectious diseases, 171
  monitoring
    fetal and early postnatal size and maturation, 127–128
    measures of later maturity, 131–132
    perinatal, 126–127
    postnatal and maturity, 128–131
    standards and norms, 123–126
  normal fetal regulation
    allometry coefficient, 4
    birthweight statistics, 2
    energy requirements of mother, 12–15
    ethnic factors, 2–3
    and maternal fasting, 9–11
    maternal glucose and fat metabolism 11–12
    maternal size and fat stores, 3–6
    normal fetal growth curves, 1–3
    optimal birth weight, 1–3
    oxygen regulation of fetal size, 4–7
    perinatal mortality, 1,2
    placental blood flow and fetal metabolism, 6–7
    preterm growth faltering, 8–9
  prenatal, and maternal nutrition, 186–195
  retardation
    and mortality, 200–201
    permanent, and early malnutrition, 197–198
  standards, secular trends, 112–116
Guatemala
  energy supplementation during pregnancy, 14
  malnutrition and growth retardation; *see* Environmental factors; Malnutrition

H

Hair, growth monitoring, 131

Head circumference
  growth monitoring, 130
  indicator of nutritional impact in infants, 196
  preterm fetal growth faltering, 8
Human milk
  amino acid content, 27
  breastfed infants, energy and protein intakes during first four months of life, 63–79
  carbohydrates, 32
  fat content, 30–32
  nonheat-treated, improved fat absorption in low birthweight infants, 50
  secretory IgA, 28
  trace substances, 35–36
Human placental lactogen, fat metabolism during pregnancy, 11
Hydrogen breath tests, lactose metabolism in low birthweight infants, 49
Hypoglycemia, maternal, and fetal growth, 11–12

I

Immune system deficits in malnourished children, 175
Immunoglobulin A (IgA)
  deficits in malnourished children, 175
  in human milk, 28,29
Infant formulas
  amino acid content, 27
  before 1972, comparison with breast feeding, 111
  and body weight, 109
  energy content, measurement of, 26
  energy and nutrient intakes, 90–94
  and immunocompetence of infants, 29
  with medium chain triglycerides, fat absorption in low birthweight infants, 50
  metabolic balance studies in preterm infants, 47
  mineral content, 55
  nutrient levels, 33
Infants; *see also* Australian growth studies
  body weight loss in early days, 129
  breastfed, energy and protein intakes, 63–79, 86–90
  formula-fed, energy and nutrient intakes, 90–94
  growth standards, 116–118
  low birthweight, nutritional requirements
    carbohydrates, 48–50
    energy intake, 52–53
    minerals, 54–56
    protein, 45–48
    rat, 50–52
    vitamin D, 56
  nutrition in healthy neonates
    carbohydrates, 32
    energy requirements, 24–26
    lipids, 30–32
    proteins and amino acids, 26–30

Infants, nutrition in healthy neonates *(contd.)*
  vitamins and minerals, 33–36
  water, 23–24
  psychomotor development, and early
    malnutrition, 201–204
  six months to one year, food intakes, 99–
    104
  small-for-gestational-age, growth
    monitoring, 126–127
  theoretical energy requirements, 73
Infections, and infant formulas with soya
    protein, 29; *see also* Environmental
    factors
Insulin
  fetal growth hormone, 7
  peripheral resistance during pregnancy, 11
Iron
  absorption, inhibition by manganese excess,
    35
  in infectious diseases, 170

K
Kala-azar, in malnourished children, 166
Kwashiorkor, and infectious diseases, 175,179

L
La Leche League International, growth curves
    of breastfed babies, 114
Lactase development in infant, 32
Lactation, infant feeding and growth, secular
    trends, *see* Breastfeeding; Infants; Growth
Lactoferrin, in human milk, 28
Lactose
  digestion, in low birthweight infants, 48–50
  in human milk, 32
Length–height, growth monitoring, 129
Limb circumference
  growth monitoring, 130
  growth standards, 113
Lipid requirements of healthy neonates, 30–32
Lumbar lordosis, and impaired fetal growth, 9

M
Magnesium, in low birthweight infants, 54
Malaria, in malnourished children, 166
Malnutrition; *see also* Environmental factors
  and child abuse, 176
  chronic
    and menarche onset, 198
    and sexual maturation in boys, 198
  early, and growth retardation
    cognitive development during preschool
      age, 204–205
    mental development, long-term effects,
      206–209
    nutritional supplementation in perinatal
      period, and cognitive function in school
      age, 205–206

psychomotor development of infants, 201–
    204
  early, and permanent stunting, 197–198
  early, and postnatal growth, 195–197
  maternal, effect on prenatal growth, 186–
    195
    caloric supplementation during pregnancy,
      187–191
    famine exposure, and birthweight, 193–
      194
    long-term stability of improved nutrition,
      194–195
    nutrition threshold, 193
    sex of newborn, role in response to
      dietary change, 192
    timing of food supplementation during
      pregnancy, 192
Maltodextrins, digestion in low birthweight
    infants, 49,50
Manganese excess, inhibition of iron
    absorption, 35
Marasmus, growth impairment, 171,175,179
Maternal
  immune system, and antibodies in milk, 28
  malnutrition, and maternal function, 204
  weight, and fetal growth, 3–6,127–128
Measles
  growth impairment, 171
  in malnourished children, 166,168,173,175
Menarche
  maturity indicator, 132
  onset, and chronic malnutrition effects, 198
Mental development, and early malnutrition
  cognitive development in preschool age,
    204–205
  food supplementation in perinatal period,
    and cognitive function in school age,
    205–206
  infants, 201–204
  long-term effects, 206–209
Metabolism, in malnourished infants, 72
Methodology, human growth standards, 123–
    132
3-Methylhistidine excretion during pregnancy,
    12
Methylmalonate excretion, test for vitamin B_{12}
    deficiency, 34
Milk, protein constituents, 28; *see also* Cow's
    milk; Human milk; Infant formulas
Mineral requirements
  healthy neonates, 33–36
  low birthweight infants, 54–56
Molybdenum, essential trace element, 35
Mortality
  and growth retardation, 200–201
  malnourished children; *see* Environmental
    factors
Multiple regression analysis, and early
    malnutrition, 207–208

Muscle, growth monitoring, 131

N

National Academy of Sciences–National Research Council, recommended energy requirements for healthy neonates, 24–25

National Center for Health Statistics (NCHS), growth standards
and breast milk intake, 65
and energy intakes, 97,112,116
percentiles, 125

National Collaborative Perinatal Project, maternal weight gain and birth size, 128

National Health and Medical Research Council (NHMRC); see Australian growth studies

Net protein utilization (NPU), 29

Nitrogen
balance
in infectious diseases, 170
in low birthweight infants, 46–47
nonamino acid, requirements of healthy neonates, 26,30
requirement for growth, 75

Nursing Mothers Association of Australia, growth patterns in breastfed infants, 151

Nutritional requirements
dietary intake, Australian growth studies, 147
and growth; see Environmental factors
healthy neonates, 23–37
low birthweight infants, 45–57

O

Obesity
childhood, Australian growth studies, 142
infantile, bottle-fed babies before 1972, 111

Office of Population Census and Surveys (OPCS), changes in attitudes toward breastfeeding, 85

Oxygen regulation of fetal size, 4–7

P

Parent height, and growth of child, 130

Perth Growth Study, see Australian growth studies

Phosphate metabolism during infectious diseases, 170

Phospholipids, in human milk, 32

Phosphorus, in low birthweight infants, 54–56

Placental blood flow, regulation of fetal metabolism, 6–7,11

Polyneonates, long chain, in human milk, 31,32

Potassium loss during infectious diseases, 170

Preeclampsia, high protein–low carbohydrate diet, 10

Pregnancy
energy requirements, 12–15
fat deposition, 11

food supplementation, and prenatal growth, 186–195

3-methylhistidine excretion, 12

weight gain, and fetal growth, 127–128

Preschool ages
cognitive development, effects of early malnutrition, 204–205
energy intakes, 107–109

Preterm growth faltering, 8–9

Prolactin, in human milk, 36

Propionic acid excretion, test of biotin deficiency, 34

Protease inhibitors in colostrum, 29

Protein
intake
breastfed infants during first four months of life, 63–65,75–78
vs. energy, and growth rate increase, 198–200
first year, Australian growth studies, 150
intoxication
in healthy neonates, 30
in low birthweight infants, 47
requirements
healthy neonates, 26–30
low birthweight infants, 45–48

Protein efficiency ratio (PER), 29,30

Psychomotor development, infants, effects of early malnutrition, 201–204

Puberty
growth monitoring, 132
malnutrition effects, 198

Pyruvate–lactate ratio, test of vitamin B_1 deficiency, 34

R

Respiratory disease, mortality in malnourished infants, 165,168

Riboflavin estimation by erythrocyte glutathione reductase, 35

Rubella, in malnourished children, 168

S

Sanitation; see Environmental factors

Selenium, essential trace element, 35

Sex differences
and birthweight response to dietary change, 192
body fat growth patterns, 131
weight and height growth, 113–114

Skeleton, measures of maturation, 131–132

Skinfold measurements
body fat monitoring, 130–131
Tanner growth standards, 113

Smoking
Australian growth studies, 145
fetal growth retardation, 6

Social class differences
  breastfeeding attitudes, 85
  dietary energy intakes, 109
  growth rates, 111–112
Sodium
  absorption, in infectious diseases, 170
  dietary intake, Australian growth studies,
    148,150
Soya protein, infant formulas, and
    immunocompetence of infants, 29
Sulfur metabolism in low birthweight infants,
    47

T
Taurine, essential amino acid for infants, 27
Temperature, ambient, and caloric utilization,
    25
The Gambia; *see* Gambia
Themogenesis, diet-induced (DIT), energy
    expenditure, 72,73
Threonine metabolism in low birthweight
    infants, 47
Thyroxine, in human milk, 36
Triglycerides
  absorption in low birthweight infants, 50,52
  medium chain, in human and cow's milk, 31
Tuberculosis, in malnourished children,
    166,173
Tyrosine metabolites in urine, vitamin C
    deficiency, 34

U
Ultrasound
  fetal growth curves, 126
  preterm fetal growth faltering, 8

V
Viral diseases, in malnourished children, 167–
    173
Vitamin B_1 deficiency, pyruvate–lactate ratio,
    34
Vitamin B_6 deficiency, xanthourenic acid
    excretion test, 34
Vitamin B_{12} deficiency, methylmalonate
    excretion test, 34
Vitamin C deficiency, and tyrosine
    metabolites, 34
Vitamin D
  deficiency 25- or 1,25-
    dihydroxycholecalciferol levels, 34
  metabolites, in low birthweight infants, 56
Vitamin K, prothrombin time measurement, 35
Vitamins, requirements of healthy neonates,
    33–36

W
Water
  absorption, in infectious diseases, 170
  percentage of body weight, 23
  requirements for healthy neonates, 23–24
  supplementation in tropical climates, 24
Whooping cough
  growth impairment, 171
  in malnourished children, 166,168

X
Xanthourenic acid excretion, test of vitamin B_6
    deficiency, 34

Z
Zinc
  excess, and copper deficiency, 35
  in infectious diseases, 170